U..iver.

Subject

http

E.
Pl

Library of Philosophy and Religion

General Editor: **John Hick**, Institute for Advanced Research in Arts and Social Sciences, University of Birmingham

This series of books explores contemporary religious understandings of humanity and the universe. The books contribute to various aspects of the continuing dialogues between religion and philosophy, between scepticism and faith, and between the different religions and ideologies. The authors represent a correspondingly wide range of viewpoints. Some of the books in the series are written for the general educated public and others for a more specialised philosophical or theological readership.

Selected titles:

Masao Abe
BUDDHISM AND INTERFAITH DIALOGUE
ZEN AND WESTERN THOUGHT

Dan Cohn-Sherbok
ISLAM IN A WORLD OF DIVERSE FAITHS (*editor*)
ISSUES IN CONTEMPORARY JUDAISM

Stephen T. Davis
LOGIC AND THE NATURE OF GOD

Padmasiri de Silva
AN INTRODUCTION TO BUDDHIST PSYCHOLOGY

Clement Dore
MORAL SCEPTICISM
GOD, SUFFERING AND SOLIPSISM

J. Kellenberger
INTER-RELIGIOUS MODELS AND CRITERIA

Khen Lampert
TRADITIONS OF COMPASSION
From Religious Duty to Social Activism

Adil Özdemir and Kenneth Frank
VISIBLE ISLAM IN MODERN TURKEY

Chakravathi Ram-Prasad
KNOWLEDGE AND LIBERATION IN CLASSICAL INDIAN THOUGHT

Joseph Runzo
IS GOD REAL?

Ninian Smart
BUDDHISM AND CHRISTIANITY

Michael Stoeber
RECLAIMING THEODICY
Reflections on Suffering, Compassion and Spiritual Transformation

Roger Teichmann
ABSTRACT ENTITIES

Donald Wiebe
BEYOND LEGITIMATION

Richard Worsley
HUMAN FREEDOM AND THE LOGIC OF EVIL

Library of Philosophy and Religion
Series Standing Order ISBN 0–333–69996–3
(*outside North America only*)

You can receive future titles in this series as they are published by placing a standing order. Please contact your bookseller or, in case of difficulty, write to us at the address below with your name and address, the title of the series and the ISBN quoted above.

Customer Services Department, Macmillan Distribution Ltd, Houndmills, Basingstoke, Hampshire RG21 6XS, England

Traditions of Compassion

From Religious Duty to Social Activism

Khen Lampert

palgrave
macmillan

First published 2005 by
PALGRAVE MACMILLAN
Houndmills, Basingstoke, Hampshire RG21 6XS and
175 Fifth Avenue, New York, N.Y. 10010
Companies and representatives throughout the world

PALGRAVE MACMILLAN is the global academic imprint of the Palgrave
Macmillan division of St. Martin's Press, LLC and of Palgrave Macmillan Ltd.
Macmillan® is a registered trademark in the United States, United Kingdom
and other countries. Palgrave is a registered trademark in the European
Union and other countries.

ISBN-13: 978-1-4039-8527-9 hardback
ISBN-10: 1-4039-8527-8 hardback

This book is printed on paper suitable for recycling and made from fully
managed and sustained forest sources.

A catalogue record for this book is available from the British Library.

Library of Congress Cataloging-in-Publication Data
Lampert, Khen.
    Traditions of compassion : from religious duty to social activism /
    Khen Lampert.
        p.   cm. — (Library of philosophy and religion)
    Includes bibliographical references and index.
    ISBN 1-4039-8527-8
    1. Compassion.   2. Compassion—Religious aspects.   I. Title.
    II. Library of philosophy and religion (Palgrave (Firm))
    BJ1475.L36 2005
    177'.7—dc22   2005049932

10   9   8   7   6   5   4   3   2   1
14   13   12   11   10   09   08   07   06   05

Printed and bound in Great Britain by
Antony Rowe Ltd, Chippenham and Eastbourne

Contents

Introduction

Compassion, in the sense of the ability to perceive the pain of another and the inclination to act to alleviate that pain, is a universal phenomenon. The majority of people – men and women, children and adults, oppressors and oppressed, tough and tender-hearted – are able to feel, recognize, and respond to the suffering and distress of others. Compassion has appeared in all cultures throughout human history. Thinkers, philosophers, and religious preachers from China to the United States, from ancient times to modernity, have presented it as a fundamental human quality to point to the inherent good of human beings and their nature as social creatures.

Throughout history, compassion has lain at the foundation of the radical cry to change the world order, to remedy injustices, and to fight for rights. It has also served, however, as a political tool for society's power-wielders, who have exploited the sense of calling compassion arouses in order to mitigate social repression and mask the immoral, belligerent, and manipulative nature of society's power structure and mechanisms.

This book engages in three discussions of compassion conducted in part concurrently. The first discussion is comparative, focusing on the different ways in which the approach to the pain and distress of the weak has been constructed in the concepts and images of different cultural traditions and in different historical periods. This discussion addresses the developmental processes of the different conceptions of compassion and the interrelationship between compassion and other concepts. In the framework of this discussion, I seek to show that the different traditions developed models of compassion that vary significantly in some aspects but are surprisingly similar in others, with discernible logical and psychological connections that cut across time and geography.

The second discussion is a critical polemic discussion that addresses the inbuilt impotency of the great cultural traditions with regard to the distress of the weak and oppressed. One of the critical claims put forth is that despite the fact that suffering is identified in every tradition as an aspect of human existence that must be fought against, the ways in which the traditions developed the concept and the praxis of compassion, bar any possibility of systematic social change. Furthermore, I will argue that these traditional concepts and praxis of compassion often serve as either an impetus or smokescreen for social and economic processes that exacerbate the distress and repression of both individuals and certain groups in society. The third discussion in the book derives from the discussions that precede it. Its purpose is to propose a somewhat different understanding of compassion, constructed around some of the shared presumptions and motifs identified in the preceding discussions. To this end, I assume the universality of human compassion, but dispute the way in which compassion is translated and explained in its various appearances in history. My claim is that the most fundamental experience of compassion encompasses an imperative for social change and this requirement is an integral constituent of both the psychology of compassion and its social import.

Traditions of compassion

Compassion as a universal phenomenon present deep in the heart of a cynical, cold, exploitative, oppressive, chaotic, and terribly unjust social reality has many times served as an optimistic point of argument in favor of humanity. The most well known applications of compassion are those found in the great religions, particularly Buddhism and Christianity, and also Islam and Judaism. These religions have made historical uses of compassion and, to this day, still present themselves, in certain senses and contexts, as the 'religions of compassion'. They maintain vast institutions for caring for the weak, poor, and downtrodden, and compassion is the hallmark of their social missionary activities (more so in Christianity and Islam and less so in Buddhism and Judaism). These religious traditions claim the notion of compassion to originate with their founders (Jesus, the Buddha) and relate to it as the highest realization of the original religious intention. Finally, they have expanded the social expressions of compassion to such practices and institutions as charity and self-sacrifice and transferred them from the moral sphere to the metaphysical sphere: compassion is presented in these religions as the path to salvation, as holiness itself.

The occupation with distress, affliction, and poverty is one of the pillars of the Judeo-Christian tradition and, certainly, of the Buddhist traditions, perhaps even of religious thought in general. From the sociological perspective laid out by Max Weber, a considerable amount of the theorization and conceptualization processes of the social-religious system can be described in terms of the different ways in which this system contends with the question of theodicy: How does the given religion explain to its faithful the existence of suffering and evil in the world? Under the Weberian logic, the possible success of a religion, its proliferation, survival, power, and influence are all to a significant extent related to its ability to offer a solution to the theodical problem. The quest for such a solution is a process of rationalization, of consolidation of a coherent worldview in which the place, source, and ways of contending with the problem are defined.

Accordingly, the appearance of compassion as a response to suffering, as an inbuilt part of the cultural world of concepts of the evolving religious tradition, was almost inevitable and self-evident. Compassion can manifest itself in two different senses. The one is as a way of observing, or distinguishing, the pain and suffering of the other. Compassion in this sense is the spectacles through which the suffering of the outcast, poor, disadvantaged, afflicted, and so on is discerned. From the moment it appears, it poses a challenge for the religious system, for it raises the need for an explanation of the suffering. This explanation is likely to give birth to a broader anthropological and metaphysical stance with regard to the status of man in the world in general. The second sense in which compassion appears is as a means to a solution: the empathetic inclination toward the suffering person can serve as the basis for action, and it holds the key to defining the scope of social responsibility of the religion. It prepares the ground for the social relations in the community of believers as well between the community and the society in general. It is the foundation on which new hope and the promise for a change of the dismal reality sprout. Its very presence has the potential to produce the catharsis for salvation.

Over the course of the book, I will show that it was the Judeo-Christian traditions that adopted the pragmatic approach, the approach of praxis, to compassion as an imminent part of their anthropological-behavioristic outlooks. Man is tested by divinity in a trial of deed: fulfilling the commandments, keeping the Word of God, and refraining from sin. Only at a later stage in history did the requirement to 'feel' or identify with the sufferer emerge in these traditions. In contrast, in the Buddhist traditions, the primary emphasis has been on compassionate observation, on the human empathetic ability, which sharpens the more a person succeeds in distancing himself from attachment to his ego and in realizing the Buddhist ideal of absence-of-self. Compassion appears in Buddhism as a type of human consciousness that takes the place of the ego, but which carries no imperative to act.

The approach to human suffering is just one example of the tension existing between the structural similarity of the religious traditions and the significant divergence in the ways in which compassion is constructed, structured, and present in the unique conceptual worlds of each of the traditions. Another example of this tension is in the way in which the religions relate to poverty. In Catholicism and Buddhism, for example, compassion frequently is closely aligned with poverty. The believer (in particular, the devoted believer) takes upon himself a life of meagerness: he withdraws from the chase after material gains, dons a monk's robe, relinquishes all property and commodities, abstains from all physical pleasure and takes an oath of celibacy, and engages only in spiritual salvation – his own and that of society. Moreover, he is also a compassionate person, who offers the wretched and oppressed his compassion and spiritual belongings. The ideal of poverty appears in Christianity in the context of the contrast between the material and the spiritual, with the material, which represents evil and the fetters of lust and desire, repressed in favor of the soul and spiritual redemption. In Buddhism, the separation of the corporal from the soul is not so straightforward; indeed, certain Buddhist sects do not even advocate celibacy for their monks. Here, the material does not represent moral evil, but, rather, desire's hold on and bondage of reality – an illusory reality, from the Buddhist perspective, that perpetuates the state of suffering. Accordingly, Buddhism calls for detachment from all things to which man is attached, whether possessions or family, as they trap him in the cycle of perpetual rebirth into the world of suffering.

Poverty in the different religious traditions is often one of the defining features of the object of compassion, in being one of the possible representatives of suffering. In this respect, Christianity and Buddhism are very similar; however, in both traditions, there is consensus that poverty is not necessarily the state of suffering that mandates change, but, rather, is likely to be the medium of purification and a basis for religious catharsis. In many senses, it is actually the pauper who is most qualified for spiritual salvation in Christianity and liberation from the cycle of suffering in Buddhism. The historical founders of the two traditions were people who consciously chose a life of poverty; their poverty enabled the appearance of spiritual insight, followed by universal compassion toward other human beings. Compassion is the bridge offered by the enlightened, the saint, to connect people with all the spiritual belongings acquired by the holy person when he gave up the material world, property, and restrictive and harmful attachment. It is the summons to salvation represented by the persona and humble lifestyle of the saint.

This similarity notwithstanding, historically, there were important differences between the two traditions in terms of their respective approaches to poverty and to the relationship between compassion and poverty. In the Christian traditions, an interesting relationship between poverty and holiness developed, to the point where poverty was conceived of as an ideal and as a holy way of life by many of the Catholic orders, which strived for a lifestyle of *imitato Christi* in light of the New Testament promise that the poor shall inherit the Kingdom of Heaven. In contrast, Buddhism evolved in a cultural environment where poverty and self-denial were integral parts of the lives of people seeking the truth and release from the Wheel of Rebirth (*'Saṃsāra'*), the fundamental representation of existential suffering in Indian terms. Buddhism, as a radical Indian movement, in fact took a rather moderate stance with regard to poverty, not setting any necessary link between poverty and suffering. The objects of compassion are all sentient beings, trapped in the *Samsaric* cycle. The poor bear no advantage to the rich in terms of potential for suffering and, accordingly, the compassion of the Buddhist.

On the socio-political level, too, it is possible to discern great similarity in the rhetoric of the two traditions, which present themselves as possessing a certain moral superiority or purity due to the simple ways and relative poverty of their disciples, monks, and monastic leaders. However, in practice, the two traditions evolved along significantly different courses. The Catholic orders, especially the Franciscan and the Dominican orders, began as poor orders, seeking a return to simplicity, spirituality without property, solitude, and the universal compassion embodied in Jesus' image. However, despite the fact that the monks in these orders did lead lives of true abstention and although many were (and still are) exemplary of compassion and generosity, the socio-political history of their orders is not one of poverty and certainly not always an expression of compassion. In a relatively short period of time, they became economic empires, and the way in which they amassed great property for the Church is the envy of any modern-day entrepreneur. But more importantly, we are hard-pressed to consider Catholicism compassionate, without immediately recalling the Church's ruthless use of its political power, the undeniable role of the Dominican order in the Inquisition, and the horrors of the conquest of South America, which at least partially were carried out with the full knowledge, guidance, and collaboration of the Church.

Buddhism took a quite different path. It did amass power and property wherever it arrived and had a dramatic, in part destructive political, impact on Tibet and certainly Burma, as well as on society and politics in China and, later on, Japan. But in Buddhist history, there were no manifestations of belligerence, imperialism, or cruel repression of the scope and magnitude perpetrated by Christianity. This is possibly related to the historical fact that Christianity was, and still is, an integral part of European imperialism, whereas Asia, the birthplace and seat of Buddhism, was one of the victims of that imperialism; in any event, the scope and strength of the political forces operating within Buddhism were less than in the case of Christianity. It is also possible that this is connected to the history of Buddhism as a religion that was driven out of its birthplace, India, to become the culture of wanderers across Asia. This culture was translated into different lifestyles in each place it arrived, absent any organized establishment and whose wealth and influence were a function of the political power of those who adopted it, not an internal part of Buddhism itself. But it is also quite possible that Buddhism as a way of life was more successful than Christianity at combining an anti-materialistic and compassionate ideology with the reality of human life.

These are just a few examples of the extent of resemblance amongst the religious traditions of compassion, as well as the divergences in how each translated and gave expression to the narrative of compassion, which is integral to their self-images.

*   *   *

Compassion had, and still has, additional manifestations in culture, which are not necessarily related to religion. Modern thought also took, and still takes, a not-trivial interest in compassion, despite the fact that it was never an important element in the self-image of Modernism, which extricated itself from the grip of the theodical problem. Modernism, insofar as it can be related to as a tradition with an identity, never set as its goal providing an explanation for suffering in the world, and in many senses it is possible to discern in its intellectual manifestations a certain degree of pleasure derived from the fact that this nuisance did not burden its thinkers. Nonetheless, even in modern thought, especially European, compassion had an important presence in accompanying the central, social, and moral dilemmas that characterized the development of the new tradition.

The general cultural ethos of Modernism, from Hobbes and Locke to Darwin and Freud, reveals extremely wide consensus with regard to human beings as creatures essentially driven by and acting to satisfy their needs. The understanding of man as an egoistic creature, who cooperates with others only out of self-interest, raised at least two central dilemmas in the history of European thought. The first one is with regard to sociability – how can we explain the social organization of human beings, the 'social contract', which, in many senses, appears to be a repression of the egoistic instinct in the interest of the general good? The second dilemma relates to altruistic behavior: How can we explain phenomena such as self-sacrifice – the willingness of certain people to act against what seems to be their self-interest?

In certain cases, it was in fact the modern thinkers who sought to propose a way to be released from the chains of dogma and ecclesiastical control and who identified compassion as the expression of a natural human inclination. The presence of compassion, according to these thinkers, could be indicative of a basic, authentic human potential, which requires no direction, guidance, or regimentation. It holds a latent possibility for laying the foundations of a just human society, with no need for Divine Grace. This understanding forgoes both the metaphysical and the paternalistic aspects of the traditional approaches to compassion, as well as the clinging to symbolic acts of benevolent charity as expressions of compassion.

This type of naturalistic approach to compassion appeared in European culture primarily amongst, for example, the work of the eighteenth-century British philosophers who proposed recognizing compassion as an inborn emotion, as the natural and, therefore, legitimate basis to building human society. This was in total distinction to their French counterparts, who clung to reason and rationality as the sole underlying rationale to Modernism's vision. In contrast, the British philosophers asserted that the existence of compassion as a human virtue explains both the need for and the success of human society and civilization, for the act of social organization should not be regarded as an act of reason (a contract or convention) but rather as an act of emotion. This stance was applied by some of the British Enlightenment philosophers, especially Adam Smith, to formulate an optimistic outlook that enables the mitigation of the incessant economic pressure of modern society: humane actions carried out parallel to the cold and often cruel free market. Compassion as a fundamental human quality can explain the social potential inherent to human beings, as well as the human responsiveness to the distress of the other – the same responsiveness that is expressed in acts of altruism and in the willingness of certain people to act for the good of others, even if it puts them at risk or clashes with their own personal interests. These familiar human actions, which challenge Darwinist and Freudian thought (in contradicting the biological survival instinct and/or psychological Pleasure Principle), can be instilled with meaning by assuming compassion to be a part of the anthropological definition of human beings.

* * *

Alongside, and in addition to, the discussion of the similarities and differences in the ways in which compassion appears in the different traditions, I will propose a critical perspective that leans on the political feasibility and advisability of compassion. Although there seems to be no need to attempt to assess the full cynical scope of the politics of compassion at this introductory stage, it is perhaps worthwhile, nonetheless, to note its central element considered from a critical perspective. At least with regard to everything related to political-institutional processes (in contrast to, perhaps, the actions and intentions of individuals), this is a politics that perpetuates the place of the oppressed and poor and allows the strong and rich a sense of morality and social responsibility. The Christian and Buddhist monks almost always worked under the aegis of strong and rich establishments, even when they led private lives of making do with the bare minimum. But they were never poor in the full sense of the word, that is, devoid of all means, oppressed, exploited, enslaved, and with a feeling of complete worthlessness and uselessness. No matter what the magnitude of the paucity of their existence, they chose this poverty; it was not imposed on them.

The politics of compassion was, and still is, paternalistic, treating compassion as a one-way relationship flowing from the strong to the weak, from the rich to the poor (even if 'rich' is defined as spiritually rich), and in fact denies the ability of the poor and needy to feel compassion, that is, to be human. This is a politics that upholds the existence of social and economic disparity, since it intentionally refrains from contending with, or taking a stance regarding, the sources of this disparity, all the while drawing its followers and power from those very social classes supposedly 'benefiting' from compassion. And finally, this is a reactionary politics that preserves social injustices: it replaces the furious and raging response to injustice, inequality, exploitation, and oppression with responses of compassion and understanding. A compassionate person is not supposed to mount the barricades, shout in protest, or undermine the social order. It is no mere coincidence that one of the most important hallmarks of compassion, in all the traditions, is the requirement to relinquish anger and to expand the scope of the empathetic capacity beyond the downtrodden to include the persecutor, insisting (sometimes categorically) that the latter be treated with understanding and compassion.

* * *

Over the course of the book, a distinction is made between four different models of compassion. These four theoretical models represent, I submit, different manifestations of compassion in different cultures and historical periods. I illustrate the nature of each of these models by pointing to their presence in the underlying infrastructure of religion or culture or else as part of the ideological mood of a specific period.

The divine compassion model

Under this model, compassion is first and foremost the response of God to the suffering of human beings and is in essence a 'supra-human' quality. Divine compassion is the possible refuge for human beings from divine wrath. It gives legitimacy to presenting human suffering and pain before God by means of prayer and the intervention of the religious establishment or spiritual guides. This compassion derives from human beings' weakness, their tendency to sin, and their inability to meet the simple requirement of following the divine commandments. Compassion, under this model, is mercy and forgiveness on the part of the strong and omnipotent toward the weak and wretched, and the poor and contemptible, and it is manifested in either concrete action or abstention from punishment. The Judeo-Christian tradition is discussed, as well as the way in which the concept of compassion developed in Catholicism, as best exemplifying the divine compassion model.

As I will demonstrate throughout the discussion of the divine compassion model in Part I of the book, this is a dynamic model, not an inflexible one, both in Judaism and in Christianity. The way in which the biblical narrator, for example, contends with the possibility of compassion reveals an antagonistic approach, almost completely hostile to the possibility of human compassion. Human beings are not supposed to act out of compassion, even when it is awakened in them and even in the context of the parent–child relationship. Compassion is an indication of weakness and cowardice, which, obviously, should be overcome. The only legitimate form of compassion is divine compassion, when God, in seeing the weakness of man, takes mercy on him. The part to be played by human beings is presented in a series of commands directed at concrete action for the welfare of the weak, poor, orphaned, and so on. There is no reference at all to our feelings or awareness of the other, but only to our actions: we are commanded to attend to the welfare of the poor and suffering, irregardless of what we feel or think.

Apparently it was the radical and widely influential appearance of Jesus that changed the rules of the game, by creating a new and different dynamic in respect to human pain – its ostensibly purifying role and the set of expectations with regard to the appropriate human response to the distress of the other. Jesus' persona created a possibility for compassion that is simultaneously human *and* divine. Divine humanity was transferred to the human sphere by means of the ultimate mediator, the Gospel. From hereon, compassion could also be said to characterize certain people: those who have been touched by Divine Grace, who are spiritually close to divinity, and whose very compassion is proof of their spirituality and closeness to God. The historical gap between Jesus' revolution and the emergence of the Christian saint and Jewish righteous is surprisingly short. These are the people who, both in their actions and in their intentionality, represent divine compassionate at its ultimate. They are those whose closeness to God, personal purity, and unwavering belief qualify them in three aspects: one, to serve as a medium for divine compassion and channel for God's abounding grace, love, and goodness toward man; two, to feel the pain of their fellow human beings and minister to them in their suffering, sickness, and poverty; and three, to bear, in a very practical sense, the sin and torments of the other and to lead her to salvation through self-sacrifice.

The discussion of the divine compassion model is divided into three parts. The first part, Chapter 1, presents the way in which compassion is construed in the Old Testament and the latter's latent reservations with regard to a human form of compassion. In this context, I relate to the appearance of the broad concept of compassion, namely agape, Christian love, which comprises compassion. In the second part of the discussion, Chapter 2, I raise the question of the possibility of human compassion that arises from the identification of Jesus with agapic compassion itself. I seek to explain why this possibility was rejected in Catholic theology, which expanded the concept and linked it to other concepts, such as grace, charity, and mercy. In the third part, Chapter 3, I submit a critical perspective of the divine compassion model, which considers the anti-compassionate elements of Catholic thought and, perhaps, of the Christian history of ideas in general.

The universal compassion model

The starting point of this model, discussed in Part II of the book, is the constant presence of pain and distress as an inbuilt aspect of the human experience in general. Suffering is not the realm of society's poor, repressed, disadvantaged, and afflicted. Rather it is a universal existential state that can be fought, first and foremost, by recognizing it. Only when we become aware of human suffering – both our own personal suffering and the general suffering of others – are we able to take action. Thus, compassion, under this model, is an awareness of the pain of the other, of her mental state, and an awareness that is fundamentally a state of consciousness (as opposed to an emotional state). Under this model, as well, the relationship between the person feeling compassion and the object of that compassion is essentially paternalistic in nature, albeit not based on a distinction between divine and human or strong and weak. Rather, it rests on a distinction between the enlightened and the ignorant, between a person who has undergone a process of exposure to truth and a person who is still trapped in the illusory reality and must be assisted to be liberated from that reality.

The Buddhist tradition, whose point of departure is the universality of human suffering, is discussed as a paradigmatic example of this model of compassion. According to the traditional Buddhist stance, the source of all pain does not lie in relationships between human beings and supra-mental entities, such as God, but rather in the human psychological structure and the way in which this structure responds to cultural-linguistic constructions, prejudices, social conventions, and so on. The ability to unravel the human psychological-cultural-linguistic constructions is inevitably contingent on empathy: the capacity to climb into someone else's skin and feel her pain, distress, and suffering is an acquired ability that is attained only through years of meditative training, mental observation, and following the Buddhist way of life.

Like the monotheistic traditions, the Buddhist tradition is not static, with discernible dynamics and evolution to its concept of compassion. Whereas the ancient concept of Buddhist compassion rested principally on the persona of the Buddha, his ability to know the pain of all living creatures, whether human or animal, and his infinite willingness to sacrifice himself for their good, over the years, the concept was expanded in certain Buddhist streams to become part of the more general characterization of the Bodhisattva – an enlightened person who reaches Nirvāṇa but chooses to return to the Wheel of Rebirth and aid others on the path to enlightenment. But not only did the attribution of the concept change, its field of reference changed as well. While, originally, compassion was a quality that was exclusive to the lone enlightened virtuous, with the development of the epistemological discourse in ancient Buddhism, compassion (meaning the ability to feel the other and look through her eyes) came to be construed as a sort of byproduct of the deconstruction process of the self and reality. That is to say, compassion emerged as a natural human phenomenon, derived logically and practically from the Buddhist training process itself. It applies universally to all human, plant, and animal life and can be felt by all.

The discussion of the universal compassion model is also divided into three parts. The first part, Chapter 4, deals with the way in which compassion appeared as an integral part of the rational theodicy of Indian Buddhism. The second part, Chapter 5, describes the development of the idea of Buddhist compassion and how it was linked to such concepts as enlightenment, equanimity, non-violence, and self-sacrifice. The final part, Chapter 6, presents a critical analysis of Buddhist universal compassion, explicating the structural impotence of this compassion, which prevents it from being transferred into concrete action to change reality for the suffering other.

Human compassion

The model of natural human compassion begins where the model of universal compassion leaves off. Under this third model, compassion is a natural human emotion that requires no training or construction: all human beings have the ability to sense the other and to feel compassion for her pain. Compassion, as a natural human emotion, is most clearly apparent in the parent–child relationship, and also is manifested in the encounter between people in distress in general, even if they are total strangers. As such, it constitutes a sort of counterweight to the radical pursuit after personal benefits at the expense of others and is even likely to serve as a barrier to repression and exploitation. No one school of thought or philosophical tradition seems to lie behind this model of compassion, a model that has appeared in different form in Buddhism (particularly Tibetan), in Christian thought (primarily in the Protestant streams of Christianity, such as Methodism), and in modern Western thought. But despite the numerous attempts to construct a model of this type, from a historical perspective, the dominant egoistic narrative of Modernism (and capitalism, which guides that narrative) has caused compassion to retreat from center stage.

Part III of the book is devoted to the fate of compassion in the modern era. The principal claim is that in later modernity, from the second half of the nineteenth century, compassion underwent a process of fragmentation, eventually being replaced by such concepts as empathy and altruism. The examination of these concepts reveals both their reduction and the almost complete disappearance of the notion of compassion.

In the final chapter of the book's discussion, Chapter 8, I will claim the imperativeness of a re-examination of compassion on the background of the demise of social welfare in the postmodern neocapitalist era and the failure to preserve such modern concepts as social justice. To this purpose, I embark on a mental experiment aimed at exploring the possibility of another model of compassion: radical compassion. The term 'radical compassion' represents a state of mind in which a person, in becoming aware of the pain and distress of another, is driven to concrete action toward changing that reality for the other. This is a natural state of mind, which potentially can be achieved by all (or most) people and cannot be categorized as either an emotion or consciousness. It is a complex of emotional, conscious, instinctual, and pragmatic aspects, and the simultaneous presence of all these aspects is what singles out this state of mind as radical compassion.

In this model of compassion, it is possible to identify traces of the previous three models, such as progression through action, which characterizes divine compassion, or the anthropological assertion regarding the empathetic capacity of the human consciousness, which characterizes the universal compassion and natural human compassion models. This notwithstanding, however, the radical compassion model differs from its counterparts in terms of both its epistemological base and the social-historical ramifications of its anthropological premises. This model necessarily binds the process of 'climbing into the skin of the other', observing reality through her eyes, experiencing her pain, and judging that reality with the imperative to take action to change the reality. The presence of radical compassion does not characterize any particular culture and is not identified with any particular historical period. On the contrary – it is universal as a conscious and pragmatic possibility and, apparently, has accompanied human history along its entire course, in all its manifestations, and parallel to the official narrative. It is quite possible that radical compassion is what lies at the foundation of the call for social change across all generations and cultures and is likely what has guided the many actions of individuals, most of which have gone unrecognized and some of which were embraced retroactively by the social institutions of the time and place – simple actions that were taken by individuals who allowed themselves to be exposed to the pain of the other and relentlessly acted to put a stop to that pain.

In the final and concluding chapter, I put forth my final claim: that there is considerable room to consider critically the presumption of the existence of a model that defines empathy, identification, and recognition of the pain of others as fundamental elements in human relations in general and, moreover, asserts that pain is necessarily accompanied by an imperative to take action to change reality. Such critical scrutiny enables a re-examination of the first three models of compassion: when compassion is construed as a basic human inclination that seeks to undermine the social order dictated by society's power-wielders and mechanisms, it emerges that the hierarchical Church (or modern nation-state), which creates, perpetuates, and participates in society's production relations as the central source of deprivation, alienation, illusion, and pain, is the social framework that is most threatened by change to the world order. And not surprisingly, it has cleverly and manipulatively adopted human compassion, the demagoguery of compassion, as the official narrative of its actions. From this analysis it follows that the traditions of compassion are an integral part of the overall anti-change social pattern and that, fundamentally, 'compassion' in the neocapitalist consumer world is an integral part of the historic trend of anti-compassion that blocks any chance of radical change.

Part I
Divine Compassion

1
The Compassionate God

The drama of Creation in the Book of Genesis is the incipient moment of compassion conceived as a response to human suffering, first in Jewish tradition and then in Christian tradition. Adam, the scion of Creation, breaches the supremely simple and fundamental contract with God, when he fails to overcome his urges and takes a bite from the forbidden fruit: he and Eve are banished from the Garden of Eden and condemned to a life of suffering. Adam's weakness as the underlying reason for this fate of suffering exemplifies the psychological depth of the Bible. Man is easily tempted, enticed precisely by what is forbidden and governed by his curiosity, and, a more complex interpretation would suggest, quickly succumbs to his awakening sexual urges. God is the omnipotent Creator: He created man and bestowed him with a carefree life, with only one, solitary prohibition. When this one rule of the game is broken, God, the judge, sentences Adam and Eve to exile from Paradise and a mortal life of existential distress and pain. Yet the passing of this divine judgment is not a perfunctory process of formality, for the punishment for eating the forbidden fruit 'of the tree of the knowledge of good and evil' was originally set as 'thou shalt not eat of it: for in the day that thou eatest thereof thou shalt *surely die*' (*Genesis* 2:17).[1] When the fateful moment arrives, God settles for what appears to be a mitigation of the preordained death sentence: Adam is condemned to die, but not immediately – he is doomed to a hard and dreary life, but left alive for the time being.

This sentence of expulsion from the Garden of Eden marks the birth of Old Testament theodicy – the explanation for suffering in the world: Man himself is the root of all suffering, for he is responsible for his banishment from the Garden of Eden (and, later on, the murder of Abel). He was saved from immediate death only by the grace of God's

3

compassion for his creatures. This existence of suffering is, indeed, punishment, but it can also be regarded as a gift from God.

Beyond the web of possible interpretations and theological and psychological ramifications entailed by the story of the expulsion, this is a problematic stance, both from the viewpoint of theodicy and in terms of the discussion of compassion. First, this view of the expulsion story leaves us with a pessimistic, fatalistic conclusion: Man's sentencing to a life of suffering, due to his own weakness, has always been and will forever be his fate. There is no hope of challenging this fate or point in trying. And where there is no hope, neither religion nor any kind of social ideology can develop. Second, the solution of expulsion as a type of collective punishment of all humanity seems unsuited to the complexities of human behavior as it unfolds in the rest of Genesis: Do Adam and Eve bear equal responsibility for the expulsion from the Garden of Eden? Cain is clearly a murderer, but what was Abel's sin? Can extenuating circumstances not be applied for certain people? And what if some descendant of Adam were to demonstrate restraint and the ability to uphold the contract with God, where Adam failed?

Third, the God of the first chapters of Genesis is presented as a complex being, riddled with misgivings and reservations. On the one hand, he wields absolute control, authority, and command, yet on the other he displays a considerable amount of fickleness, indecisiveness, and perhaps even compassion:

> And God saw that the wickedness of man [was] great in the earth, and [that] every imagination of the thoughts of his heart [was] only evil continually.
>
> And it repented the Lord that he had made man on the earth, and it grieved him at his heart.
>
> And the Lord said, I will destroy man whom I have created from the face of the earth; both man, and beast, and the creeping thing, and the fowls of the air; for it repenteth me that I have made them.
>
> But Noah found grace in the eyes of the Lord.
>
> *Genesis* 6:5–6:8

The relationship between God and man evolves over the entire course of the biblical narrative: Abraham challenges divine judgment, pleading for compassion for the inhabitants of Sodom and resolutely negotiating with God to ease their harsh sentence. God reacts to Sarah's distress over her barrenness and intervenes in the couple's fertility problems. Abraham obeys the divine order and prepares Isaac for sacrifice, but God intervenes and rescinds the original command, revealing a manipulative aspect to divinity and divine command as a sort of test to be passed, with a reward given for demonstrating faithfulness. Divine judgment varies with the extent to which people obey that judgment, a tendency that evolves throughout the Bible, particularly after Mount Sinai and the setting of the Mosaic Laws, when the rules of obedience and faithfulness become absolutely clear.

As the biblical story progress, additional, more elaborate images quickly begin to appear. The story of Abraham and Sarah, the historic originators of the Judeo-Christian tradition, presents the paradigmatic forging of a certain type of relationship between God and man. Abraham is called upon by God to found a new world order – with a Chosen People, faithfulness to God, covenants with God, burnt offerings – and, in return, the promise of fertility, success, continuity, protection, and political and economic prosperity for Abraham's progeny, the same Chosen People. The medley of images woven into the chronicles of Abraham and Sarah present humanity in a more intricate light than its appearance in the Garden of Eden tale. In the former, people are divided into three distinct groups. The first are the righteous, faithful to God. This is the group that upholds God's covenant with Abraham and who are responsible for the preservation of the continuous link between the People of Israel and God. The second group comprises the waverers, who represent the overwhelming majority of the Israelite Nation. They recognize God and are familiar with the covenant with him, but their weaknesses, urges, and fearfulness consistently prevent them from doing 'right and good in the sight of the Lord' (*Deuteronomy* 6:18). The third group is composed of all those not included in the covenant between man and God. These are the grievous sinners, heretics, and pagans, who refuse to accept the word of God or else are ignorant of it.

The righteous, the first group, are, as a rule, supposed to be rewarded with a good and prosperous life. The difficulty is that, according to Old Testament logic, radical piety, a near impossibility, is the only possibility of becoming a member of this group. Even Moses, the bearer and founder of the Hebrew Law, did not achieve the status of full righteousness. Moses' flaw was in doubting God, and thus the biblical narrator does not let him enter the Promised Land. Moreover, the idea of the righteous only prospering and never suffering is ultimately rejected in the Book of Job.[2]

The third group, the sinners, heretics, and pagans, represents the ultimate enemy, an integral part of the Bible narrative. This group is unique in the punishment it receives: usually a death sentence and no possibility for mercy.

The wavers, the second group, are the most interesting: first, because they represent the majority of people, or at least the majority of the Israelites whose story the Old Testament tells; and second, because his treatment of this group reveals God's compassion, which is manifested in the Bible in two principal ways. The first is in the guise of the possibility of penitence, forgiveness, remorse and mitigation of the divine decree. The Priests are the Nation's intermediaries, pleading for divine mercy by evoking the covenant with Abraham and vowing a change of attitude toward God. The second manifestation of God's compassion is when God responds and acquiesces to individuals' direct appeals to him to acknowledge and identify their pain and to intervene to remedy the situation. This became the dominant expression of God's compassion in the later periods when traditions were being shaped and appears mainly in the form of prayer.[3]

Indeed, God is the Great Merciful One. His compassion is a fundamental aspect of his essence and the basis of humankind's hope, of the possibility for people to make grave errors and yet be saved and win divine benevolence. This compassion flows in one direction: compassion from the Great, the Omnipotent – of God – to the weak, wretched, and idle – human beings. This compassion is conceptually synonymous with mercy: it defines the way the powerful relate to the weak, the omnipotent to the impotent, the healers to the suffering and afflicted – this is divine compassion.

The Old Testament concept of compassion links divine mercy to judgment and justice, both human and divine. Compassion is the prerogative of the judge. Compassion is where pleas for the mercy of the court are heard. For man, compassion is part of what the Bible would deem his flawed system of judgment and justice: King David's love for Absalom led him down the path of forgiveness and blinded him with regard to the good of Kingdom, as he chose to spare his son from death despite Absalom's betrayal of the Kingdom. For God, however, the Supreme Judge, compassion is an intrinsic tool of judgment and constitutes simultaneously the greatest hope of sinners and the protection given to the righteous:

> When morning dawned, the angels urged Lot, saying, 'Up, take your wife and your two daughters who are here, or you will be swept away in the punishment of the city.'

But he hesitated. So the men seized his hand and the hand of his wife and the hands of his two daughters, for the *compassion of the Lord* [was] upon him; and they brought him out, and put him outside the city.

Genesis 19:15–19:16[4]

In addition to mercy for sinners and protection for the righteous, compassion encompasses the notion of absolution:[5] the Children of Israel are most in need of God's compassion precisely when they need to be forgiven for their sins. Under the very simplistic structure of Old Testament logic, all sinners are condemned to death and only divine compassion can mitigate the terrible punishment to a lesser sentence of 'mere' misery. This lays the foundation for the clear connection between absolution and compassion and for the evolution of prayer as a recognized and legitimate means of appealing to God's compassion. The Hebrew concept of *nihem*, which means 'to console' and from which the Hebrew word *nehama*, 'consolation', is derived, represents, in the Old Testament, God's change of mind, his relenting, and, sometimes, his decision to mitigate the punishment he has set:

But let man and beast be covered with sackcloth, and cry mightily to God; yes, let every one turn from his evil way and from the violence that is in his hands. Who can tell if God will turn and relent, and turn away from His fierce anger, so that we may not perish? Then God saw their works, that they turned from their evil way; and God *relented from the disaster that He had said He would bring upon them, and He did not do it.*

But it displeased Jonah exceedingly, and he became angry. So he prayed to the Lord, and said, 'Ah, Lord, was not this what I said when I was still in my country? Therefore I fled previously to Tarshish; for I know that You are a *gracious and merciful God, slow to anger and abundant in loving kindness, One who relents from doing harm.* Therefore now, O Lord, please take my life from me, for it is better for me to die than to live!'

Then the Lord said, 'Is it right for you to be angry?'

Jonah 3:8–4:3[6]

In the majority of cases in the Old Testament narrative, divine compassion is revealed in its full splendor on the background of a concrete threat of impending death: either an external threat is posed by heretics, enemies, or pagans (Assyrians, Babylonians, Philistines) and, hearing the pleas of the Children of Israel, God acknowledges their apprehensions, acquiesces, and comes to their avail, or alternatively, divine judgment mandates mortal punishment for sinners, but God, in his goodness and compassion and for reasons known only to him, pardons the wrongdoer (usually the Nation) and spares him from death. However, it is important to note the two sources from where divine compassion derives its force. The one source of legitimacy is the general rigidity of divine law, which does not allow any deviation from its dictates: alongside his 'gracious and merciful' nature, God, who is 'slow to anger and abundant in loving kindness', is first and foremost a stern judge, abounding in wrath, who does not balk at meting out harsh punishment:

> Let us lift up our heart with [our] hands unto God in the heavens. We have transgressed and have rebelled: thou hast not pardoned. Thou has covered with anger, and persecuted us: thou has slain, thou hast not pitied.
>
> *Lamentations* 3:41–3:43

The second source of the great force of divine compassion is related to the problem of theodicy noted above. The Old Testament narrator does not hide the empiric contradiction of the biblical logic of punishment-and-reward: Life is supposed to proceed according to a simple system of 'the righteous prosper and the wicked suffer', and in both the text and the subtext there is the explicit promise that '[t]he Lord [is] nigh unto all of them that call upon him, to all that call him in truth. He will fulfil the desire of them that fear him: he also will hear their cry, and will save them' (*Psalms* 145:18–145:19). But in practice, this is not the face of things, for indeed

> [t]here is a vanity which is done upon the earth; that there be just [men], unto whom it happeneth according to the work of the wicked; again, there be wicked [men], to whom it happeneth according to the work of the righteous: I said that this also [is] vanity.
>
> *Ecclesiastes* 8:14

The pinnacle of the incongruity between the punishment-and-reward structure and the virtue of righteousness is, of course, the case of Job, who is subject to terrible decrees, due to no fault on his part and for no justifiable, logical reason. Indeed, Job's trials and tribulations are a sort of test that God imposes on him in a compassionless wager with Satan. We see that divine compassion is not guaranteed to the righteous, despite the fact that at the beginning of the tractate, it does, indeed, seem to be. Just as God's great wrath and divine punishment appear at random, capriciously and inexplicably, so too does divine compassion: it is not perpetually present, and it is subject to considerations far beyond human comprehension. Divine compassion is part of the possible solution to the problem of theodicy, but it remains a mere possibility, since the Bible does not offer a full solution to the problem.

Another completely different aspect of compassion in the Old Testament appears in the context of social and familial relations. The set of divine dictates that are manifested in the commandments (which constitute the biblical Hebrew Law) requires the Children of Israel to care for the weak, orphaned, widowed, slaves, and strangers and, ultimately, the poor and impoverished in general. The divine command is particularly strong in this context, because it includes two themes that do not appear in other social laws: the first, the implied consideration of the mental state of society's weak, as those who suffer torture at the hands of others; the second, God's unique willingness to act as the direct protector of orphans and widows. In fact, only with regard to the latter group does God make any explicit commitment to always be heedful of their distress. It is interesting to note that there is a sort of mixed divine response to distress: God first attends to the punishment of the victimizer and only afterwards does any possibility of compassion for the victim arise.

> Ye shall not afflict any widow, or fatherless child. If thou afflict them in any wise, and they cry at all unto me, I will surely hear their cry; And my wrath shall wax hot, and I will kill you with the sword; and your wives shall be widows, and your children fatherless.
>
> *Exodus 22:22–22:24*

And He continues:

> If thou lend money to [any of] my people [that is] poor by thee, thou shalt not be to him as an usurer, neither shalt thou lay upon him usury. If thou at all take thy neighbour's raiment to pledge, thou shalt deliver it unto him by that the sun goeth down: For that [is] his covering only, it [is] raiment for his skin: wherein shall he sleep? and it shall come to pass, when he crieth unto me, that I will hear; for I [am] gracious.
>
> *Exodus 22:25–22:27*

God in fact commands the Children of Israel to demonstrate a type of compassionate activism toward anyone who has been dealt a cruel fate, unveiling the possibility of *human* compassion. This possibility has far-reaching implications, from both a theological perspective and the perspective of theodicy. For example, it can be understood from this command that the poor and suffering are not at all sinners and are entitled to social support – raising yet again the question of the reason for suffering, particularly when we consider that God undertook to always be attentive to this group's cries of distress. Though this issue is beyond the scope of the present discussion of compassion, what is noteworthy is the fact that the biblical story brings to light the possibility of human compassion of a *formal* nature: it is a *form* of behavior, an act that one is obliged to perform, unconnected to any emotion or empathy or to any acknowledgement of the suffering of another. Even if we despise the person suffering, we are still obliged to come to her aid. Compassion as a prerogative is the exclusive domain of God; human beings, in contrast, are obligated to perform the practical actions that are the consequence of divine compassion and, as such, require no explanation.[7]

Here the question arises as to whether compassion, or mercy, is, indeed, the exclusive domain of God or, rather, does the biblical narrator acknowledge the presence and power of compassion as a basic human way of relating to others. The answer to this question is not a simple one. On the one hand, the Bible acknowledges that, as a rule, in human relations, especially familial relations, there is a kind of emotional interaction whereby one person responds to the pain and suffering of another. On the other hand, in almost every instance in which a biblical hero is expected to demonstrate a degree of humanity and mercy, the story requires of him or her to overcome any sense of compassion and mercy and to act in accordance with God's command or the dictates of society or logic. There is no question that compassion exists, but in the human sphere, unlike the divine sphere, it is a sign of weakness, submission, yielding – all of which are forbidden by the biblical narrator. The most famous example is the sacrificial offering of Isaac by Abraham. Despite the fact that no mention is made of Abraham's emotions in the theoretical text, it is undeniably clear that the father is gripped by great apprehension and raging emotions. It is in fact the reader's awareness of the possible emotional storm engulfing the father about to put his son to death that makes the story of the offering of Isaac so dramatic, with this drama reaching its climax when Abraham is required to overcome his emotions and kill his son. What is remarkable is that this episode highlights the presence of compassion not in the biblical protagonist, but in the reader of the story. This compassion exists in the subtext, in the external interaction between the story and its audience, and it is what gives the story its vitality.

One of the ways in which the relationship between God and the People of Israel is presented is by analogy to the father–son relationship. Despite the fact that this is not a dominant motif and, in many respects, is very problematic theologically,[8] it nonetheless contributes to the overall image of a compassionate God. The father–son motif begins in *Exodus*: 'Thus saith the Lord, Israel [is] my son, [even] my firstborn: And I say unto thee, Let my son go, that he may serve me: and if thou refuse to let him go, behold, I will slay thy son, [even] thy firstborn' (*Exodus* 4:22–4:23). The imagery continues and develops through the text, emphasizing the Children of Israel as God's Chosen People: 'Ye [are] the children of the Lord your God...the Lord hath chosen thee to be a peculiar people unto himself, above all the nations that [are] upon the earth' (*Deuteronomy* 14:1–14:2). It stresses the filial duty to obey one's father ('Let my son go, that he may serve me', *Exodus* 4:23) and laments the rebelliousness of sons and their failure to live up to paternal expectations ('I have nourished and brought up children, and they have rebelled against me', *Isaiah* 1:2).[9] But the Prophet Malachi makes most significant use of the imagery: 'A son honoureth [his] father, and a servant his master: if then I [be] a father, where [is] mine honour?' (*Malachi* 1:6). And after being disappointed in his demand for honor (that is, obedience to his commands) from his son, the father's response is, '[A]nd I will spare them, as a man spareth his own son that serveth him' (*Malachi* 3:17).

The father–son imagery in the context of God's relations with the People of Israel primarily stresses God's historic commitment to the Nation and its duty to fulfill his commandments. This imagery does not, however, sidestep the response to disobedience of the commandments and, in this context, stresses God's compassion in relation to his 'sons': the father's compassion is directed at his son, who is sometimes a good son, that is serves the Lord, as we see in *Malachi*, and sometimes a wayward son, with the combination of sinner and son enabling God to give expression to his compassion.[10]

Quite distinct from God's paternal compassion for his nation is the human bond between parent and child in the biblical stories. The latter paints a very gloomy picture of the message conveyed by the biblical story. Parents in the Bible are required to conquer their emotions and put their children to death whenever there is a clash between emotion (which represents weakness) and logic (which represents the law).

The Offering of Isaac: Abraham is commanded to sacrifice his son as a burnt offering. He follows God's command to the letter, showing no trace of the excellent bargaining skills he demonstrated when pleading for the people of Sodom and Gomorrah. Without questioning God's will, he leads Isaac to the mountain, overcomes his (assumed) emotions, and only divine intervention (compassionate or manipulative, depending on the interpretation) saves Isaac's life.

Jephthah's Daughter (Judges 11:30–11:40): Jephthah, setting out for the battlefield, vows that if God delivers the children of Ammon into his hands, as a sign of gratitude he will offer as sacrifice the first person who comes forth from his house to greet him upon his return from victory. And indeed the first to come forth is his only daughter, greeting him 'with timbrels and dances'. Jephthah's grief is devastating ('when he saw her . . . he rent his clothes, and said, Alas, my daughter! thou hast brought me very low', *Judges* 11:35). But despite his love for his daughter and aided by her, he resists his powerful emotions, and his daughter, loyal to him, sacrifices herself so that Jephthah will not break his vow to God.

David and Absalom (2 Samuel 15–17): David finds himself at war with his son Absalom, who has rebelled against the Kingdom. Despite his deep love for his son, David finds himself his own son's enemy, something he did not choose. Absalom had fled in the past when he killed Amnon, who had raped Absalom's sister Tamar. But David forgave him and welcomed him back into the fold. This time, too, David is willing to endure the threat to himself and the entire Kingdom as long as his beloved son is spared from harm. The tragedy culminates when Joab, David's Minister of War, disobeys the King's order and kills Absalom. Here, Joab represents the voice of reason and the law, which triumph over David's paternal sentimentality.

These three examples shed light on the biblical approach to human compassion and empathy: in a clash between empathy and compassion and the dictates of a divine command, the law prevails over emotion. The secret to the biblical hero's strength lies precisely in his ability to overcome his feelings and obey the divine mandate (both David and Jephthah need external help to succeed at this: Jephthah from his daughter and David from Joab). Moreover, the three stories represent the three biblical contexts in which people are required to discard compassion, when they are expected to put aside even parental sentiment and compassion, for human compassion is no more than an expression of the basic weakness of humanity. The first context is the explicit requirement to fulfill a direct divine command that is part of an act of epiphany – as was experienced by Abraham – regardless of the contents of the command. The second context is the requirement to uphold an oath made to God – similar to Jephthah's vow – with the oath taking precedence over fatherhood. Even though the vow was made of Jephthah's own initiative, without any direct request from God, it was an explicit pledge made by the man to God. The third context, perhaps the least rigid, is represented by the dilemma faced by David: Is he, first and foremost, a father or king? The biblical answer to David's agonizing is unequivocal: Absalom betrayed the kingdom and therefore must die. Even David is required to act against what his emotions would dictate.

There are also instances in the Bible where even though human compassion does not clash with a divine command or the law, it takes at least a backseat to reason. Two of the more prominent examples of such instances also arise in the framework of familial relations.

Joseph and His Brothers (Genesis 42–44): Joseph is Egypt's Governor of Land. His brothers appear before him, but do not recognize him. They feel great emotional distress and shame when Joseph tells them of their imminent meeting with their brother Joseph, whom the brothers think they murdered. Witnessing his brothers' distress arouses Joseph's sense of mercy, especially after seeing his youngest brother Benjamin, and he goes to his chamber to weep. 'Now his heart yearned for his brother; so Joseph made haste and sought somewhere to weep. And he went into his chamber and wept there. Then he washed his face and came out; and he restrained himself...' *(Genesis 43:30–43:31)*.[11] When Joseph returns to his brothers, he continues through with his original plan. Thus, even when compassion poses no threat to the fulfillment of an oath or the law, the Bible still prefers the execution of the rational course of action, rather than its unraveling under the emotional pressure of human compassion. Only at a later stage, after his plan has been carried out, does the tale allow Joseph and his brothers to give vent to their intense emotions *(Genesis 45)*.

Solomon's Judgment (1 Kings 3): In one of the most familiar biblical tales, Solomon is required to determine which of two women is the mother of a baby and orders that the baby be divided into two. The woman who immediately gives expression to her emotions and declares her willingness to relinquish her claim to the baby as long as he is not killed is proclaimed the true mother by Solomon. In this story, maternal emotion is granted full legitimacy. It does not clash with the law; on the contrary, it is precisely Solomon's insight into the structure of maternal emotion that enables him to ensure that justice is administered. However, a closer reading of the tale shows that there is no actual deviation from the general paradigm: one means of upholding justice is to recognize human weakness, and maternal compassion is just one such human weakness, which is exploited by Solomon, albeit for a worthy cause.

Thus, it appears that two distinct modes of compassionate behavior emerge in the biblical narrative. The one is God's forgiving, paternalistic attitude toward human weakness, especially that of the People of Israel. This divine compassion is the all-important glimmer of light in the relations between God and humankind, for it offers perpetual hope of salvation or leniency after sinning. In contrast, we find human compassion – an emotion people feel for a friend, relative, or child in distress or facing disaster. This latter compassion is a type of human weakness that should be conquered since it poses a threat to the fulfillment of divine commands and laws, as well as earthly sovereign laws. Yet this human weakness proves also to be extremely beneficial to the Israelites – the compassion of Pharaoh's daughter enabled the Nation's redemption and exodus from Egypt. Her decision to break the law of the land and save the baby Moses, whom she found floating in the ark of bulrushes, wrought a terrible catastrophe upon her own nation and culture (again, the recurring theme of the danger inherent in succumbing to compassion), but from the perspective of Jewish history, this human compassion was the key to a new stage for the Hebrew Nation, climaxing finally and ultimately at Mount Sinai. Thus we see that human compassion – paternal, maternal – is a recognized and even understandable phenomenon in the Bible. But it is also the two-edged sword of biblical history, for it is a perilous weakness that is likely to bring disaster upon the Kingdom.

Finally, we see that the ultimate source of divine compassion is the socialist commandments in the Bible: those commandments requiring the performance of a variety of acts, regardless of people's wants or inclinations. As the biblical narrative develops, a pedagogic aspect to these commandments emerges. Since these commandments originate in divine compassion, their mere fulfillment can be assumed to produce a transformation in the person fulfilling them and lead her to feel, understand, and, perhaps, in some way participate in divine compassion.

* * *

The two traditions that evolved on the background of the biblical narrative in its entirety, Judaism and Christianity, construe the text in completely different ways, as well as its status vis-à-vis the faithful and its central themes, such as divine compassion. From the perspective of Judaism, the text embodies detailed and specific divine instruction for the faithful as to the correct way of life. And since there is a need to supplement the biblical instructions so that they are suited to life in all its facets and social complexity, expansions on the divine commandments have appeared throughout Jewish history: beginning with the Oral *Torah*,[12] which supplemented the Written *Torah* given at Mount Sinai and was passed down to the Rabbis by oral tradition and later formulated as the *Mishnah*[13] in the third century BCE; and culminating with the *Tosefta*[14] and Babylonian *Talmud* and Jerusalem *Talmud*,[15] formulated from the fourth century to the ninth century BCE. These supplements represent the Jewish search for the will of God and the process of consolidating a tradition of detailed textual and legalistic interpretation that gives presence to the divine decrees in every detail of day-to-day life. The Jewish emphasis on the biblical text as the Book of Laws had ramifications for the way in which different expressions in the biblical story, such as compassion, were manifested in the later traditions. For example, for the Jewish believer, the most important and concrete manifestation of divinity is the law itself. In Judaism, the law's status can be equated to that of Jesus in Christianity. A life conducted in accordance with the divine laws – that is, a life of obeying the commandments – is an expression of the will of God in the truest form. Thus, the commandments to practise benevolence and charity, to care for orphans and widows, to console mourners, and to visit the sick are the worldly manifestations of divine compassion. The legalistic dimension to the Jewish tradition (that is, the strict requirement to follow all the commandments to the letter) and the scrutiny of all behavior through the legalist prism are completed by the implicit promise that in the very performance of all the required acts a person discharges his or her duty; that is, ensures the presence of divine compassion in human society.

It seems that, in early Jewish tradition, the focus on obeying the social commandments was external in regard and did not attribute great significance to the internal, emotional, and intentional aspects to follow them. Despite the importance of the commandment 'Love thy neighbor as thyself', the operative connotation given to the expression in present times (whose source is Christian tradition) was almost totally lacking in the early Jewish interpretation (until the period of the *Talmud*). The commandment was construed as calling for a type of action and social attitude, not an emotional response. The focus on intention and emotion appeared only at a much later stage, in fact crystallizing in the seventeenth century in the framework of the Jewish *hassidic* tradition.[16]

But this notwithstanding, it is important to understand that alongside the formal-rational aspect, Jewish law embraces and develops an extremely impressive narrative of compassion, which begins with the argument between Abraham and God in *Genesis*:

> Peradventure there be fifty righteous within the city: wilt thou also destroy and not spare the place for the fifty righteous that [are] therein? That be far from thee to do after this manner, to slay the righteous with the wicked: and that the righteous should be as the wicked, that be far from thee: Shall not the Judge of all the earth do right?
>
> *Genesis* 18:24–18:25

Abraham appeals to God to refrain from punishing the sinners in order to prevent the punishment of the innocent – and remarkably, God is swayed! At least on the face of things, we encounter here a deity who operates according to a code of ethics, who can be persuaded by reason that derives from that same code and that binds him. This ethical principle became one of the cornerstones of Jewish law (and, in its footsteps, modern law), appearing in different forms in the Book of Laws and in *talmudic* interpretation. But the principle does not relate only to favoring the innocent – it also requires that the trial be conducted with mercy and grace: 'He loveth righteousness and judgment: the earth is full of the goodness of the Lord' (*Psalms* 33:5). 'I [am] the Lord which exercise lovingkindness, judgment, and righteousness, in the earth' (*Jeremiah* 9:24). This is conveyed through the linking of mercy and grace with love, which originates in the biblical text itself: 'I remember thee, the kindness of thy youth, the love of thine espousals' (*Jeremiah* 2:2). This association is impressive in light of the fact that the virtues of mercy and justice are not necessarily commensurate with the legalistic bias toward exhausting all legal proceedings – indeed, at times, they even work against this inclination – with the association adding a tinge of compassion to the formalist biblical messages. The combination of the principle of favoring the innocent and administering justice with mercy, grace, and, perhaps, love with the socialist commandments produces a type of compassionate and protective approach that necessitates considering the interests of society's vulnerable and weak, and limits the authorities' ability to act against those interests. This is a legislative principle whose essence is in the protection it provides: uniform, equal protection with all the advantages of legalism – objectivity and equality before the law and autonomy from the whims and capriciousness of the ruler and establishment.[17]

The supplementary aspect to the Jewish laws set in the *halakhic* literature[18] (and, prior to that, in the *Midrash*[19]) is that it adds the practical, pragmatic component of caring for the poor and weak, expressed in the concepts of charity and benevolence. Charity and benevolence emerge from the rabbinic literature as Jewish praxis: caring for orphans, visiting the sick, dowering brides, burying the dead, consoling mourners, and giving to the poor. There is serious debate in the *Talmud* and modern Jewish exegesis over the differences between charity and benevolence (which is preferable, which takes priority, if there is really any difference between the two), but wide consensus over the fact that giving is a commandment to be obeyed absent any intention whatsoever of receiving something in return. Both are evidence of the centrality of the social aspect to the consolidation of the Jewish tradition. Insofar as compassion is concerned, on the one hand, Jewish law and custom can be regarded as representing formal compassion, that is, the acknowledgement of the objective social distress of human beings and the commitment to alleviate that distress. On the other hand, there is an anti-compassionate aspect to the same law in the fact that the very adherence to the law curbs empathy and emotional involvement. First, the legal custom provides an *a priori* definition of distress and does not leave any opening for someone who is in pain and suffering but does not meet the 'objective' criteria set by charity and benevolence. Second, the law itself already attends to justice and compassion, thereby effectively releasing the individual from that burden.

The theoretical-religious development of Christianity took a different course from Jewish tradition. I will address this development by way of two biblical concepts whose evolution over the course of the New Testament narrative endowed them with new meaning and status: the idea of love and the idea of divinity, both of which are closely linked to compassion.

Despite the fact that the early Christians regarded themselves as Jews and followers of the Jewish traditions and that the Hebrew Bible was accepted by the nascent Christian Church as holy scripture,[20] the Old Testament did not constitute the textual underpinning of the new religion. The New Testament makes almost no direct reference to the Hebrew Bible. Jesus is portrayed in the New Testament as imbuing certain commandments with new meaning (*Mark* 2:23–2:28, 3:1–3:6) and, at times, rejecting or dismissing others.[21] The idea of using the Hebrew Bible as binding law was in effect rejected by the New Testament itself, based on the assumption that the appearance of Jesus as Messiah changed the rules of the game. The dramatic change, in terms of the present discussion, appears in the reduction proffered by Paul in his *Epistle to the Romans*: only love is necessary to fulfill God's law.

Owe no man anything, but to love one another for he that loveth another hath fulfilled the law. For this, Thou shalt not commit adultery, Thou shalt not kill, Thou shalt not steal, Thou shalt not bear false witness, Thou shalt not covet; and if [there be] any other commandment, it is briefly comprehended in this saying, namely, Thou shalt love thy neighbour as thyself. Love worketh no ill to his neighbour: therefore love [is] the fulfilling of the law.

Romans 13:8–13:10

Thus, in Christianity, the Jewish quest for God's precise intention ended with Jesus' appearance. The Word of God is embodied in the Messiah, and this embodiment enabled the cessation of both the precise, focused analysis of the commandments, and the expansion of the commandments to all areas of life of the community of the faithful. Instead, the Ten Commandments are reduced to 'Love thy neighbor' (a reduction that later appears in Jewish exegesis), one of the most important distinguishing features of the evolving Christian identity and what came to be the foundation of Christianity's general self-image as a religion of compassion.

But the Christian innovation of love (agape) as the central message of the New Testament cannot be dismissed as mere reductionism. The very notion of love undergoes radical change in the Christian Bible, acquiring new contours, even when Jesus seems merely to be quoting the original biblical source:

Master, which [is] the great commandment in the law? Jesus said unto him, Thou shalt love the Lord thy God with all thy heart, and with all thy soul, and with all thy mind. This is the first and great commandment. And the second [is] like unto it, Thou shalt love thy neighbour as thyself.

Matthew 22:36–22:39

The first part of Jesus' answer in this passage is a reference to Deuteronomy: 'And thou shalt love the Lord thy God with all thine heart, and with all thy soul and with all thy might' (Deuteronomy 6:5).[22] The source of the second part is an earlier, no less 'famous' appearance of love in the Bible: 'Thou shalt not avenge, nor bear any grudge against the children of thy people, but thou shalt love thy neighbour as thyself: I [am] the Lord' (Leviticus 19:18). But Jesus in effect proposes three innovations vis-à-vis the love commandments in the Bible. First, the New Testament text promises the faithful that the Kingdom of Heaven is imminent ('And as ye go, preach, saying, The Kingdom of Heaven is at hand', Matthew 10:7) and presumes that this imminence is expressed in Jesus and in the Incarnation, the demonstration of God's boundless love for all people. That is to say, the text extends the concept of divine compassion to encompass the idea of divine love. Jesus, the manifestation of earthly divinity, is also the manifestation of divine love of man. Love is not merely another exclusive command that people must follow in relation to God, but, rather, it is an attribute of divinity itself, as expressed in the persona, actions, and the Incarnation of Jesus.

Second, in the above passage from Matthew, Jesus depicts a close bond between love of man and love of God. He links the two and suggests that they be understood as similar in nature; indeed, certain passages in the New Testament portray an even derivative connection between the two (1 John 3:17, 4:20). Yet if we understand the biblical concepts of love only in their practical sense, that is, that love is the indicator of a certain type of behavior, then there can be no resemblance between love of God, which is expressed in rituals and fulfilling the commandments, and brotherly love, which, in its Old Testament sense, is refraining from punishing, avenging, and coveting. It is in the mental-experiential sphere that a resemblance between the two types of love can emerge. In creating a link between love of God and brotherly love, the New Testament text gives love a new sense: as the indicator of a psychological state, of an emotion, not of behavior. Thus, even when the behavior diverges, a similarity in feeling can be identified.

Third, whereas the commandment to love God reappears in the New Testament almost to the letter (excluding what seems to be a printing or transcription error), the commandment to love one's neighbor seems to be taken out of its Old Testament context. The original passage explicitly refers to Israelites refraining from vengefulness or bearing a grudge toward other Israelites as part of the social relations within the community. No mention is made of a more general love for all creatures. Yet when Jesus is asked who the neighbor that we must love is, he answers that it is the person who has been harmed, robbed, stripped of all his clothes, and abandoned in his loneliness. Jesus recounts how the Priest and Levite passed by such a person and recoiled, 'but a certain Samaritan, as he journeyed, came where he was: and when he saw him, he had compassion [on him]' (*Luke* 10:33). In other words, the New Testament notion of brotherly love presented in the image of Jesus has a universal quality; its essence extends beyond the Israelite community to the injured and suffering. Love is the perception of another's distress and action to assist that person: in other words, love is compassion.

But the New Testament goes even further in expanding the Old Testament notion of love. The concept appears in two other novel forms, neither of which is an interpretation of Old Testament conceptions and both of which are prominent in the Christian narrative.

The first form appears in Jesus' defiant challenge of the biblical wrath toward the enemies of the Israelites. In the famous passage from *Matthew*, Jesus propounds, 'Ye have heard that it hath been said, Thou shalt love thy neighbour, and hate thine enemy. But I say unto you, Love your enemies, bless them that curse you, do good to them that hate you, and pray for them which despitefully use you, and persecute you' (*Matthew* 5:43–5:44). This passage, like others from this key chapter, presents a loose interpretation of an Old Testament passage (nowhere in it is commanded to 'hate thine enemy'), followed by Jesus' call to extend the scope of love: there is nothing exceptional in loving one's friend, even the tax collectors and gentiles do that – the real value of love emerges when it transpires in non-reciprocal circumstances. This passage, in conjunction with Jesus' counsel that 'whosoever shall smite thee on thy cheek, turn to him the other also' (*Matthew* 5:39), produces one of the great myths of Christian thought: that Christian faith means tolerance, forgiveness, and, most particularly, the absence of wrath and anger, both toward people who 'smite' you and those who appear to be your enemy; that Christian love is expressed in relating to another precisely when that person does not reciprocate that love and has the additional sense of a passive endurance of pain, a willingness to accept, forgive, and devote oneself. This myth is reinforced by Jesus' powerful claim that he does not appeal to the righteous but, rather, to the sinners (*Matthew* 9:13). In response to the claim made by his foes, the Pharisee priests and elders, that he is the friend of tax collectors and sinners, Jesus declares, 'Verily I say unto you, That the publicans [tax collectors] and the harlots go into the kingdom of God before you' (*Matthew* 21:31).[23] Jesus' explicit request is to love one's enemies and sinners without expecting that this will make them righteous.

The second innovation, of particular relevance in our context, appears in the guise of a third type of love, one that deviates from love of God and brotherly love: 'A new commandment I give unto you, That ye love one another; as I have loved you, that ye also love one another' (*John* 13:34).[24] This seemingly simple request in fact encompasses at least three elements that eventually became integral parts of the Christian concept of love–compassion: First, the very assertion that this is a new commandment makes it patently clear that the original Old Testament commandment to love one's neighbor is not sufficient. From the Christian perspective, the primary flaw in the original commandment lies in the fact that brotherly love is based on self-love: love thy neighbor as *thyself*. Indeed, it can be understood as instructing people to love themselves, so that they will be able to love others as well. The new commandment does not entail such self-love: you must love your neighbor in a way that is analogous to 'my' love for you, independent of how you relate to yourself. Second, the construction of God's love for man in Christian tradition is derived from John's conception of the death of Jesus as an act of sacrifice made out of love and for the purpose of man's salvation (*John* 3:15–3:17). Accordingly, under this understanding, the crucifixion is the strongest and most tangible expression of love, and the analogy drawn between brotherly love and Jesus' love implies a willingness for total self-sacrifice for the good of others. Third, since Jesus is conceived of as divine in nature in mainstream Christian tradition, that is, as intrinsic to the concept of divinity, the analogy in fact highlights divine love as the model for human relations. This conception of divine love is also a departure from the Old Testament (and Jewish) paradigm of God as a passive father who is not called upon to do anything but uphold his historic commitment to the Nation of Israel and to absolve his wayward children here and there. In Christian tradition we see a very active fatherhood, manifested in the explicit divine intervention in the form of Jesus for man's salvation. Moreover, the salvation narrative redefines the biblical concept of pain and distress as well: pain and distress in Christianity are not only represented by poverty, widowhood, and orphanhood but also by the absence of the divine gospel, forgiveness, and the chance to enter the Kingdom of Heaven. Thus, Christian love, which is, in fact, tantamount to compassion, means the possibility of relief from spiritual distress or, in other words, salvation.

The concept of agape was constructed from this array of new meanings that Christianity infused into the Old Testament concept of love by means of the persona of Jesus and from the great assortment of inter-pretations and myths regarding this persona. As we have seen, the concept of compassion and the concept of Christian love overlap are in fact almost identical: from the Christian perspective, any perception of another person's pain and any act to alleviate, prevent, and so forth, that suffering are encompassed in agape. However, it can be argued that the concept of Christian love is broader than the concept of compassion, mainly because it incorporates meanings and references that the narrow concept of compassion does not include. In other words, compassion is, indeed, evidence of the presence of love, but not vice versa. Thus, for example, love is an emotion that can emerge in moments of happiness and spiritual awakening and not necessarily in times of pain; and divine love can be claimed to constitute the primary and central basis for every form of love, including the joyful love one feels for one's friends. These possibilities show that compassion is not a two-way street: God relates to man with love and compassion, but man relates to God with a different love – it includes wonder and marvel, awe and reverence, admiration and veneration, and so on. Here we see again the analogy to the parent–child relationship: The parent's love for her child encompasses compassion in the sense of acknowledging the child's distress, identifying and bearing its pain and suffering. The child, in turn, loves the parent in a different sense, one that, according to this logic, also is based on numinous relations. The unidirectional working of compassion extends also to more socio-economic relations: compassionate people are distinguished from those for whom compassion is felt. The Good Samaritan is a compassionate person, whereas the person who is robbed is the object of compassion. Catholic theology has been required on more than one occasion to decide on the matter of which is preferable from the perspective of faith: to be a victim (and resemble Jesus in his divine sense) or to be the person who feels compassion for the victim (and resemble Jesus in his human sense).

A feature of the history of the evolution of Christianity, especially Catholicism, is the appropriation of the role of the compassionate person by the Church establishment. For example, in a variety of ways, the Church took upon itself the role of the Good Samaritan and even constructed ceremonial, psychological, and pragmatic procedures for responding to human distress and for channeling that distress to the

Church. Alternatively, an idealization and mythologizing of the persona of the compassionate person evolved in Christianity, with its ultimate expression in the granting of official status of sainthood to people whose work represents the ideal of Jesus' compassion.

A firm textual basis to the linking of the concepts of love and compassion could be found in the Christian Holy Scriptures long before it evolved in the scholarly theological discussions of these concepts. Paul's assertion in the *First Epistle to the Corinthians* sets the groundwork for equating the two:

> And now abideth faith, hope, and charity, these three:
> but the greatest of these [is] charity
>
> 1 *Corinthians* 13:13

If the most important commandment in the Bible is love and the most important value in Christian doctrine is charity, then love is synonymous with charity or at least charity is the most significant expression of love. The substituting of the concept of love with the concept of charity signifies a clear evolution of the concept in Christian thought. When this substitution is considered in conjunction with the tale of the Good Samaritan, a vibrant and clear image of love in the sense of relating to the distress of others emerges. And to this image, we can add Jesus' famous promise, which specifies the practical aspects of charity, categorized in medieval theology as 'Works of Mercy':

> Come, ye blessed of my Father, inherit the kingdom prepared for you from the foundation of the world:
>
> For I was an hungred, and ye gave me meat: I was thirsty, and ye gave me drink: I was a stranger, and ye took me in:
>
> Naked, and ye clothed me: I was sick, and ye visited me: I was in prison, and ye came unto me.
>
> *Matthew* 25:34–25:36

And the promise was accompanied by a rebuke:

> Depart from me, ye cursed, into everlasting fire, prepared for the devil and his angels:
>
> For I was an hungred, and ye gave me no meat: I was thirsty, and ye gave me no drink:

I was a stranger, and ye took me not in: naked, and ye clothed me
not: sick, and in prison, and ye visited me not.

Matthew 25:41–25:43

This explicit translation of feeling into praxis formed the basis for the
development of the Christian social aid system and, specifically, of the
Catholic institutionalized arrangement of charity. It is important to
recall that despite the fact that the formulation as it appears in the
New Testament supposedly relates to only the pragmatic aspects of the
act of charity or mercy, already in the text itself, when the disciples
ask why they are accused of failing to render assistance, for never has
such a thing occurred, Jesus explains that the physical distress he
mentioned is nothing more than an analogy for true spiritual distress;
for hunger, thirst, the lack of clothing, and so on, occur in the soul
(*Matthew* 25:44–25:46). In accordance with these understandings, the
Catholic tradition distinguishes between corporal works of mercy
(feeding the hungry, giving water to the thirsty, clothing the naked,
harboring the refugeless, ransoming the captive, burying the dead)
and spiritual works of mercy (instructing the ignorant, counseling the
doubtful, admonishing the sinners, suffering wrongs patiently, forgiving
offences willingly, comforting the afflicted, praying for the living and
deceased).

*   *   *

This chapter has shown that part of Jesus' revolution, or reform, as it
appears in the Gospels is manifested in the expansion of the conception
of the compassionate deity from its limited sense (at times) of forgiveness
or relenting to a sense of a more actively 'loving' God, with its accompanying possibility of spiritual redemption. And since the realization of
this possibility, under the Christian paradigm, is embodied in Jesus and
since Jesus represents the corporeal materialization of divinity, it would
perhaps be reasonable to expect that Christian logic would entail
understanding compassion as a human quality rather than a divine
one. Yet such a revolutionary conceptual switch did not transpire in
Christian thought. As I will claim in the next chapter, the 'relegation' of
compassion to the worldly sphere, to the concrete reality of human life,
in fact highlighted the divine nature of compassion and hindered any
possibility of understanding it as a natural and simple human quality.

2
Human Divinity

Against the background of the Old Testament's lack of unambiguousness regarding the divine nature of compassion and the narrative's latent call to surmount human compassion and its dangers, the Judeo-Christian traditions of the post-biblical period weave a more complex and intricate picture. It may well have been the dramatic appearance of Jesus, the story of his crucifixion, the debates over his divinity, and the persecution of Christians in the first few centuries of the Common Era that laid the groundwork for the search for a tangible and concrete manifestation of compassion in human existence. Both in Christianity and in Judaism, figures began to appear, whose lives and actions embodied compassion, endowing them with the special status of good, pure people, and, later on, saints. In Christianity, these were people directly connected to Jesus – the apostles, the martyrs, and, especially, Mary, who, in the evolving world of Christian imagery, received the unofficial status of representative of all-embracing, unconditional, all-forgiving maternal compassion.

In Judaism, as well, traditions began to surface relating to compassion as a positive and definitive quality of key figures in the culture (Hillel the Elder, for example, whose historical persona was constructed analogously to Jesus' compassionate persona[1]). One of the most interesting such traditions was built on the story of the matriarch Rachel from the *Great Commentary on Lamentations*.[2] The *Commentary* tells of God's great grief over the destruction of the Temple and what he regards as the breaking of the covenant with the People of Israel; in his great anguish and fury, he decides to sever the tie with the Nation. Appearing before God are Judaism's greatest figures and patriarchs, who try to convince him to relent in his anger. Abraham, Isaac, Jacob, and Moses all expound on their many great acts and unwavering faithfulness, but God is unmoved. Then, in the middle of Moses' placating speech, Rachel interjects and begins to tell her own tale, a tale of compassion. She tells of her passionate love for Jacob and of the signals that they set so that he would be able to identify her at the wedding altar and not be duped by her father, who intended to swap Rachel's older sister Leah for her and marry Leah to Jacob instead. But Rachel, who could not bear to witness her sister's pain, was flooded with compassion and decided to sacrifice herself and her love for her sister's sake. Her self-sacrifice reached its peak when she hid beneath the bed on which Leah and Jacob lay and conversed with Jacob so that he would hear her voice and not realize the deceit. According to the *Commentary* story, Rachel's compassion and self-sacrifice vanquished God's rage, and he decided to deliver the Nation from its plight.

Thus, human compassion prevailed over the primary virtues presented by the Hebrew patriarchs and became an element in the paradigm of female-maternal emotion, which, at its height, is translated as the 'maternity' that saves the entire Nation. The story in the *Lamentations Commentary* highlights the sharp cleavage between human compassion and divine compassion, as well as illustrating how human compassion can precede, both logically and chronologically, divine compassion and even be its trigger, as Rachel's compassion triggered God's compassion toward the People of Israel. This is the unique aspect to the story, since it bears the latent claim (which has no parallel in the Christian narrative, for example) that human compassion has an independent – legitimate and powerful – existence that is not necessarily the product of divine compassion. Yet, nonetheless, the compassion described by Rachel is of didactic value only because it leads to *divine* salvation. From the story, it is not at all clear what the status of this compassion is in relation to human-social life, for example, or whether it can influence the legal system, which is subject to the biblical commands.[3]

The compassionate personas in Christian (primarily Catholic) tradition and the attribution of holiness to their works of compassion usually did not represent the emergence of new images of distinctly human compassion, with Jesus the primary example of this. Indeed, the central theological interest was in developing *divine* compassion, related to the evolution of the concept of divinity with the appearance of Jesus and its didactic extension to desired forms of human behavior. Nonetheless, despite the fact that the source of genuine compassion remained divine, the very extension of the concept of divinity to the human, embodied by Jesus, opened (at least seemingly) the Christian options for human compassion.

In many senses, the Christian concept of divinity is the direct continuation of the Old Testament concept – namely, the understanding of God as a personal divinity, as the Creator of the World and Mankind, Father of History, as Judge of Humankind, which was created in his image. But the Christian version of the concept added new and unique dimensions, some of which stemmed from or were derived from the image of Jesus and the way in which his persona was understood and structured in the Christian contexts. The belief in God as it appears in the New Testament cannot be detached from the belief in Jesus. The man, his dogma, behavior, and personal history all embody, in one way or another, the new senses of divinity in Christianity. Jesus himself not only preached belief in the Biblical God, the God of Abraham, Isaac, and Jacob and of Mount Sinai, but also regarded himself as the Messiah, the Son of Man, the herald of God's Kingdom, which was immediately translated by the Synoptic Gospels into one meaning his being the Son of God. Indeed, in prayer, Jesus appealed to God using the designation *abba*, an Aramaic word meaning father that took root in Hebrew as well. The use of this appellation implies great closeness between Jesus and God, creating an *a priori* sense of intimacy between them, which augmented the ancient (albeit very marginal) biblical image of the paternal God. Christianity's combination of this familial relationship with Jesus' messianic aspect led to the identification of his doctrine (Christology) as the authentic and new doctrine of God (theology).

The Christian Church doctrine asserts that Jesus is the Son of God, born to Mary, his mother, and fathered by the Holy Ghost: he had a body of flesh and blood and was raised from the dead in bodily resurrection by God and infused with the Holy Spirit (one of the vaguest concepts in Christian theology); he is one of three personae of the divine Trinity, the unit of divine substantiation. The official doctrine, as it was formulated at the First Council of Nicaea in 325 CE, professes Jesus' absolute divinity alongside his full human existence. This problematic credo, declared on the background of the great dispute in Christianity at the dawn of the Middle Ages, in effect left the matter of whether Jesus' behaviors, statements, and qualities are divine or human open for interpretation. Despite the fact that monophysitism (the Christological stance that Jesus is exclusively divine in nature) was not sanctioned by the central streams of Christianity (the Catholic and Orthodox Churches), the general trend in Catholic thought was to a large extent dictated by the theological need to relate to Jesus first and foremost as a divine entity and only thereafter as a human God (based on the assumption that divinity logically precedes humanity and, at times, the view of humanity as deriving from the divine).

The Christian-Catholic vacillation and eventual stance with regard to compassion exemplifies well the problematic determination of divine status. Christianity asserts that Jesus is the complete and ultimate embodiment of the ideal of fatherly compassionate love and of the divine desire to love and embrace humankind. But is this divine compassion or in fact human compassion, or even both? The answer is in no way simple or straightforward. At least potentially, Jesus' ongoing presence has far-reaching ramifications for how compassion is understood. For example, we can assume that Jesus' flesh-and-blood embodiment of divine compassion on Earth should give it a human aspect. It is therefore possible that human beings – especially those who believe in Jesus, embrace him, and 'let him into their hearts' – can be compassionate and that compassion is their personal trait. This is no longer the distant, one-way, and one-sided divine compassion of the Old Testament stories, but rather a compassion that is manifest in the lives of human beings and, at least theoretically, can perhaps be considered a human quality. The history of Christian thought, however, is more complex than this analysis would suggest. While the idea of compassion was brought significantly closer to the human reality, this was construed in the Christian context as a divine imminence, not as a new conception of human beings and their qualities.

The crucifixion of Jesus and the understanding that accepting Jesus as a sort of empathetic identification with his torment and suffering thus marked a new view of the status of the concept of compassion, which joined the additional senses with which the Christian concept of agape had imbued it. Whereas previously, compassion had flowed in only one direction – from omnipotent God to suffering, impotent, and sinning human beings – now God himself was understood as suffering as well, suffering for the salvation of human beings.

> Neither pray I for these alone, but for them also which shall believe on me through their word;
>
> That they all may be one; as thou, Father [art] in me, and I in thee, that they also may be one in us: that the world may believe that thou has sent me.
>
> And the glory which thou gavest me I have given them; that they may be one, even as we are one:

I in them, and thou in me, that they may be made perfect in one; and that the world may know that thou has sent me and has loved them, as thou has loved me.

...

And I have declared unto them thy name, and will declare [it]: that the love wherewith thou has loved me may be in them, and I in them.

John 17:20–17:26

From this point the concept of compassion developed in Christian tradition at a dizzying pace, until the forging of the all-encompassing Christian paradigm under which Jesus, in his suffering, bore upon himself the burden of human beings' sins, with the intention of bringing them closer to salvation. This suffering is part of the definition of Jesus as the Savior and his own understanding of himself as divine. This is not only a God who suffers for his son, but a God who is himself crucified in the form of Jesus as part of overall divine activism and his decision to take concrete action to lead humankind to salvation. Thus, when someone embraces Jesus, she casts herself at the feet of the suffering crucified entity, she feels his pain and suffering, or in other words – the divine receives empathy and compassion from the human! Thus, here, compassion is a two-way relationship and, with regard to the crucifixion, a truly mutual one between the believer and the divinity. This is a declaration of genuine intimacy that can be understood as an invitation to closeness, dialogue, and experience, and which has quite a number of expressions in Christian mysticism. This type of intimacy, which stems directly from the switch in the object of compassion, would be absolutely inconceivable in the Jewish traditions.

This change also had a decisive impact on the resolution to the problem of theodicy, and when considered from the perspective of the explanation for suffering in the world, it takes on a rather reactionary, conservative light: all known types of human pain and distress become trivial from the moment God's incarnated image climbs onto the Cross and chooses suffering and from the moment that this suffering is recognized as bearing absolute significance both in terms of its content (as the agony of corporeal death) and its status (as God's suffering due to his *choice* to suffer for mankind). The wonderment and anger at the obstacles and whims of fate and at what seems to be outrageous injustice and the need to justify them in light of a God who is absolute goodness and is supposed to do only good all fall from the agenda of the suffering person, whose own woes pale in comparison to the torment of the Crucifixion.[4] This added another dimension to the understanding of human compassion as legitimate and necessary. This compassion stretches beyond the model of the Good Samaritan and includes identifying being a Christian with the acceptance of Jesus, equating this acceptance with identification and empathy with and awe of the torments of the Cross, and understanding all of these as the basis to a new eschatology.

This development should not, however, be understood as the dawning of a new anthropological concept of man or of his status in relation to God. In many important respects, it is precisely the transporting of divine compassion into the range of human options that paradoxically signifies the *non*-humanity of compassion and its specifically divine nature. To clarify, the Christian anthropological stance, like its Jewish counterpart, is based on the biblical assertion that man was created in God's image in conjunction with God's selection of man (in Judaism, his covenant with man) as the favored creature, through which he can realize his rule over the world. From this status it can be deduced that, at least potentially, human beings have qualities that are divine in essence, a sort of divine 'genetic' baggage that allows them to perform at least some of the divine tasks. For example, man can assign names to animals and plants; he can listen to and understand the word of God; he can use his reason ('eternal intelligence' in Aristotelian theology) to find some type of heavenly kingdom; and he can serve as judge over other human beings, at least in matters pertaining to this world and life. The problem is that, from the theological point of view, man does not fulfill his latent divine potential. It is irrelevant as to whether this non-realization of potential is a primal state rooted in the Original Sin or part of a long historical process of a failure to withstand temptation and of poor choices in a life of sin. The fact remains that the overall historical performance of the human race is antagonistic to the divine qualities, whether out of (poor) choice (the preferred explanation in Judaism and certain Christian streams) or due to capitulation to God's great adversary, Satan.

The great message of Christianity, and the great hope accompanying this message in the form of Jesus, is precisely the understanding of his appearance as divine intervention intended to enable human beings to realize more successfully their inherent potential as the chosen species created in God's image. Jesus gives human beings an additional 'portion' of divinity: the fullest meaning of Jesus' incarnation in human beings is their acquisition of new and additional divine energy, not the use of the worn-out qualities that have already shown themselves to be mere potential and unfeasible without belief in and acceptance of Jesus. In other words, according to Christian theological logic, man cannot be good in the full sense of the word (that is, in the Christian sense, which is, of course, a circular assumption) without belief in Jesus and the acceptance of Jesus both out of faith, and physically, ceremonially, and spiritually. In effect, man requires divine infusion in order to be free of sin. This infusion is acquired through a person's love of God/Jesus and divine grace and is translated into a real possibility of being allowed entry into the Kingdom of Heaven – all of which, in its precise sense, means simply being a person who loves God, loves her neighbor, and is compassionate toward the weak, abused, and outcast. In other words, human compassion in its optimal manifestation is none other than a form of divine love–compassion.

Accordingly, man cannot be compassionate without Jesus – just as he cannot be a judge, enter into the Kingdom of Heaven, suffer the torment of the Cross, fulfill his social and religious duties, be moral and pure, withstand temptation, or experience justification. In short, he cannot be a human being in the full sense of the word without belief in Jesus. Any measure of compassion that may be discerned in the non-believer in heretic lands, for example, or in the relationship between children and parents is not genuine compassion, namely Jesus' compassion when he chose to bear man's sins and purify mankind through his love and own suffering, creating a new world order and the new and immediate chance for man to enter the Kingdom of Heaven. The belief in and acceptance of Jesus, therefore, are the conditions for the existence of divine compassion in man; and whatever the case may be, divine compassion is forever preferable to human 'natural' compassion, the compassion that animals experience in their relations with their offspring.

The way in which the concept of compassion was constructed in Christian thought, especially in the scholastic theology, points to two seemingly contradictory trends in the understanding of compassion. On the one hand, the jumble of concepts that relate to compassion and are arranged along different hierarchical scales presents compassion as a byproduct of the larger configuration of agape; at least seemingly, compassion is placed amongst such prominent Christian concepts as alms, mercy, grace, charity, and so on. On the other hand, it is precisely this set of concepts through which theologians have attempted to present agape in its entirety as evidence of the centrality, presence, and importance of the divine love embodied in the Savior, that is indication of the proximity, to the point of complete overlap, between the concepts of love and compassion in Christianity. Indeed, the translation of love into grace, charity, and mercy means that love begins and ends with the concern for the physical and emotional welfare of the other and includes accompanying that other through his greatest suffering.[5]

The equation of love with charity and the positioning of charity at the top of the scale of values as a synonym for agape raise two issues about which there has not always been concurrence amongst theologians. The one is whether the source of charity is divine or human; the second is how charity relates to the other values. With regard to the first question, almost all the important Catholic thinkers have agreed that divine infusion is the source of charity. The *Catholic Encyclopedia* gives the following definition of charity (which is based primarily on Thomastic theology):

> a divinely infused habit, inclining the human will to cherish God for his own sake above all things, and man for the sake of God.

The problem with this definition is twofold. First, there is the matter of free will: if even the source of faithfulness is divine infusion, then this is absolute determinism that reaches into the most intimate regions of the soul, and such a presence is of no moral value. The second problematic point is consistency with reality, for at the empiric level, it is most certainly possible to find people whose behavior shows most of the elements of charity but who are not at all religious and may not even have heard of Jesus' Gospel.

But the most difficult problem with regard to understanding the divine source of charity–mercy–compassion was created with the embracing of Aristotelian philosophy in the Middle Ages. This meant that in order for certain qualities to be recognized as 'worthy', that is, as qualities that are evidence of their possessor's potential to behave in a desirable Christian manner, they must receive the status of substantial qualities – they must be presented as virtues. But the hitch was that, according to Aristotle, a virtue is in fact a natural human quality, an inborn characteristic and not exactly the result of divine infusion.

Further complicating matters is charity's problematic and disputed status vis-à-vis the other values. The scholastic theology recognizes mercy as a value parallel to charity. Indeed, the majority of Catholic theologians placed mercy under the category of values related to justice, not as a derivative of charity, as they understood the concept of mercy as relating to the social link between human beings and not the relationship between God and human beings. But later interpretations pointed out the difficulty presented by this approach. First, because the Christian relationship of neighborly love must necessarily be presented as a derivative of love of God, if the source of the love of God is divine infusion of charity, then the source of mercy must also be as such. Second, the problem with regard to inconsistency with reality becomes more acute in the context of mercy: it is in fact the isolation of mercy to the sphere of social relations that excludes it from the theologian 'game' in many important ways.

The theological wavering and struggling with regard to the status of charitable love is apparent in Aquinas' great canonical *Summa Theologica*. One by one, Aquinas analyzes the objections to Augustine's idea of divine infusion and attempts to give a response to each one that preserves both the authority of Augustine his Platonic bias, and the Aristotelian ethical naturalism, as well as the divine status of at least some of the values. The authoritative summary of the Thomastic stance was as follows:

> It is therefore evident that all virtues are in us by nature, according to aptitude and inchoation, but not according to perfection, except the theological virtues, which are entirely without.
>
> *Summa Theologica*, Part II, Ch. 1

Accordingly, charitable compassion, as the theological value of primary importance to Christianity, is defined as follows:

> [C]harity is a friendship of man for God, founded upon the fellowship of everlasting happiness. Now this fellowship is in respect, not of natural, but of gratuitous gifts, for, according to Rm. 6:23, 'the grace of God is life everlasting': wherefore charity itself surpasses our natural facilities. Now that which surpasses the faculty of nature, cannot be natural or acquired by the natural powers, since a natural effect does not transcend its cause.

> Therefore charity can be in us neither naturally, nor through acquisition by the natural powers, but by the infusion of the Holy Ghost, Who is the love of the Father and the Son, and the participation of Whom in us is created charity, as stated above.
>
> *Summa Theologica*, Part II, Ch. 2

Now all that remained was to extract mercy from the problematic framework of human relations (where it was placed by Augustine, under the concept of justice, and, in his footsteps, by the majority of scholastic theologians) and transfer it to the world of values whose source is divine infusion. Accordingly, Aquinas asserted that mercy is a virtue that affects the will of human beings to feel compassion and, to as great an extent as possible, to alleviate the distress of the other:

> Mercy signifies grief for another's distress. Now this grief may denote, in one way a movement of the sensitive appetite, in which case mercy is not a virtue but a passion; whereas, in another way, it may denote a movement of the intellective appetite, in as much as one person's evil is displeasing to another. This movement may be ruled in accordance with reason, and in accordance with this movement regulated by reason, the movement of the lower appetite may be regulated.... And since it is essential to human virtue that the movements of the soul should be regulated by reason, as it was shown above (I-II, 59, A4, 5), it follows that mercy is a virtue.
>
> *Summa Theologica*, Part II, Ch. 2

And, of course, there is no questioning of Thomas Aquinas' authority.

*   *   *

The Protestant streams in fact emphasized the importance of divine grace (which was proposed by Augustine as the basis for the notion of infusion). The Protestant logic rejects the Church establishment as a meaningful expression of divine presence and, correspondingly, significantly diminishes the importance of the established actions, such as charity expressed in acts of mercy. Moreover, the Catholic effort to present compassionate love as part of the 'natural religion' and as rationally derived from understanding God was rejected in the wake of the anti-rationalism tendency of the leaders of the Reformation. This change in approach combined with the Reformation leaders' and their successors' understanding of Jesus' command of neighborly love as guidance vis-à-vis reciprocal responsibility amongst human beings and social commitment based on individual choice,[6] to form a model under which compassion is not necessarily a function of infusion or divine grace.

This shift had a significant impact on the status of compassion. First, under the Protestant conceptions, man cannot affect divine decisions. The relationship between God and man is essentially one-way in direction, obligating only man and not the Divinity. The Calvinist logic, for example, which is the most radical in this respect, establishes that man must act morally, but this does not ensure any salvation – the determination with regard to salvation is divine and subject to divine logic, which is beyond the grasp of man. All that man can expect is a touch of divine grace, which is also granted by divine decision and, in fact, often seems arbitrary or mere coincidence. From this we can derive that faith does not offer any grounds for compassionate behavior: such behavior is extraneous to the dialogue with divinity. Second, we can further derive that the place of compassion as it was demonstrated and instructed by Jesus is in the framework of the social–communal relationship, that very unit that replaces the ecclesiastical establishment and where certain patterns of behavior that reflect the relationship between Jesus and his flock of faithful are reproduced. Third, two final conclusions can be drawn: either there is no need for compassion to serve as a basis for salvation and, instead, it is simply a directive regarding social behavior (as in Judaism, for example[7]) or, alternatively, this is a new status for compassion – a type of basic human tendency, completely unconnected to faith. In the latter sense, Jesus is the proper model of compassion, precisely because he was a worthy and moral person and not because he is divine. Thus, under this model, compassion remains a matter of personal choice for the believer. Moreover, in this type of model, ethics – or more precisely, the Protestant ethic in its Weberian sense – takes the place of divine compassion. In its most extreme form, which appeared during the Enlightenment, as a deontological rational code of ethics, not only was compassion unwelcome, it was even regarded as a hindrance to the rational imperative (referring, of course, to Kantian ethics).[8]

In order to complete the model of divine compassion, it is important to note two further uses, or senses, of compassion in the Christian-Catholic tradition, both of which emphasize its divine supernatural nature.

Compassion and holiness

The idea of compassion as a divine infusion of grace has also been widely used in its reverse formulation: when a person demonstrates primary virtues, this is indication that he has accepted Jesus into his heart, that he has been blessed with the touch of the divine hand, that he has received a portion of divine grace. Or, to rephrase this, a person who acts with compassion, cares about the distress of others, behaves as a Good Samaritan, whose passion is for God and God alone, who withstands the temptations of the flesh, and so on, is a person who realizes her inherent divine potential – in short, a saint. In the history of Christianity, there is no shortage of examples (in fact, they are countless) of the folkloric use and, in its wake, institutionalized use of compassion as a tool for attributing sainthood to people. This sainthood, which means great closeness to divinity, is expressed empirically in miracle work attributed to the saints. With the institutionalization of the canonization process in the Catholic Church, unequivocal evidence of the occurrence of miracles by the saint or in his or her immediate surroundings was necessary in order for him or her to be recognized as such.

The origins of the supernatural aspect to compassion lie in the New Testament account of how Jesus, assisted by the Holy Ghost, performed miracles. In many Gospel stories, and certainly in the later Christian literature, which was based on the Gospels, Jesus appears as worker of miracles, as controlling both the natural and the supernatural forces. In all the stories, he acts to help his followers in distress, to heal the ill, to exorcise demons, to restore vision to the blind, and to even raise the dead. Moreover, his work amongst the masses also was acts of welfare: it is told of how he fed 5000 people with five loaves of bread and two fish and turned water into wine at a wedding celebration; when he calmed the waters of the raging Sea of Galilee, he did so to alleviate the distress of his apostles whose boat was about to sink in the storm. These stories, which glorified Jesus and were responsible for a considerable part of his attraction for his followers (as the Gospels themselves attest to), highlight the supernatural and superhuman character of compassion. Both openly and subliminally, they weave a narrative of admiration and self-deprecation toward a person who acts out of compassion and stress the impotence of the simple believer. In certain respects, what we see in the New Testament stories is an expansion of the Old Testament miracle or wonder from the realm of proving the existence of God and displaying his power and ability into the realm of aid, welfare, and concern for the other.[9] This expansion is the pillar of the Christian concept of miracle: from this point on, a miracle constitutes an act of compassion, and the presence of compassion is proof of the holiness, divinity of the person exhibiting compassion.

The Christian ritual of sainthood perhaps best exemplifies these dynamics. Despite the fact that the Church periodically tried to fight the folk aspects of the ritual, especially anything that appeared to be chiefly blasphemy, and despite the fact that from a historical and socio-logical perspective, it seems the Church was almost forced to concede to part of the public's demand for a sainthood ritual; in actuality, the existence of saints and their work formed an integral part of Christian ecclesiastical culture.[10] In the sociology of Christianity, there has been a long-running debate as to the status and importance of the stories of the saints in Catholicism. On the one hand, there are those who claim that these stories, with all of their rich imagery and concrete uses in shaping Catholic culture in general, are merely a tool in the hands of the Church for constructing and implementing its power and control over the community of faithful and, at times, for converting heretics into followers. In this sense, they are didactic stories that promote values and ideas that the establishment is interested in fostering. On the other hand, quite a number of researchers have shown that the stories of the saints form a rich and vibrant body of literature that cannot easily be reduced into a didactic 'scheme', as it were. In many important ways, this literature presents radical narratives that at times stand in contradiction with the Church's purposes and even undermine them.[11] But what is of particular relevance for our matter is the strong presence of compassion in these stories, which set interesting and novel connections between compassion and concepts such as sacrifice, holiness, and poverty. At times, these links served the ecclesiastical establishment's interest in power and control; but at times they seem to have subverted Church authority by re-forging the persona of the saint in the image of Jesus himself and thereby serving as a channel for 'bypassing' the Church.

During the long history of the crystallization of Christian culture, there were a number of shifts in emphasis, with new forms and patterns of sainthood emerging: the Christian martyrs, who set the tone in the first century CE on the background of the harsh persecution of Christians, demonstrating self-sacrifice and adherence to faith in the face of torture and death in an attempt to imitate the magnitude of the Savior's sacrifice; the desert ascetics and the ascetic monasteries that developed in the early Middle Ages, which created the strange yet quite familiar connection between 'spiritual purity' and physical self-denial and morti-fication; the miracle workers, healers, and seers who not infrequently embarrassed the Church institutions when they (and, thereafter, their remnants buried in the basilicas) defied the laws of nature and produced wondrous supernatural cures and remedies (and, of course, drew thousands of followers, which was successfully exploited by the Church); and the saints of the late Middle Ages, who tend to evoke the image of teacher, theologian, pope, or businessmen, in a period in which the narrative that stressed medical miracles and grandiose practices was eclipsed by the more spiritual narrative of prayer and theology.

The stories about St Francis of Assisi are perhaps the best example of how the concept of compassion was expanded by way of the biographies of saints. In 1209, St Francis abandoned his life of material comforts in order to realize the ideal of imitating the life of Jesus, which, for him and his Franciscan brothers, meant a life of poverty, humility, self-deprivation, and strong literal adherence to the Holy Scriptures. The biographical tales of St Francis of Assisi, some of which were compiled by the official Church biographers and some originating from different sources within the Franciscan Order itself, portray a unique image of a person who succeeded in leading an exemplary life of humility, acceptance, innocence, and adherence. What was unique about St Francis was that he represented an integration of a number of different elements of sainthood in Christian history; the amalgamation of these elements into one whole and coherent pattern of behavior constituted the backbone of the Franciscan social image and self-conception. Indeed, St Francis linked self-sacrifice to asceticism, the ideal of poverty to the renouncement of property, self-deprivation and even self-mortification to the possibility of a spiritual form of salvation, and obedience and faithfulness to joyfulness and love. He supposedly drew these values directly from the Holy Scriptures and affixed them to the image of the Savior's life and teachings, an image that, in turn, attached itself to St Francis and (especially in the eyes of the members of his Order) turned into the direct successor of the Savior. St Francis of Assisi was, without a doubt, the saint with the highest 'ratings' in the history of Catholicism. According to Thomas of Celano, a disciple of St Francis and his official Church biographer, he and his followers

> sought to be where they would suffer persecution of their bodies rather than where their holiness would be known and praised, lifting them up with world favor. Often mocked, objects of insult, stripped naked, beaten, bound, jailed, and not defending themselves with anyone's protection, they endured all of these abuses so bravely that from their mouths came only the sound of praise and thanksgiving.[12]

St Francis' precepts were extreme and had far-reaching ramifications. He set the uncompromising requirements and directives for acceptance into the Order of modesty, self-deprivation, a willingness to happily endure any degradation or pain, relinquishment of all property,[13] and refraining from holding money (even for the purpose of collecting donations) and to never 'worry about tomorrow'.[14] It was this zealousness in the rigid maintenance of poverty as a way of life and holy ideal ('holy poverty') that preserved St Francis' image as pure and innocent throughout Christian-Catholic history – even when the Franciscan Order was shaken at a certain point in time, with the tainting of its integrity and righteous reputation and accusations that it had strayed from the original path and had submitted to the dictates of the Church. This zealousness also contributed significantly to the formulation of the way of life in the monasteries and Christian churches, as well as impacting the internal debate in Christianity between the ascetics and the hermits (who represented the *vita passiva*) and the priests who actively ministered to the community and worked with the Church establishment in the big cities (*vita activa*), by showing how the two can be integrated.

A great part of St Francis' power derived from his serving as a personal role model throughout his life, especially with regard to his compassionate treatment of his Franciscan brothers, of Christian believers in general, and even of animals. According to the biographical stories of his life, even when he was ill (which happened frequently throughout his life), he was troubled by the distress of those who were concerned for his welfare, and not by his own personal suffering:

> During those days and in the same place, after he had composed the Praises of the Lord for his creatures, St. Francis similarly composed some holy words with a tune for the greater consolation of the poor ladies of the house of San Domingo, especially as he knew that they were very grieved at his illness. . . . As St. Francis knew that from the beginning of their conversion they had led and were still leading a very hard and poor life, both by choice and by necessity, his spirit was always stirred with compassion towards them. Therefore, in his message he asked them, as the Lord had gathered them together from many parts into one congregation dedicated to holy charity, holy poverty, and holy obedience, always to live and die in these virtues.[15]

St Francis was not the first to suggest imitation of Jesus as the desirable way of life for a Christian; indeed he merely offered his own version of *imitato Christi*. And he most certainly was not the first to promote a radically humble existence by setting a personal example, despite the fact that his version of this lifestyle deviated from the desert ascetic model and bore absolutely no resemblance to the hermitic seclusion chosen by St Anthony (as portrayed by Athanasius of Alexandria), for example. St Francis also was not the first to suggest relinquishing all property for the good of the poor, a condition of acceptance into the Franciscan Order and a requirement that can be traced back to the Holy Scriptures themselves. Rather, his innovation was in being the first to integrate all of these elements and inject them into the very heart of the Catholic establishment, by attaining Pope Innocent the Third's official blessing and constructing what would one day become one of the strongest and largest orders of the Catholic Church.

From a political perspective, the establishment and fortification of the Franciscan Order had a decisive impact on the history of Catholicism. This began with Pope Innocent's supposedly daring approbation of the Order and its problematic Rule, which in fact was a classic exercise of co-option aimed at drawing the Order into a bear hug and thereby smothering the problematic folk elements of Christianity so prevalent at that time. This continued with the sprouting of the mendicant orders, which, in time, spearheaded the Catholic missionary effort and its war against the Reformation. Finally, the process culminated with the sowing of the seeds of 'calamity' in the form of the legitimization of the possibility of achieving personal salvation beyond the bounds of the Church hierarchy.

But alongside this political-historical process, the image of St Francis influenced and shaped the world of Christian imagery and the linking between compassion and holiness, more than perhaps any other figure in Christian history. This linking commences with the Franciscan's conscious decision to relinquish all property, status, prestige, and pleasure and to set forth on the path of *imitato Christi*. From this point onward, he begins to acquire a new type of property – the so-called 'spiritual possessions' that will be available to him in the Kingdom of Heaven. Indeed, with the very physical and spiritual acceptance of Jesus into his midst, the Franciscan, like any believer, develops the ability to serve as a vehicle for divine qualities; and this is holiness itself – the ability to feel compassion, to love, and to identify with the pain of another, which are simply components of the divinity embodied in the believer. The Franciscan version of compassion (in fact a sophisticated form of the Dominican theological logic) therefore focuses on a practical display of control over the process of divine infusion. The ability to achieve infusion is acquired by embracing holy poverty, with the Franciscan thereby stepping into Jesus' enormous footsteps. Thus we see that the Franciscan intention was to turn its followers into replicas of Jesus himself, although this was never explicitly stated, for it would have been denounced as blasphemy.

One of the immediate costs of this kind of practical theology is the discarding of the conception of compassion as a basis for action. If the purpose of the Franciscan way of life is to achieve and realize the ideal of poverty, and if this leads to the acquisition of divine qualities including compassion, then compassion is an outcome, not a cause. In order to be considered a worthy Christian, a person must show lack of world attachment, modesty, and so on and so forth; if he meets all the requirements of the Franciscan Rule, then he becomes a saint (at least in the Augustinian sense, according to which saints are members of the community of faithful). Only from the moment that this objective is attained do the divine qualities, including compassion, appear. Thus, the didactic emphasis must be placed on the *way* and not the *outcome*. In effect, there is no point in instructing people to feel and act with compassion who have yet to undergo the process of detachment from all worldly entanglements.

Compassion and salvation

One of the important reasons for Jesus' compassionate treatment of sinners, as it is frequently portrayed in the New Testament, is related to his belief in the imminence of the Kingdom of Heaven. The very fact of the impending End of Days provided the basis for a relatively tolerant approach to worldly evil, for soon the problems of suffering, pain, and distress would be resolved: with the ascent of the Kingdom of Heaven, the righteous will receive their proper reward and the evil their punishment. 'Blessed [be ye] poor: for yours is the kingdom of God. Blessed [are ye] that hunger now: for ye shall be filled. Blessed [are ye] that weep now: for ye shall laugh' (*Luke* 6:20–6:21). Thus, there is no difficulty with the fact that God does not distinguish between the righteous and the evil, that 'he maketh his sun to rise on the evil and on the good, and sendeth rain on the just and on the unjust' (*Matthew* 5:45), for salvation is fast approaching, and this salvation in any event bears with it absolute divine justice.

However, the New Testament understanding of the concept of the Kingdom of Heaven as referring to the imminent end of the world and the dawning of salvation is not as simple as it might initially appear. Does this mean the end to 'evil' political rule, of Roman rule, for example, relevant to the New Testament context? Or does the end of the world refer to a general cosmic change that will forge new laws of nature or reinstate the genesis state of chaos, as God sought to do before the Flood? Alternatively, will the salvation be spiritual in nature at the 'expense' of the material world, that is to say, entailing the complete destruction of the material (death?)? Or perhaps the spiritual salvation will be manifested in the eradication of all human evil and the salvation of humankind from sin?

Each of these options can be derived from the texts attributed to Jesus, but Catholicism made a clear choice to focus on the final understanding. This understanding emphasizes that part of Jesus' dogma that assumes that, in a certain sense, the Kingdom of Heaven is already present, here and now. This is not the same Kingdom of Heaven that appears in Jewish tradition, which refers to an exclusive rule of God over the entire world, but rather a Kingdom of Heaven that designates a special spiritual domain for the followers of Jesus. In effect, the congregation of faithful is already present in the Kingdom of Heaven, which exists alongside evil in this world, and only those who accept Jesus can enter the gates and inherit God's Kingdom – for sinners, no entry can be gained.

> Verily, verily, I say unto you, He that heareth my word, and believeth on him that sent me, hath everlasting life, and shall not come into condemnation; but is passed from death unto life.
>
> *John* 5:24

Thus, under this interpretation, the Kingdom of Heaven is the exclusive domain of those who have been saved through belief in Jesus; its materialization, by spreading throughout the world, constitutes the materialization of the messianic salvation of the congregation of faithful. The tangible manifestation of the Kingdom of Heaven, which seeks to purge the world of 'evil', is, of course, the Christian Church, particularly the Catholic Church. The Church serves as chief headquarters in the battle to implement the rule of the Kingdom of Heaven throughout the world, which, in its precise sense, means the deliverance of humankind from sin.

Grasping the full breadth of the concept of salvation in Christianity sometimes seems an impossible task, and, indeed, I will not even attempt such an endeavor. Instead, I will conclude by mentioning briefly three familiar appearances of compassion presented as part of the wider project of salvation.

The first is the institutional appearance of compassion, which relates to the central place of the community of faithful and, in particular, the Church (under the Catholic version) in giving compassion presence in the world. Jesus' command to love the sinner and forgive the evildoer is turned into an instrument in the general program of salvation and spreading of the Kingdom of Heaven. It is manifested in the missionaries, who, echoing the spirit of the Paulinian Mission, venture beyond the protected, safe, divine domain of the Church into the world of evil and heresy, to spread the Gospel and bring salvation. And since one of the most important tools in achieving this goal is compassion, a global network of missionaries has been deployed whose work is broken down into a series of acts of aid and welfare on behalf of the Church for the general public, including the poor, hungry, and suffering.

The second such appearance of compassion is connected to the conception of the Kingdom of Heaven as spiritual salvation and is illustrative of the Christian linking of compassion with absolution for sin. Jesus' command created a link between evildoers and sinners, and forgiveness, love, and compassion; that is to say, the strongest expression of compassion will be found where sin resides. The process of the institutionalization of the Christian Churches, and (again) of the Catholic Church in particular, was a significant factor in the construction of the bond between the Church and the faithful through the recognition of sin, confession, and penance. The Church shaped its image as God's assigned judicial authority, as well as setting the formal procedure for others to identify it as such. This formal judicial aspect is expressed in, amongst other things, the emphasis of sin in the relationship between the believer and the Church establishment. Pain and suffering are seen through the judicial prism as the result of sin – as a sort of punishment of man imposed by Heaven. The role of the judicial system is to translate what appears to be the punishment meted out by human hands into causational terms of reward and punishment in the context of the relationship between God and man. This familiar process, which, over the years, became the signature mark of Catholicism and of Christianity in general,[16] is essentially built on the association of the process of purification, penance, and absolution with the compassion and divine love that is embodied in Jesus – a process that, from a theological and eschatological perspective, is equivalent to spiritual salvation itself. Indeed, the explicit condition for entry into the Kingdom of Heaven is a high level of purity: 'Whosoever shall not receive the kingdom of God as a little child, he shall not enter therein' (*Mark* 10:15). And the path to achieving the pure and chaste status of a child is via confession and absolution. Viewing compassionate love as a means of achieving salvation creates a necessary bond between compassion and sin, with compassion ceasing to be the response to pain and becoming a response to sin. The spectacles through which people are seen as suffering, poor, and oppressed are exchanged for spectacles that show only sinners, heretics, and evildoers; their sin – not their distress! – makes them candidates for compassionate treatment. In other words, the vision of pure salvation from sin, switches compassion (in the sense of feeling another's pain and distress), for absolution, which signifies a willingness to recognize human weakness, wretchedness, and almost certain submission to the temptations of Satan. Compassionate paternalism is replaced by self-righteousness, with the forgiver now superseding the forgiven, both hierarchically and in terms of spiritual purity.

Finally, the third appearance of compassion is the revival of Jesus' (God's) compassion in the believer herself, whose personal process of salvation leads her to realize Jesus' presence in her and to become a compassionate person. The process of salvation, as it was presented in later periods of Christianity (especially by the Protestant streams, which rejected the Catholic and the Orthodox sainthood rituals and preached the rebirth of Jesus in believers themselves), rests on a renewed forging of relations between the believer and the God as a direct continuation of the Paulinian theology (justification), usually a short and immediate event that occurs the moment Jesus is accepted and the believer joins the community of faithful, and on the believer's development of spiritual holiness, which is a long and ongoing process (sanctification). These two spiritual occurrences, which represent the basis of spiritual salvation, are expressed in, amongst other things, an emotional awakening in the believer and are translated into compassion toward fellow members of the community of believers and, sometimes, even toward those yet to embrace Jesus' Gospel. It is in fact possible to derive from the understanding of the Kingdom of Heaven as having concrete and immediate presence in the world a connection between compassion and community – compassion takes on the sense of a type of social relations and of person's ability to become aware of, identify with, or show empathy for the distress of the other, that is, the acquisition of social skills. Under this understanding, which, again, was greatly stressed by the Protestant streams and, in the modern era, by the Free Church, the Christian believer, striving for and nearing salvation, is a social person, considerate of others, willing to contribute to their community, and loyal and responsible toward that community. But, not surprisingly, even to this day, this is still also expressed in reverse logical order: being a good citizen, good friend, loyal family person, worthy member of the community, and so on, is contingent on being a Christian.

3
Seeds of Anti-compassion

In Chapter 2, I described the development of the divine compassion model in Catholicism, with all its different meanings and its unique Catholic field of reference. In this chapter, I present a critical perspective of this model, although this is not to say that in other streams of Christianity (Protestantism and, in a certain sense, also Easter Orthodox), the different models of compassions that evolved are not 'deserving' of criticism. The reason for the focus on the Roman-Catholic church is twofold. First is the fact that Catholicism is the better representative of the divine compassion model, which constitutes the basis for both its activity and its ecclesiastical structure. Second, Catholicism, more than any other stream of Christianity, identifies itself as the 'tradition of compassion'. Compassion is an integral part of its self-image as well as its official narrative.

The long history of the aid and welfare activity in Christianity is truly impressive in its immense scope, systematic nature, and determination. One of the greatest (if not the greatest) social systems in the world, the Christian aid system reaches almost every corner of human distress, responds to every disease, famine, and plague across the globe. There is almost no place – from famine- and plague-stricken Africa, to the poverty-stricken neighborhoods of Sao Paulo and Mexico City, to the gutters of Bombay and Calcutta – where Christian priests, missions, shelters, medical workers, or some other presence or activity for the needy cannot be found. The Christian aid system encompasses almost every known form of social institution that accompanies a person from birth to death: hospitals, medical clinics, schools, institutes of higher education, soup kitchens, shelters for the poor, needy, abused, and homeless, the elderly – the list is endless.

Moreover, the religious, missionary passion for work with the needy accompanies to this day a great deal of social activism in general – beginning from public and political crusades, to local and international organizations espousing public causes, to the activities of individuals, both volunteer and professional, who devote time, energy, and effort to the struggle for rights, for a change in social priorities, for more just allocation of resources, and for any reform of the current reality that will improve the state of the abused, oppressed, and deprived. A considerable number of these movements and organizations owe a direct debt to the convictions of their founders, whose work was often motivated by profound Christian belief and who sought to actively implement a certain interpretation of agapic compassion: from the attempts to realize different types of moderate socialism and the forms of social organization dominant in the nineteenth century, to the campaign against the slave trade and the struggle to establish public education systems for underprivileged children, to the organizations that connected the works of mercy and the political struggle for legislation of social aid for the poor; and culminating with current enterprises that have revived St Francis of Assisi's love and concern for animals and translate this love into a crusade for animal preservation and ecological activism. But even when these movements are not affiliated with the religious establishment or supported by Church bodies and whose members are not, in fact, Christian believers (and, in many cases, are actually self-sworn atheists acting out of socialist commitment or in the name of universal humanism), they are frequently driven by a fervor that recalls, to a great extent, religious missionary zeal. Thus it would not be completely unfounded to point to a presence in the overall narrative of their works of imagery and concepts that are no more than a metamorphosis of Christian agapic compassion.[1]

All things considered, however, it is still difficult to ignore the ugly side of Christianity, as a cultural force that rendered social damage that was, and still is, massive and caused suffering and pain throughout history that far exceeds the relief it provided. Indeed, there has been an intolerable discrepancy between Christianity's lofty and noble declarations and intentions and the miserable outcomes in practice that eradicated all hope for multitudes. Christianity's double messages were particularly evident in the vast contradiction between its uncompromisingly strict judgmental attitude toward all, Christian or otherwise, and its commitment to compassion, acceptance, and forgiveness, with the balance always tipping in favor of the former, yet while cynically employing the terminology of compassion. Religion in general and Catholicism specifically always played into the hands of society's power-wielders (with the Church a prominent occupant of that stratum), while breeding acceptance, submission, and even happiness where there should have been anger, protest, and a social struggle for change. All this places Christianity in the light in which its accusers see it as an opium for the masses, a sedative force that not only fails to offer salvation (even the rather odd type of salvation it offers), but also systematically strips most people of any chance of improving their dismal, alienated, and suffering existences. Christianity has to its dubious credit a long history of social injustices – supporting slavery and upholding racism, anti-Semitism, and intolerance for the other; granting divine status to the privileges and prerogatives of the ruling classes; burning the so-called 'heretics and witches'; waging supposedly holy and justified religious crusades; entering into strange covenants 'with the devil'; and amassing great wealth and political power, which it refuses to relinquish to this day.

Thus, critical scrutiny of Christianity today, even without Marxist or Liberal spectacles, reveals that although the Christian churches deserve great credit for their work in alleviating such social miseries as hunger, disease, and homelessness, a considerable part of their activity is decidedly harmful. They promote relentlessly the Bible as the most absolute and appropriate guide for human life, though it includes notions and behaviors that are patently illegal and certainly not moral – extracting teeth and amputating organs, preventing medical treatment, encouraging oppression and violence toward children and women, and the like. Furthermore, the churches act as a barrier to any possibility of social openness by applying political pressure that ranges from censorship of books, movies, and scientific thought, to opposing abortion, to fighting the separation of state and religion. They also, paradoxically albeit not surprisingly, block any possibility of the world's weakest populations securing greater control over their lives – beginning with their persistent opposition to birth control to their alignment with the reactionary political right-wing and 'historical' resistance to anything that whispers of socialism.

To complete this Part's discussion of divine compassion, it is necessary to consider those elements of Christian theory, practice, and motivation that do *not* facilitate the manifestation of compassion as I have defined it. Is Christian agapic compassion in fact a direct awareness of the pain of the other? Is the world of Christian terminology indeed a tool that fleshes out the human endeavor to feel the pain of others, interpreting and shaping it in a way that stimulates that type of experience? Do the processes of the institutionalization of Christianity support or hinder the possibility of experiencing compassion? Does the Christian tendency to understand agapic love as charity, and charity as action indicate that

Christian compassion is of an active kind and intended to change the reality of the poor and suffering? In order to respond to at least some of these questions, I will present the elements present – the seeds that have been sown – in the underlying structure of Christian thought and institutions that act as an internal counterbalance to the possibility of compassion.

The emasculation of human compassion

Thus far, I have pointed to the Christian commitment – rooted in the biblical texts and carrying on to the later theology – to understanding compassion as a quality, or possibility, exclusive to God. Compassion does not belong to the sphere of human beings; rather it is a heavenly domain. Only through Jesus' mediation and, subsequently, mediation by the saints and the institutional (and no less holy) mediation of the Catholic Church, as authorized by the Pope, can human beings touch divine compassion, and even then they do so only as the objects of compassion, not as subjects. This prerogative of being a compassionate person is reserved, first and foremost, for those who reach the highest level of sainthood, which can be achieved in one of two ways. The first way is by leading an ascetic and pure lifestyle, a path that underwent a process of institutionalization over the history of Catholicism, for it involved a considerable amount of public veneration for the holy person and thus could not be left outside the reach of the establishment's control. This is a familiar and well-known path, culminating with Catholic canonization, which leaves in the hands of the Church and its leaders the final and decisive ruling as to a person's degree of holiness.

The second way of achieving the status of a compassionate person is by serving in an official religious position under the aegis of the Church, with progression in the Church hierarchy meaning coming nearer to the heavenly territory. The closer one is to this realm, the greater the compassion, with the Pope the greatest bestower of compassion after Jesus. Of course, this is not to say that Christianity refutes the possibility of 'natural compassion', which most certainly exists between human beings in interpersonal relations, particularly between a mother and her offspring, but this is supposedly 'simple' human compassion and is a mere pale and usually rather unsuccessful imitation of divine compassion. Man's predilection for the material and his known weakness in the face of Satan's temptations obviously do not allow him to feel naturally the full scope of divine compassion. Just as man substitutes divine agape with pathetic and superficial Eros (and even dares to call this love!), so he cultivates irrationally his set of emotional bonds. Only through divine infusion can he feel compassion. And herein lies the trap: in order to receive this infusion, this divine energy that turns someone into a good person, that person has to be worthy – that is, a good Christian to be awarded divine grace. Thus we see that from the original biblical narrative, which asserts that man is not a worthy believer in the full sense of the word if he does not feel compassionate love toward his neighbor, Christianity created a commitment to the opposite narrative: a person cannot feel compassionate love without being a good Christian believer.

The immediate implication of this commitment is the diminishment to the point of delegitimation of human compassion. At least on its face, this inclination seems staggering considering that it relates to a culture whose historical self-image was to a great extent constructed on compassionate love. But under critical scrutiny, we see that human compassion at its ultimate is likely to be a hurdle and even threat to many of the principles of Christian faith and politics. If we assume that human beings have a natural ability to be compassionate, then there is no need to accept the Gospel in order to fulfill Jesus' commandment of neighborly love (and, indeed, Jesus himself gave the example of the Good Samaritan, in which someone who did not belong to the community of faithful behaved in the appropriate human way). Thus, acts of mercy do not require Church direction and instruction and can originate in simple human whim or impulse, without constituting any representation of the abundance that flows from the image and embodiment of Jesus. Thus non-believers, those who have not accepted the Gospel, can, and in practice actually do, act out of compassion toward others.

But in fact, human compassion represents the greatest danger of all to the Christian approach to human suffering, for it tends to give immediate priority to eradicating human suffering. It is likely to cast doubt on the ideas of future salvation, of acquisition of spiritual possessions for the next life, of prayer and absolution as a practical and concrete response to suffering, of happiness arising from the mere acceptance of Jesus as Savior. It is likely to challenge all of these notions, part of the concept of divine compassion, as completely groundless and detached from the simple human desire to stop the suffering of the other. Moreover, if compassion is a human quality, what is to ensure its presence specifically in clergymen or those who deem themselves good Christians? Why does the priest, bishop, or archbishop enjoy the guaranteed status of a compassionate person? Since, as individuals, they have no greater tendency toward compassion than the shoemaker or doctor, what is the implication of such a distinction being tied to church hierarchy, which draws most of its power from its control over the ritual and interpretation of Jesus' commandments and which claims that only by accepting these three elements can compassion be given earthly presence? And, finally, what are the ramifications of a here-and-now solution to human suffering likely to be for the resolution to the problem of theodicy? For a true war on human distress entails the belief that it is possible to provide a person with immediate ease, and even if happiness or welfare cannot be attained for everyone, it is certainly possible to advance in that direction without any need for recourse to the Kingdom of Heaven. Thus, from the Christian perspective, awareness of another's pain is unwelcome and must be subdued, both conceptually and practically, if it is not anchored in the world of concepts shaped by Christianity, if it does not bear a sense of divine compassion embodied on earth, and if it is not subject to the hierarchical structure of Church-sanctioned sainthood and Church power.

The opening words of St Francis' last Testament tell of how before he repented, he was strongly repulsed by the mere sight of lepers. They did not arouse his 'human' compassion, but rather his disgust. The biographic stories, both by Thomas of Celano and those in the *Legend of the Three Companions*,[2] also recount the tale of the encounter between St Francis and a leper early in his conversion process, and the saint's initial response of repugnance at the leper's appearance and smell; he managed to overcome this repulsion once he realized he was turning away from God by turning his back on the leper. Only after God had led him into their midst, St Francis told, could he perform acts of grace. These acts (at least according to the biographical tales) amounted mainly to embracing or kissing the hands of the lepers and perhaps giving them alms.

St Francis' compassion, which, as described in the previous chapter, served as the paradigm for ultimate Catholic compassion, was not stirred by the sight of mere suffering. Rather, it emerged only with *a posteriori* divine intervention. The simple person, prior to her conversion to Christianity, can experience no compassion for the suffering of others, especially not toward lepers, who, in the conceptions of the period, epitomized the idea of the spreading of illness through the body as a reflection of a person's sins.[3] And moreover, the suffering person (in this case, the leper) was a mere instrument in the hands of St Francis to demonstrate the intervention of Divine Providence, to enable his holy transformation toward true conversion, and to reinforce the symbolic status of his purification and sainthood. As Wolf elucidates in his critical analysis of the encounter between St Francis and the leper, the leper himself in fact gained no benefit from this encounter:

> What did the leper get out of his contact with Francis? – the answer is: precious little, especially when one considers the enormous spiritual and social benefits that Francis took away from the encounter.[4]

The glorification of poverty

One of the frequent accusations directed at Christianity (one with more than a shred of truth) is that the Christian ethos on the whole sanctifies suffering and poverty rather than fighting them and trying to eliminate them. According to this line of criticism, Christianity has always had an interest in the persistence of poverty, since this ensures the continuation of the social and personal distress of broad sectors of society from where Christianity draws believers: this distress is the impetus that drives people into the arms of the Church in search of deliverance.

The classic example of the glorification of poverty is the saints' interpretation of *imitato Christi* as choosing a life of poverty and paucity. No one better exemplifies this than St Francis. What is interesting about Francis' approach to poverty is his presentation of poverty as holy ('holy poverty') and relentless insistence on the Franciscan brothers being in a perpetual state of poverty greater than that of anyone else, including the homeless or the most miserable of beggars. This insistence on poverty – to the point of expressly instructing the Franciscans to never eat or take alms beyond their needs for that same day, to don capes more meager and uncomfortable than the garbs of a beggar or vagabond, to make do with paltry and unprocessed food, to relinquish all material possessions – turned St Francis and the brethren of his Order into objects of veneration, and, not surprisingly, they successfully collected donations and charity from the rich, who were always happy to support a poor monk as opposed to a street pauper.

St Francis himself showed no particular interest in alleviating the existence of the poor. Indeed, his principal interest was to create more poverty, albeit poverty out of choice, in his Order. In effect, Wolf claims, in making entry into the Order contingent on relinquishing all property and choosing a life of poverty, Francis created two problematic phenomena. First, those who joined the Order were, *a priori*, people from the middle class, with property to relinquish. Those who had no property to give up, on whom poverty had been imposed through no choice of their own, could not and were not permitted to enjoy the fruits of holy poverty, for they could not create for themselves a 'measure of grace' by means of renunciation or transformation. Second, the desire to identify with the poor was quickly transformed into an odd type of competition with them. For if poverty itself is holy and I seek to be a Franciscan, I am clearly required to be poorer than the poorest pauper in order to come as close as possible to the holiness of Jesus. Accordingly, the Franciscan's encounter with poverty on the street – actual, imposed poverty, poverty through which the pauper cannot obtain any spiritual possessions in this world or the world to come – does not facilitate compassion and does not arouse any drive for change, but rather creates only a baseline for comparison: Have I reached the desired level of poverty and degradation? Have I succeeded in suffering more than this person suffers? In other words, this is an encounter that is immediately subordinate (albeit perhaps unwillingly) to the process of the personal salvation of the monk without any necessary link to the state of the pauper, who serves here only as an instrument of salvation.

> Once when St. Francis was going through one of the provinces preaching, he happened to meet a very poor man. While he reflected on the greatness of his poverty, he said to his companion: 'This man's poverty puts us in great shame and much rebukes our poverty.' His companion answered: 'In what way brother?' He replied: 'It is a great shame to me when I find anyone who is poorer than I, as I have chosen holy poverty for my lady and for my bodily and spiritual delights and riches, and this voice has resounded through the whole world saying that I have professed poverty before God and men. . . .'[5]

This instrumental approach to the poor excludes them from the bounds of compassion under my definition – as an empathetic way of relating that mandates recognizing and knowing the other as a subject, not an object. This could well be the reason that, not surprisingly, both from the tales about St Francis and from his own letters, we learn much of his great compassion toward his Franciscan brethren striving for salvation, but little of his compassion toward the unwilling poor and needy.

In the thirteenth century, during St Francis' era, the Italian cities in which the speedy and dramatic process of pre-capitalistic economic development occurred experienced a great concentration of social phenomena that were unheard of in the European cities of the Middle Ages: the first hints of the Renaissance in the world of the upper classes; an unprecedented strengthening and consolidation of the Church as a political force;[6] and rapid urbanization (in the wake of the burgeoning sea trade with the East), which was synonymous with the birth of socio-economic disparities and poverty in the street and the urban deprivation, hunger, and disease that became the signature mark of society's under-classes. On the background of all these phenomena, many in Italy (mainly on behalf of Christian groups connected in some way to the Church) worked in giving aid and support, raising funds and resources, volunteering in hospitals and shelters, and directly assisting the poor who crowded the streets. Priests and preachers delivered piercing and profound sermons to the rich, appealing to them for charity; nuns treated the ill and lepers; and the churches distributed food. In a certain sense, it can be said that during this period, the operative foundations of the Catholic social system were laid.

Thus, St Francis was not the only one, and certainly not the first, to propose participating in the suffering of the poor as a worthy way of life for Christians. In Italy of his time, many Christians (some of which were eventually canonized) actually lived among the poor and sick and nursed them in their suffering and afflictions, while taking very high personal risks. In his book, Wolf describes many of these individuals who devoted themselves and everything at their disposal to the relentless battle against poverty, out of a clear commitment to making a genuine change in the lives and economic and physical states of society's weak and to even improving their political state. According to Wolf, these unique individuals, who came from every walk of life and sector of society, were not necessarily from the ranks of the Church (despite the fact that later on it granted them and their work official approbation), most prominent of which was Raymond Palmario of Piacenza, who was a pilgrim in his youth and later became a wandering preacher. These people all demonstrated through their lifestyles, their devotion and commitment, and their struggle for the welfare of the needy the possibility of realizing the Christian command to love thy neighbor in more impressive ways than St Francis did.

How, then, did the Franciscans achieve such prominence, both as a legitimate order of the Catholic Church and, in the Christian consciousness even to this day, as the supreme example of a life of humbleness, purity, holiness, and, of course, compassion?

The explanation offered by sociologists relates to the excellent service the Franciscan model of poverty rendered to the political dominance of the Church. For example, this model assisted in creating the humble image and reputation of one of the most powerful and richest establish-ments in the world, which reaped both the support and the money of the members of the affluent classes.[7] In addition, the Franciscan poverty paradigm conforms well with the idea of transformation, the pillar of the Church's missionary power base, for the affluent person (as St Francis was prior to his conversion) who forfeits all material benefits and becomes, out of choice, a beggar in the service of the Lord is both the allegory and the moral of the Christian sanctification process.[8] Moreover, St Francis had to his advantage extraordinary verbal skills, which may have been the result of his background as a merchant; and as a result of his great charisma and skillful political handling of his Order's affairs (for example, attaining Papal approbation of the Order's Rule), he avoided the mistakes made by the Waldenists before him and succeeded in acquiring for his Order the legitimacy that had eluded them. It is also quite possible that the Franciscans were well served by the convergence of their interests with the political and personal interests of Pope Innocent III, who sought to smother the problematic elements of Christianity (with the Waldenist movement at the top of the list) breathing down the Church's neck.

All these explanations notwithstanding – most of which have a compelling logical basis – there is another explanation that is of greater relevance to our context, namely that stemming from the Christian narrative of compassion that has been presented thus far. The Christian translation of agapic compassion into social activism, which begins with the understanding of Jesus' command of neighborly love as the basis for providing concrete aid to the needy, should lead to a general understanding of the essence of Christian love as a war on poverty – that is to say, to a commitment in practice to stamp out poverty. But such an interpretation, when combined with the emotions aroused in those actively engaged in aid by the distress and pain they witness, is likely to generate a tangible threat to the Church establishment. As already noted, this summons to undertake radical activism which deviates substantially from the array of options, images, and interests of the Church, which, as a powerful economic and political institution, would be categorically opposed to any change in the world order, seeking rather its fortification. The best way to remove the war on poverty from the public agenda and, at the same time, meet the Christian requirement of neighborly love and social aid is by presenting poverty as a 'non-problem'. Here we find the huge advantage to the glorification of poverty: poverty, rather than a problem, is presented as a wonderful platform for salvation since it holds the potential for drawing close to Jesus – for, indeed, salvation belongs to the poor! But only certain people (those who have undergone transformation) are candidates for sainthood and glorification, for holy poverty exempts the Church from defining every pauper as a religiously worthy person. Under the formula conceived by St Francis, the Church can continue to differentiate between the worthy and the sinners irregardless of their economic state. Indeed, the Franciscan model facilitates what is seemingly impossible from a logical and practical perspective: on the one hand, to claim that poverty presents no problem in itself; and on the other hand, to continue to treat the poor as worthy objects of compassion and activity on the part of the Christian establishment. It is precisely here that the reactionary aspect to Christian agapic compassion is exposed in full colors. This is a compassion that entails objects, since it is a religious duty. It is inconceivable that a genuine or successful war would be waged against the social phenomenon of poverty, since this would literally be chopping off the branch on which the essence of the faith itself rests. A significant diminishment of human agony and distress or, Heaven forbid, the complete disappearance of paupers would spell doom for agapic compassion: Who will be its objects through which the Gospel can materialize?

The Franciscan model, under which the pain of the poor, dying, lepers, and afflicted should be shared and according to which this sharing brings relief and joy first and foremost to the person assisting them, does not call for healing pain, exterminating poverty, or, of course, eliminating distress.[9] Pain and suffering are important matters, and we should therefore rejoice in them.

'Mother Teresa, what do you hope to accomplish here?'
'The joy of loving and being loved.'
'That takes a lot of money, doesn't it?'
'It takes a lot of sacrifice.'
'Did you teach the poor to endure their lot?'
'I think it is very beautiful for the poor to endure their lot, to share it with the passion of Christ. I think the world is being much helped by the suffering of the poor people.'[10]

If we take this logic one step further and assume that human history is the reflection of the realization of power interests, we quickly reach the conclusion that if Christianity has an interest in poverty and if it is an institution of power in the sense that it is capable of crafting history, it clearly not only rejoices in poverty, but also creates poverty – whether directly or indirectly.

Masochistic theodicy

Hovering in the background throughout the discussion of divine compassion have been the problem of theodicy and the connection between the cultural construction of the concept of compassion and the need to respond to the matter of the existence of suffering in the world. Is it possible that the Christian path for contending with the problem of theodicy – by presenting compassion as a type of armor that can protect human beings from pain – in fact bears the seeds of anti-compassion?

Peter Berger has defined successful theodicy as that which 'permit[s] the individual to integrate the anomic experience of his biography into the socially established nomos and its subjective correlate in his own consciousness'.[11] According to Berger, what is unique about successful theodicy is not its ability to create a reality or even perception of happiness for the individual. Rather, its great power lies in its instilling the pain with meaning, even in the most difficult moments of suffering. It is certainly likely that precisely in such moments, the afflicted person will seek to understand 'Why?', and this query, claims Berger, is of no less critical existential-psychological importance than the alleviation of the pain itself.[12]

What is interesting about Christian theodicy is the ambiguity it creates with regard to the answers to two questions: What is the reason for suffering, and how can suffering be stopped? Seemingly, the answers should be remarkably simple, rooted in the New Testament: the reason for personal and social suffering is man's sins, and the best way to contend with this suffering is to accept Jesus, feel his suffering, love, and forgiveness, and thereby gain entry into the Kingdom of Heaven. In practice, however, things are not quite so simple, for a person who sins does not necessarily endure greater personal suffering than a righteous person. On the contrary, oftentimes it seems that the empiric reality completely negates any presentation of the world as a moral place. Thus, it is necessary to amend the presumption with regard to the morality of reality and to assume two different levels of reality. The one is the sphere of the worldly reality, the material world of human beings as we know it, which is, indeed, tainted by (perhaps the original) sin. This world does not function in accordance with a moral logic, and therefore we at times find the righteous suffering and cannot gauge the extent of present suffering or happiness as a correlate of sin or right-eousness. Only in the second sphere of reality, the divine reality, is there a direct correlation between sinning and righteousness, and punishment and reward. Thus, in the face of the causal chaos of the material world, Christian theodicy offers a certain latent temptation: it is quite possible that the suffering that people feel in this world is preparation for the good life in the heavenly reality. It is precisely this suffering, like poverty as discussed above, that is the indicator of the great potential for nearing the Kingdom of Heaven, since it brings man closer to the experience of Jesus. That is to say, from a Christian theodical perspective, the reason for suffering is not at all clear (for only God knows the solution), but this lack of clarity should be understood in positive terms as preparation for life in the world to come and for a life of holiness in this world (assuming that, in a certain sense, the Kingdom of Heaven is already present here).

There is no clear answer to the question of the cessation of suffering either. In the previous chapter, I showed that the Christian religious-social criterion, the nomos, must be met in order to be able to accept Jesus and to reap the benefits of faith in him and of his infinite love, which is the closest thing to happiness that Christianity can promise. But meeting this requirement, which includes fulfilling the command of neighborly love, entails divine infusion; and as we saw, those who are able to benefit from this infusion are in fact not necessarily the most needy. Thus, the circularity of agapic compassion, the social and institutional dangers of active compassion, and the inbuilt contradiction between the desire to embrace and help the needy and the need to perpetuate their neediness do not add clarity to the idea of salvation in the gutters.

According to Berger, the route Christianity chose for dealing with the complex of contradictions and dilemmas relating to the problem of theodicy was to develop what he terms 'masochistic' theodicy. A masochistic attitude amounts to total self-denial in the face of an (fictitious or actual) entity that is perceived as absolute and omnipotent:

> Its key characteristic is the intoxication of surrender to an other-complete, self-denying, even self-destroying... 'I am nothing – He is everything – and therein lies my ultimate bliss' – in this formula lies the essence of the masochistic attitude.[13]

The masochistic attitude is defined by Berger as a pre-theoretical tendency that precedes the conceptual forging of the social reality. It is a distinctly irrational tendency and, in many senses, clouds and even presents an obstacle to determining a rational solution to the problem of theodicy. This attitude appears in many contexts – in interpersonal relations (sadomasochism), in the revitalization of patriotism in social frameworks (equating patriotism with willingness to die for one's country), and in the monotheistic religions, which developed different types of masochistic theodicies to contend with the trivial question that emerges in the face of horrors and indescribable suffering: 'How could God let this happen...?' Berger maintains, following the lines of Camus' famous claim that the pinnacle of the masochistic attitude is represented by Catholicism.

In that Christ suffered, and had suffered voluntarily, suffering was no longer unjust and all pain was necessary. In one sense, Christianity's bitter intuition and legitimate pessimism concerning human behavior is based on the assumption that over-all injustice is as satisfying to man as total justice. Only the sacrifice of an innocent god could justify the endless and universal torture of innocence. Only the most abject suffering by God could assuage man's agony. If everything, without exception, in heaven and earth is doomed to pain and suffering, then a strange form of happiness is possible.[14]

The question of the Christian attitude toward the suffering divinity is interesting in itself: To what extent did Christian thought allow itself to view Jesus' divine suffering as a substantive part of man's way of relating to divinity? As stressed in Chapter 2, the very formulation of this question indicates the possibility of a two-way interaction between divinity and man. Even if we accept the Berger–Camus claim above that human distress retreats in the face of the terrible suffering of the Divinity, which was caused by man and was taken from him by Jesus for the sake of man, there is still a possibility that God will be the object of some sort of human compassion. This possibility has not been embraced in the history and theology of Christianity. First, as already indicated, the source of compassion in Christianity is divinity itself, and therefore it is not possible for human beings to have the ability to be compassionate toward God without this being facilitated by God himself. Thus, even if the Christian believer finds herself feeling compassion for Jesus, obviously this emotion is of merely didactic value and its source divine grace – it is not a human reaction to the pain of another. Second, the tendency to place the suffering of Jesus the Divinity at the heart of the understanding of Christian theology and theodicy is characteristic of the later theological and theodical trends and of the interpretation from the last two centuries. In fact, until the Age of Enlightenment, the idea of a suffering god was not a legitimate possibility in Christian thought.

The notion of a masochistic theodicy has, however, other implications with respect to Christianity's anti-compassionate tendency. The paling of human suffering in the face of divine suffering carried with it also the fading of compassion. Identification with and awareness of the distress of the other are no more than a flimsy reflection of true compassion, divine compassion, which not only identifies the suffering and recognizes the pain, but also continues to burden Divinity itself with this pain. Accordingly, the road is short to the delegitimation of human compassion altogether and the declaration of divine compassion as the sole possibility, to complete the anti-compassion processes described above.

If we take the Berger–Camus logic one step further, we can distinguish a model that the masochistic tendency imposes on the individual: every human action – beginning with the motivation to perform the action, to the feelings and awarenesses involved in the action, and culminating with the execution of the material act – is subject to the paradigms of meaning that reach man externally from the omnipotent entity. In fact, within a masochistic (or, more precisely, sadomasochistic) configuration, there is no need for any meaning to an action in itself. It is sufficient that the action is demanded by the patron, with the entire meaning of the act lying in the fact that the demand to perform it came from 'above'. Thus, there is no meaning to the content of the command to take action: it is irrelevant whether man is required to be compassionate or to murder – what is important is that the demand is external and that its fulfillment satisfies the entity making the demand. Psychological-sociological direction of this kind is especially forceful in the context of the masochistic theodicies of the monotheistic religions, because the demanding entity is not present and because the relationship that cancels out the individual exists between her and an abstract, distant entity. The individual can only guess the demands of the omnipotent entity with the help of mediators who do not always concur with one another and who work on behalf of social institutions that have their own agendas. This situation creates a reality in which the contents of the act of satisfying the omnipotent entity are likely to change dramatically and frequently. A person is likely to find herself performing actions 'in the name of the Lord' that clash with one another (for example, aiding the poor in the morning and killing heretics in the evening), but they are all subject to the same paradigm that is expressed in the social ethos of loyalty to the Word of God.

This situation *a priori* undermines any possible ethical meaning to human action. A person assists her friend not because she loves him or because she has decided to behave in accordance with the imperative of her reason, but rather because she has been so ordered to act. Under this model, if, tomorrow, the social ethos dictates a different interpretation of God's will – say, one that commands people to alienate others – the individual will adhere to this just as strongly and will derive the same degree of satisfaction and meaning from her action.

Christianity, as an example of masochistic theodicy in its ultimate form, is the most extreme of the monotheistic traditions in this respect, not only because it is based on the torment of the Lord, as Berger and Camus claim, but also because it encompasses an explicit command and a complete social ethos that govern not only one's actions but also their emotions. The requirement – or command – to 'feel', to 'love', illustrates, on the one hand, the enormous power of the masochistic theodicy and its great presumptuousness in dictating the way in which people feel about the other and, on the other hand, the great weakness of agapic love – as a love that we are commanded to feel and not as a feeling that awakens in us when faced with the distress or joy of the other. This is a command that evokes a considerable amount of frustration: first, because it is doomed to failure – it is impossible to summon emotions (although it is possible to socially create them) and certainly to command their appearance; second, since the very failure, which is well anticipated by the guiding institution, rebounds directly on to man himself for not having met the requirement and for having failed to satisfy God, that is, for not having been faithful 'enough', for not making enough of an effort or perhaps not attaining the desired level of allegiance to the Lord. All of these serve to systematically reinforce the masochistic attitude.

With this discussion as background, it is perhaps possible to understand the ability of the Inquisitors of the Middle Ages to present torture, infliction of pain, and sadistic cruelty as acts of compassion toward their victims (as 'freeing' the souls of the sinners, as it were). It is perhaps possible to explain the effortless waiving of agapic compassion in the Christian wars against heretics, in the crusades and conquests carried out in the name of the European Christian Empire, for example. We can see the origin of the ability of priests to witness the acts of murder and atrocities carried out by the Spanish soldiers and adventurers in South America and then suggest different modes of the so-called 'compassion' toward the natives (for example, advocating strangulation instead of burning at the stake); similarly, we can understand the Church's clumsy political response to the atrocities of the Nazi regime in

Europe (quite in contrast to the actions of lone Christian individuals, local Christian groups, and monasteries to save Jews, for example). All of these illustrate well how, from a certain perspective of the logic described above, the masochist becomes the sadist, while taking the empty place of the omnipotent entity in a sophisticated social version of role swapping.

Part II
Universal Compassion

4

Indiscriminate Compassion

The religious and intellectual traditions of India pose a unique challenge to the idea of compassion, despite the fact that they developed through a systematic occupation with the suffering and transient existential state of human beings. The point of departure for this concern with human suffering is its presentation in the framework of a chaotic cosmic reality – ever-changing, fleeting, and lacking all purpose – of miserable and fragmentary human existence in which pleasure and satisfaction of needs have no meaning:

> In this ill-smelling, unsubstantial body, which is a conglomerate of bone, skin, muscle, marrow, flesh, semen, blood, mucus, tears, rheum, feces, urine, wind, bile, and phlegm, what is the good of enjoyment of desires? And we see that this whole world is decaying, as these gnats, mosquitoes, and the like, the grass, and the trees that arise and perish...Among other things, there is the drying up of great oceans, the falling away of the mountain peaks, the deviation of the fixed pole-star...
>
> In this sort of cycle of existence (*saṃsāra*) what is good of enjoyment of desires, when after a man has fed on them there is seen repeatedly his return here to earth?
>
> *Maitri Upanishad*[1]

Under Weberian sociological logic, the way in which Indian religious thought has dealt with the problem of suffering and its explanation for the existence of suffering in the world (the problem of theodicy) are rooted in the internal logic of the *karma–Saṃsāra* theory. The successful linking of *karma* – the law of causation that governs all actions in the cosmos – with the *Saṃsāra*, the Wheel of Rebirth, produced an under-standing under which every phenomenon that seems chaotic, inexpli-cable, and random (especially one evoking pain, injury, or distress) is integrated into a comprehensive and coherent composite of a logical and systematic reality. Every human action has necessary consequences that will materialize in the future; thus, everything that a person experi-ences in the present is merely the outcome of her actions in the past in this or a previous incarnation, even if she has no memory of them. Such an action can be verbal, reflect ive, or physical, but what deter-mines its *karmic* quality is the intentionality behind it. If this intention-ality conforms with the eternal essence of the soul (*ātman*), then the action that derives from it will bring its owner closer, in her next incar-nation, to her soul's eternal destination: a better life, whether in the form of rebirth into a higher caste or ascent to the height of holiness, which can be manifested in a release from suffering. Thus, under the *karmic–Samsaric* logic, human beings bear sole responsibility for their fates and for what happens to them, leaving nothing inexplicable in principle (which, in Weber's view, is what characterizes religious thought in India as particularly rational in nature).[2]

Peter Berger, in his discussion of the Indian solution to the problem of theodicy, quite rightly notes that it is precisely at this point that the conservative quality of Indian religious thought is most conspicuous, in that it gives expression to the ideology of the governing social class in India – the Brahmin caste. Indeed, the most important social manifesta-tion of the *karmic–Samsaric* configuration appears in the claim that a person can only lessen the suffering entailed by the Wheel of Rebirth if she behaves in accordance with the *dharma* in the Hindu sense of the concept, namely follows the social norms, particularly the rules of the Indian caste system. Thus, the outlook embodied in the Indian *Laws of Manu*,[3] which represents Brahmin ideology at its ultimate (though it is not clear to what extent and how this form of ideology was applied in practice in Indian social life), presents the social division into castes (especially the cruel reality of being born into a lower caste lacking all social, religious, and political rights) as the product of the acts of the people themselves. Thus, according to Hindu ruling class logic, you do not suffer because someone exploits, oppresses, or degrades you, but, rather, because of the necessary and inevitable consequences of your own deeds in the past.[4]

From this it follows that the solution to the problem of suffering is not a social one, nor does it involve people who can alleviate the suffering, be compassionate, or actually act for the good of others: the problem is the individual sufferer's and hers alone! The Indian folk traditions supported this logic, developing an amazing and extensive assortment of customs, rituals, sorcery and mystic practices, and communication with different types of divinities, all of which were summoned to ease the heavy personal burden imposed by the *karmic–Samsaric* system on the individual. These traditions evolved despite the fact that the gloomy and even repulsive picture of human existence painted in the *Upanishads*[5] was certainly not the reality experienced by the ordinary people.

In fact, the trap of the Wheel of Rebirth, including the 'punishment' of being born into a lower caste, can be escaped by following one of two routes, both of which have been prominent in the history of Hindu religious thought: either by adhering to custom and practice and following the *dharma* path or else by embracing a vision of liberation with mystic connotations, which, not surprisingly, constituted the pillar of the majority of the traditions that evolved out of the *Upanishads*.[6] In the *Upanishads*, we find the identification of the *ātman* ('breath', the self, the soul, the personal consciousness) with Brahman (the god, the principle or unifying entity that lies at the foundation of all phenomena) as the basis to this vision of liberation:

> Be pleased to deliver me. In this cycle of existence I am like a frog in a waterless well. Sir [Sakayanya, one who knows the true nature of the *ātman*], you are our way of escape – yea, you are our way of escape!
>
> *Maitri Upanishad*[7]

But whether this is a type of escapism or a transformative liberation theory, it clearly leaves no room for compassion, at least with regard to the theodicies of suffering and liberation. The only possibility for compassion is in the framework of the behavioral and social principles of the *dharma* itself, in its capacity as a code of ethics that preserves the social order, on the one hand, and ensures the realization of the individual's *karmic* potential on the other. In this vein, the great seventh-century philosopher Kumārila Bhutta suggested an understanding of the *dharma* as the 'good deed', as a sort of moral act that creates 'potential' energy that accrues to the credit of the person in the *karmic* process. Under Kumārila's approach, the *dharma* as a moral virtue need not be manifested in a concrete action taken for the good of another; rather it can be based on intentionality alone, on sharing in the suffering of the other.

The implication of this type of outlook is that compassion can bear significance in preserving the *dharma* and the presence of compassion offers a certain potential for *karmic* 'class improvement'. However, compassion is not an integral part of the theoretical conception of liberation from the Wheel of Rebirth and does not advance a person toward liberation. Compassion can operate within the cosmic structure of the *karma–Saṃsāra*, and certainly it holds advantages for the private individual. But it does not lead to liberation in the sense of a mystical melding with the *ātman–Brahman* existence – that is, the cessation of the painful and unremitting cycle of perpetual rebirth and the entry into an ontological/conscious state of static, quiet, indiscriminate unity, lacking all sense of self. None of these are attained through compassion. Rather they are the product of practice, belief, and ritual (each Indian school and its particular system), which facilitate the radical transformation of the consciousness/reality.

The Buddhist traditions presented a different and more extreme approach to the *karmic–Samsaric* configuration, as well as to the concept of compassion and its role in relation to the possibilities for liberation. According to Weber, Buddhism in fact represents the most radical rationalization of the Indian *karmic–Samsaric* model.[8] Ancient Buddhism, especially in its more theoretical manifestations in certain parts of the Pali Canon,[9] in effect eradicated the importance of the *karmic–Samsaric* system, with all its traditional accompaniments in the Indian religious imagination: the metaphysical account of the cosmos as being in a perpetual state of creation and annihilation; the presence of gods, demons, and entire Hindu mythological worlds. All of these either disappeared (to reappear later in the folkloric traditions in some form or another) or, at the very least, became irrelevant.[10] Only the person as an entity was left in place, in a reality composed of concrete elements (*dharmas* in the Buddhist sense), by means of the human psyche and the creation of an illusory reality that leads to attachment and suffering. The Buddhist understanding of the *karmic–Samsaric* system casts doubt on the causal structure of the model as representing a possibility for approaching the eternal, authentic, fundamentally cosmic essence of the soul. In Buddhism, essences of this type disappear along with the negation of a metaphysical interpretation of reality – a redundant interpretation that inevitably leads to great suffering. The Buddhist understanding of the *karmic* system, similar to the approach espoused by Kumārila (who was influenced by the Buddhist tradition), rests primarily on the moral quality of actions as based on intentionality. According to the Buddhist sense of rebirth, a person's *karmic* status or impact, discernible in all of their actions in this life, generates a new form of life. But since, by definition, every form of life is necessarily doomed to some sort of suffering, liberation from that suffering is in fact tantamount to liberation from the Wheel of Rebirth of the *karmic* system. This possibility for liberation is contingent on a person's ability to know and understand the underlying laws of the illusory reality. All else is completely irrelevant in the unique understanding of the *karmic–Samsaric* system offered by Buddhism, which is based primarily on what became the general Buddhist paradigm – the Four Noble Truths of the Buddha.

The first Noble Truth is that life is replete with suffering (*dukkha* in Sanskrit). This is perpetual, tangible, existential pain that accompanies man from birth to death (both painful moments in themselves). This Truth, as the analytical departure point, directly binds Buddhist anthropology to the question of theodicy. The Buddha's identification of life with suffering, definition of suffering as a problem in need of solution, and proposed diagnostic process for identifying the source of the suffering and providing a solution for it all reveal Buddhist thought to be, in essence, a type of rational theodicy.

The second Noble Truth is that the source of pain is desire, or craving (*tanha*), or, more precisely, the attachment to objects of desire. Desire is an integral part of human existence, as it enables that existence, makes it possible – without desire, there would be no sexual relations, for example, and thus no perpetuation of human existence. From the Buddhist perspective, desire is the very driving force of life – the impetus behind the cycle of death and rebirth, impelling human beings to continue to be reborn into new incarnations, into unending states of suffering. Desire, however, is also the yearning for what cannot materialize. This creates the peculiar situation in which man is attached to objects of his desire (which can be anything – a material object, an emotion, a person), attempting to possess them and grasp them, consume them and exploit them. Desire is thus founded on a perpetual lack of satiation and the need to satisfy what is missing, which can never be accomplished – and in this way, desire causes pain.

The second Buddhist Noble Truth thus is the formal presentation of the diagnosis of perpetual existential pain, pointing to suffering as both a problem and the impetus for a specific psychological and social human reality. Here we can discern the radical nature of Buddhism, in transferring the causal logic of the *karmic* configuration from the metaphysical realm to the therapeutic sphere. But this is accompanied by a distinctly conservative bent, in the attribution of the cause for suffering to the person themselves, their actions, traits, and tendencies (although it is not clear to what extent they are in the person's control).

The Third Noble Truth is the assertion that a person's pain and suffering can be brought to end only by eliminating desire. This, in turn, will lead to the cessation of the attachment to the objects of desire and yearning, which, from both practical and theoretical perspectives, amounts to the cessation of the life of suffering, of perpetual rebirth, and the attainment of the ultimate goal of Nirvāṇa. This Truth, therefore, represents the passage from diagnosis to cure: suspending or wiping out the cause necessarily leads to the elimination of its outcome as well. This is an interesting and, again, double-faceted claim. On the one hand, it distances us from the logic of the *karmic* configuration in declaring that precisely those things that are the most intimate and authentic identifiers of human beings are what delays us, obstructs us, and prevents us from attaining liberation. On the other hand, this assertion is the product of a long tradition in India that stretches back to the Vedist sources, a tradition that is an integral element of the very logic underlying the *karmic* model: in order to achieve holiness, liberation, Nirvāṇa, a person must overcome his urges and drives, conquer his desire, and repress his emotions.

In order to accomplish this, according to the Fourth Noble Truth, the person must adopt a lifestyle that is governed by what is known in Buddhism as the 'Eightfold Path to Enlightenment'. This lifestyle comprises eight moral, intellectual, and pragmatic elements that enable a person to attain liberation from his cravings and reach Nirvāṇa, which, in its precise etymological sense, is the 'extinguishing of the flame'. The intellectual elements of the Path are a *right understanding* of the Buddha's principal teachings (including the Four Noble Truths, the law of *karma* – good deeds lead to happy states, bad deeds to miserable ones – and the three aspects of existence – suffering, impermanence, and absence-of-self) and *right thought* (thought free of ill-will, cruelty, and lust). The moral elements are *right speech* (abstaining from lying, harsh or malicious speech, and gossiping); *right action* (abstaining from killing (including animals), stealing and unlawful sexual acts such as rape or adultery); and *right livelihood* (abstaining from any occupation that would involve the breaking of the five precepts, such as a butcher). The final three elements are *right effort* (avoiding or overcoming unwholesome states, such as losing one's temper, and developing and maintaining wholesome states, such as equanimity) and *right mindfulness* and *right concentration*, which relate to two approaches to meditation vital to one's spiritual development.

This Fourth Truth could be seen as the most disappointing of the Truths, at least in terms of providing a formula for salvation that in the long run clarifies how, in practice, the complicated task of disconnection from objects of desire can be carried out. Indeed, this long-awaited formula would close the rational cycle described by the Buddha and would offer a clear alternative to the *karmic* system. But instead, the Buddha chose to leave the answer open to interpretation. And indeed, an abundance of varying interpretations of the practical requirements of the Path to Enlightenment ensued and came to constitute the backbone of Buddhist thought across the generations and different streams of Buddhism, each offering a different understanding of the eight elements of the Path. Yet it is important to note that, in refraining from prescribing a specific formula and, instead, choosing a general, sweeping formulation, the Buddha in fact left a considerable opening to understanding the solution as an overall and total transformation in all parameters of human life – at both the psychological and social levels.

Alongside the Four Noble Truths, Buddhist philosophical tradition espouses two radical claims, both of which can be traced to the Buddha's doctrine and have appeared in Buddhist intellectual history in different formulations. The one claim relates to the absence-of-self: human beings have no constant mental state, either lofty or simple, that consolidates within them into perceptions, thoughts, or emotions. There is also no such thing as a mental 'supra-framework' by which a person comes to know himself as of uninterrupted identity, continuous over time. A person's consciousness, like his body, is, under the Buddhist conception, in a constant process of change, and any attribution of 'self' as a permanent and constant entity is mere illusion and deception. In effect, a person is no more than an assortment of psychological-physical components, separated into groups of corporal elements, emotional elements, perceptions, thoughts, and so on, with each group in a constant process of change and existing autonomously, with no causal connection to the other groups.

The second claim pertains to the illusory nature of the external reality. Reality as we perceive it (the phenomenal world) is merely an assortment of conventions that are based on the illusion of the self, on the one hand, and the established use of language, on the other. Together, these two create in human beings the illusion of an actual reality with continuity, permanence, constancy, and cyclicality. But in fact, reality, just like the self, is no more than a random and shifting assortment of perpetually transitory elements. Behind these claims lies the assumption that the immediate consequence of liberation from the grip of the self, just like release from the grasp of the illusory reality, is liberation from suffering, for how can suffering exist if there is no subject to feel it? And how can desire exist without objects of reality to yearn for?

These two claims, when considered in conjunction with the Four Noble Truths, elucidate the nature of illusory life as a life of suffering and present an alternative in the form of a quest for the 'truth', namely that uncovering the illusion of reality, recognizing the self's absence of actuality, and leading a moral lifestyle composed of study and meditation, all of which loosen the hold of the illusions of the self and reality, are the key to bringing an end to suffering.

Parallel to and in conformity with the Buddhist philosophical conception of liberation, different and varied techniques of meditation developed in Buddhism, which were intended to sustain the 'right' way of life. Some of these techniques were aimed at directly facilitating the 'melting' or extinguishing of the self and, concurrently, the negation or at least diminishment of the ontological status of the objects of reality. The Buddhist meditator trains himself over the course of years to attain a special concentration that enables him to 'transform' the ego and the world, pushing them away and diminishing their status in his field of consciousness. In certain streams of Buddhism, the ultimate purpose of this process is to attain an empty consciousness, or 'absolute voidness', whose precise meaning is Nirvāṇa. The fundamental meaning of the term 'Nirvāṇa', which represents the teleological aspect of Buddhist practice and thought in general, is 'obliteration' or 'extinguishment'. Nirvāṇa is a sort of quenching of the fires of desire, lust, anger, and attachment, as well as the overcoming of prejudices, false concepts, and instinctual ignorance. Its philosophical meaning is the correct view of reality as it 'truly' is; its psychological-existential meaning is release from suffering and the Wheel of Rebirth. Nirvāṇa, as a central concept in Buddhist culture, has a wide field of reference and has been the subject of different analyses in the Buddhist literature and the Buddhist and commentarial traditions, beginning with its understanding as a regulative ideal that does not necessarily represent a consciousness in its accepted sense (that is, in the intentional sense of a consciousness 'of' something), to its understanding as a state of joy and grace, to its presentation as a mystical experience of totality.

Together, the Four Noble Truths and the claims of absence-of-self claim and need for extinguishing the illusory reality combine to form a most radical transformative structure. This model assumes that the source of a solution to the problem of suffering cannot be any of the familiar elements of reality, since in the final analysis, they are always likely to emerge as part of the problem itself. The solution can exist only in unanimity, understanding, and perpetual practicing of deconstructing reality. The great debates in classical Buddhist thought frequently revolved around the attempt to explain the meaning of the deconstruction process and its effects: Is it the consciousness negation of reality and opting for an alternative life of absolute voidness, of intentional absence of consciousness? Or is it a relinquishment of attachment and abandonment of perpetual sensual movement across the transient and impermanent components of a fleeting reality, similar to how a leaf floats in the wind? Perhaps the intention is to the stripping of the spurious masks forced on us by the social-linguistic-cultural reality into which we are born and the decision to lead a life of perpetual quest for authenticity, which, though unattainable, is preferable to being trapped in the illusion of stability (similar to what the existential philosophers were to propose far away in time and place). All of these possibilities (and many others) can be derived from the words of the Buddha and from the overall Buddhist canon, and all appear in some form in Buddhist history and in later commentaries on that history.

For the purposes of the present discussion, there is no need to decide on an answer to the above questions. What is significant to our context is the fact that Buddhism defines human suffering as a problem that must be resolved – indeed, the Buddha presented himself as a type of healer or therapist, not as a metaphysicist. Similarly, it is important to understand that Buddhism proffers a kind of idealistic logic according to which it is possible to change reality by manipulating the consciousness – that is to say, the most rudimentary Buddhist logic asserts that reality is in many critical respects consciousness-contingent.[11]

Lying in the background of this brief description is another element of Buddhism: compassion. Under the Buddhist approach, compassion is the ability to feel the pain and suffering of the other, as well as being a way of relating that is universal in two senses: First, it can be experienced by all people, especially those who have been liberated from the illusory conceptions of the self and the world. The melting of the ego and the emptying of reality enable one to enter into the world of the other and to discover the final, surviving element after the deconstruction of the worldview – compassion, revealed as the ultimate and, accordingly, most authentic substance, which defines man for what he is. Second, compassion is universal in that it is directed at every person, without distinction – rich and poor, child and adult, and so on. In fact, from the Buddhist perspective, compassion is a way of relating also to all animals, plants, and so on, and is not designated for human beings alone. This lack of discrimination is, of course, rooted in the Buddhist fundamental view of life, in all its forms, as suffering.

The Buddhist motivation to fight ignorance – from the Buddhist perspective, the flames of desire that lead to attachment and suffering or, alternatively, the false concepts that tighten the grip on the illusory reality – originates with the journey of the Buddha himself, first to enlightenment and then to expanding the circle of enlightened by marking the way for the unenlightened and suffering (that is, for everyone). The Buddha's compassion is, first and foremost, a willingness to share with all forms of life trapped in ignorant desire in their suffering and desperate need to be rescued from the cycle of suffering. It is not clear from the ancient canonical Buddhist literature (which tells the story of the Buddha and his teachings) whether this compassion refers to an identification with the suffering of others who have yet to attain enlightenment, based on the Buddha's personal experience along the winding and unpredictable path to enlightenment, or if it is an extremely radical and fundamental anthropological conception of all human beings as immediately discerning the suffering, bondage, and tragedy of life in the *Saṃsāra* as soon as they correctly observe reality. What is indisputable is that the Buddha himself had the ability to be compassionate and this ability was the ultimate basis both for his decision to show the way to liberation and his assertion that the Path of Enlightenment necessarily leads through empathy for the suffering of others. One of the most familiar expressions of this empathetic stance as an inherent part of the essence of Buddhist teaching in general appears in the famous (and frequently quoted) passage from the *Sutta-Nipa-ta* commentary that deals with the Buddha's discourse on loving kindliness (*metta*):

One who knows the state of well-being, who seeks that place of peace, should live thus: able, upright, truly upright, of noble speech, gentle, humble.

Knowing sufficiency, well-content, with few wants and simple tastes, With senses calmed, discreet, not arrogant, not attached to blood-relations, Not pursuing the least thing for which one could be censured by the wise.

May all things be happy and safe, may they all be truly happy.

Whether they are weak or strong, long or large, medium or short, without exception, Seen or unseen, dwelling far or near, born or yet unborn, May all things be truly happy.

Let no one deceive another, nor look down upon another anywhere, ever. Let no one wish harm on any other, in anger or ill will.

As a mother would protect her only child with her whole life, let one cultivate such a boundless mind towards all beings.

Let this kindly heart, this boundless mind, embrace the whole world. Above, below, across, unobstructed, free from hatred, free from ill will.

Standing, walking, sitting, lying down, while awake, cultivate this mindfulness, This it is said, is the sublime dwelling place.

Not falling into wrong views, living virtuously, replete with insight, overcoming delusive desires, such a one will not enter the cycle of rebirth.

Metta Sutta[12]

Ancient Buddhist logic sets compassion as an integral, even inbuilt part of the process of liberation that leads to Nirvāṇa, on the basis of four insights, each of which appears in the Pali text cited above. First, there is the anthropological assertion that supplements the definition of life as suffering. A person on the way to enlightenment succeeds in freeing himself and in ridding his thoughts of ignorant desire and illusory concepts and finds himself to be a compassionate person. That is to say, compassion is the fundamental definitive characteristic of human beings, the quality that survives the test of the deconstruction of reality. Second, there is a didactic quality to compassion in that it enables concentration on emotional elements and elements of consciousness with positive contents, which constitute a sort of counterweight to the deconstruction process. Positive contents – regulative or concrete, logical or analogical – are imperative for a workable didactic for a process of refutation, annihilation, negation, and so on, that needs to be translated into a general way of life. Third, the presumption of compassion must inevitably be universal in scope and apply to all spheres of ignorance and suffering (including animal and even plant life). The entire force of the Buddha's contention (encompassed in the Four Noble Truths and the accompanying claims) rests on relating to life, in all its forms, as a problem in need of a solution. From this it follows that every person, even someone who does not experience immediate distress, is trapped in the illusory web, whose meaning is suffering, even if he or she does not know this truth at present. Fourth, the universal pursuit of happiness and the commitment to the welfare of all are not presented as commandments or dictates, but rather as a counsel to be consciously accepted as an aspiration or a hope. The combination of commitment to the other and free choice points to the ethical and social connotation of the Buddhist claim of compassion as well as the possibility of a utopian social vision supplementing the process of individual liberation.

The first two points – the anthropological and didactic insights – highlight the necessary link forged by the Buddha between the concepts of liberation and compassion. Compassion is simply a conscious-emotional stage on the way to Nirvāṇa and is situated very close to Nirvāṇa, perhaps even identical to the state of Nirvāṇa. And since this compassion is universal, it possesses the features of the radical totality of the Nirvāṇa consciousness:

> Making the whole world of being the object of these minds endowed with compassion, we will continue to relate to the whole world with minds that are like the earth – untroubled, free from enmity, vast, enlarged and measureless.
>
> *Majjhima-Nikāya* I:127[13]

Nonetheless, compassion, like Nirvāṇa, cannot be automatically and instantly achieved. It requires cultivation and fostering; a person must train their mind to become compassionate. This didactic aspect is immediately apparent in the *Metta Sutta* passage cited above. On the one hand, in order to reach Nirvāṇa, a person must disconnect himself from all attachments – amongst other things, by alienating themselves from familial relationships. On the other hand, this requirement is completed by the notion of compassion, which offers a 'new' basis for human relations as well as imagery to aid us in attaining such relations. Thus, three lines after asserting the need to detach oneself from family ties, the text presents the relationship between mother and child – the strongest family bond – as the proper and correct imagery on which compassion should be based.

In a similar vein, the Buddhist commentator Buddhagosha offers the following interpretation of the *Aṅguttara-Nikāya* collection of discourses:[14]

> When a youth is in the womb, the parents think with a compassionate mind, 'When will we see our son healthy and endowed with all major and minor limbs?'. Then, when this tender creature lies on his back and cries or wails because of being bitten by lice or fleas or

because of being bothered by troubled sleep, the parents hear this noise and feel simple compassion. Furthermore, when the parents observe the youth in his most desirable years...their minds become tender, like a hundred fluffy balls of cotton soaked in the finest clarified butter.[15]

Thus, not only is parental compassion successful didactic imagery for advising empathy toward all living creatures; it also can be used to describe the evolution of the consciousness at different stages of the progression toward spiritual liberation and serenity, analogized to the parental sensitivity that evolves with the growth of the child. And the likening of the development of compassion to the desirable evolution of the consciousness makes clear the link between compassion and Buddhist liberation itself, as well as the therapeutic value of compassion in supplying a remedy for the problem of suffering. As was asserted by Buddhagosha,

> The liberation of the mind is love and compassion. It is compassion as it relates to all sentient beings with the wish for their welfare. Moreover, since the mind conjoined with compassion is liberated from all adverse factors such as the hindrances and so forth, it is called a liberation of the mind. Specifically, one becoming possessed by anger, compassion is the liberation of the mind.[16]

The supplementary aspect to the ideal of compassion of ancient Buddhism was set by the Buddha in the form of the social commitment and motivation to improve the lives of human beings. In the teachings attributed to him, no real comprehensive social agenda, utopian social vision, or even practical plan of action is pronounced, mainly because these would entail taking a stance preferring the interests of one group over those of another and this would have stood in contradiction to the motif of universal compassion itself. Yet the desire to put an end to the social and economic distress of different groups in society is clearly distinguishable in the *Digha-Nikāya* collection of the Buddha's discourses, as is the call to the Buddha's disciples and pupils to undertake social responsibility for decreasing crime and violence:

> [T]he Buddha suggests that, in order to eradicate crime, the economic condition of the people should be improved: grain and other facilities for agriculture should be provided for farmers and cultivators; capital should be provided for traders and those who are

engaged in business; adequate wages should be paid to those who are employed. When people are thus provided for with opportunities for earning a sufficient income, they will be contented, will have no fear or anxiety, and consequently the country will be peaceful and free of crime.[17]

The two supplementary motifs of Buddhist compassion – compassion as therapy that leads to the evolution of the consciousness and Nirvāṇa and compassion as a type of social duty – pose a difficult intellectual challenge for Buddhist thought. At the outset of the discussion on Buddhism in this chapter, I pointed to rationality as the Buddhist route for solving the theodicy problem; the commitment to this route lies at the methodical and technical core of the Buddha's teachings. However, the inclusion of compassion as a central and necessary part of Buddhist learning, at least on its face, gives rise to two internal contradictions. The first is in the clash between the need to subdue emotions and overcome desire and the fostering of emotional responsiveness to the distress of the other. In fact, certain parts of the Buddhist writings interpreting the intention of the Buddha describe compassion itself in terms of yearning:

> Compassion is the state of desiring to remove the suffering and misfortune, with the thought 'May they be liberated from these sufferings', and so forth. Love is the state of desiring to offer happiness and welfare with the thought, 'May all beings be happy'...
>
> *Visuddhimagga* VI:158, 162[18]

Clearly this advocating of emotion and acknowledgement of a certain type of desire, even the desire to witness the happiness of others, are not commensurate with the requirements of detachment and conquering emotions, setting a rather thorny anomaly.

The second internal contradiction relates to compassion as a way of relating to the other. If we assume that the Buddhist process of deconstructing the consciousness involves the annihilation, melting, or negation of the self and that this process is based on the unraveling of that self into its fundamental components, then from the perspective of the Buddhist practitioner, there is no meaning to the concept a 'person'. In effect, the Buddhist on the way to enlightenment does not see people at all, but rather a collection of impermanent, fleeting elements interrelating coincidentally (or causally, depending on the school of Buddhism) with one another. How is it possible, then, to feel compassion toward a random collection of 'atoms' of matter or thought (one of the senses of the concept of *dharma* in Buddhism)? Who in fact are the objects of compassion – those same conscious entities that feel and refer to themselves as 'human beings', who are none other than the very creatures deemed fictitious and whose actuality is refuted? Conze gives the following explanation of the Buddhist sage's compassionate gaze:

> Although Avalokita is aware of the suffering of all beings, and suffers with them, making his pains their own, nevertheless, when he casts his glance at this swarming multitude of men, animals, ghosts and angels, all more or less ill at ease, he does not see any persons or beings at all. Where ignorance imagines a personality or a living being, wisdom beholds but *five heaps* [*skandhas* in Sanskrit].[19]

It is in fact the very concept of universal compassion that offers the key to contending with these incongruities (or at least to mitigating their inherent methodical problematics). To begin with, it is relatively easy to present compassion that is all-inclusive – that is, applies to all people without distinction – as not necessarily a specific feeling directed at a specific person, but, rather, as a more general state of consciousness unaccompanied by any emotional connection to a given person. Compassion's motif of desire seems less threatening, or less problematic, when directed at the entire human race or all life forms, and not at a specific other. Such intentionality does not stand in open conflict with the recommendation not to become attached to specific people or objects and allows a 'holding of the stick at both ends' (a typical Buddhist tendency, which is related to the Buddhist approach to the mystical). Second, if Buddhist compassion is understood as mandating the absolute applicability of compassion to every possible object of the consciousness and if we assume a link between compassion and Nirvāṇa, which is the consciousness of totality, then the fact that no 'person', in the conventional, *Samsaric* sense of the word, appears before the Buddhist does not in fact present a problem, but rather an advantage from the viewpoint of Nirvāṇa. For indeed, Nirvāṇa is not comprehensible as a conscious state to someone not in that state, but, rather, is a sort of enigma that, *a priori*, does not lend itself to rational analysis since it assumes the obliteration of reason. Accordingly, the inability to grasp how the Buddhist sage can see the other, or people in general, is self-evident when the person trying to understand this is not a Buddhist sage herself. The incomprehensibility of the state of compassion is not necessarily a shortcoming, but rather, an advantage for any system that poses a gradated developmental challenge, with every stage in the process understood only when it is reached. Thus, in order to understand what genuine Buddhist compassion is, we must become Bodhisattvas – Buddhist monks who have progressed to the highest possible level approaching Nirvāṇa.

Thus, we see that the universality of Buddhist compassion is not only deeply rooted in the ethical motivations of the Buddha himself, but is also an integral part of the internal logic of the overall Buddhist philosophy and therapy. This universal nature is imperative for mitigating the internal inconsistencies in the epistemology and alleviating the tension between personal salvation and social commitment. In fact, *only* compassion of universal application can be introduced as a concept into the basic methodology of Buddhism. This concept of universal compassion relates to the scope of the objects of compassion, as including all people (suffering and happy, poor and rich, aggressors and victims, rapists and raped, oppressed and oppressors) as well as all other life forms, and to the essence of the compassion itself, as a unique state of consciousness – non-specific, a-personal – that does not represent an emotion, in the sense of yearning for an object, but rather general sympathy that is apprehensible primarily to the person who has approached and touched Nirvāṇa.

* * *

The spread of Buddhism through Southeast and East Asia led to the emergence of different Buddhist traditions, which often developed their own at times significantly deviating and even opposing conceptions of the Buddhist *dharma*. Buddhist compassion also took on different faces and forms over the course of history and through its journey across the Continent – from India, the birthplace of the Buddha, to faraway Japan, where primarily Chinese versions of Buddhism arose in the form of Zen Buddhism. To give just a slight sense of the internal Buddhist interpretational disparity, I will describe three of the later manifestations of compassion, all of which are derived from different understandings of the same Buddhist text, the *Lotus sūtra*. This *sūtra*, translated into Chinese from Sanskrit in 406 CE by the Buddhist scholar Kumārajīva, became one of the most popular and influential Buddhist canonical texts of all time across East Asia, with a genuinely mystical impact.[20] What is most interesting is that every interpretation of this text presents compassion in a different way and highlights a different aspect of compassion.

One manifestation of compassion is in its 'folk' form: compassion as it appears in the folklore, beliefs, and imagination of the people who live in the lands where Buddhism has had a massive presence. Buddhism's rational appearance at the doctrinal level and the Buddha's objection in principle to metaphysical speculations and the Indian phantasmal traditions of his time in no way hindered the flourishing of supernatural motifs, tales of miracles, and the summoning of the powers of the different incarnations of the Buddha to aid people in their distress. These phenomena, widespread even during the lifetime of the Buddha, particularly thrived following his death and reincarnation into different and strange forms, by which he continued to instruct and aid the people and demonstrate his great compassion. This extramental aspect was present at every level of Buddhist tradition. It had a tremendous impact on the Buddhist concept of compassion, which underwent a process of personification, taking, in the traditional imagery, the form of the Buddha and his successors, who themselves attained the status of deity.

One of the more familiar figures personifying the Tibetan-Indian tradition of compassion is Avalokīteśvara, the Buddha of Compassion. The chapter in the *Lotus Sūtra* that formed the basis for Avalokīteśvara's persona was granted the status of a separate and independent *sūtra* (Chapter 25 of the *Lotus Sūtra*), becoming so popular that it reached the level of cult worship of the God of Compassion. According to Williams' presentation of this text,[21] this *sūtra* tells how Avalokīteśvara responds to the appeals and pleas of its readers and saves them from disaster, primarily natural disasters such as fire, flooding, and storms, and also disasters caused by human and superhuman entities (murderers and robbers, ghosts and spirits). Avalokīteśvara also saves those who appeal to him for assistance in the face of evils caused to them by their own tendencies; he dissipates desire, anger, and stupidity, ensures fertility, and even can decide on the sex of unborn children. Avalokīteśvara appears in different embodiments and ways, always in accordance with what is necessary and appropriate for aiding and rescuing sentient creatures, for assisting them in seeing the correct path, and for listening to or freeing humanity. He can appear as a Buddha, as a landlord, a monk, a beggar, a teacher, a child, or a woman, or, alternatively, an all-powerful deity. In the Tibetan traditions, he also appears as a bird to impart the words of the Buddha to animals,[22] as well as appearing as the Dalai Lama himself. Above all, Avalokīteśvara is the embodiment of compassion: all of his actions are motivated by compassion, and he works tirelessly in the service of all creatures – rescuing them, comforting them, bringing them peace and serenity, and showing them the path to salvation.

Williams further explains that, in the supplementary texts that refer to the Indian roots of the God of Compassion, Avalokīteśvara appears as a mighty god, creator of the world and other gods and designator of their positions and statuses. In many senses, the Buddhist folklore endows Avalokīteśvara with the status and image of the Indian god Shiva. Interestingly, when the God of Compassion arrived in China, he changed gender to become Kuan Yin, the Goddess of Compassion in Chinese Buddhism.

There are two possible meanings to the deification of compassion in terms of the development of the Buddhist ideal of compassion: either this is a personification of compassion, accompanied by the deification of the Bodhisattva (the ramifications of which are the distancing of compassion from the human experience and its shift to the supernatural, phantasmal sphere, as the only place where it can exist), or, alternatively, this is a didactic popularization of the notion of compassion, which assists in shaping the Buddhist world of imagery, especially the image of compassion – the implication being that compassion is ever-present everywhere and always accessible. This notwithstanding, compassion appears in the world in the form of the Bodhisattva – a powerful, desired, multi-achieving persona, bearing an aura of holiness and the supernatural.

A second well-known manifestation of compassion (which also stems from the *Lotus Sūtra*, is found in the commentary of Nichiren, a prominent Japanese scholar (1222–82). Nichiren advocated a radical social vision and influenced tremendously the shape Japan took in the thirteenth century CE, a particularly difficult period there following the country's social, political, economic, and religious decline. He constructed his interpretations of Compassion primarily on the parts of the *Lotus Sūtra* that relate to the Buddha. According to the Chinese-Japanese-Buddhist tradition, this *Sūtra* was in fact the Buddha's last discourse before he disappeared from the world. Nichiren regarded himself as the Buddha's successor, his incarnation, and, with profound self-conviction, stressed the *Lotus Sūtra* as the most important of the Buddhist scriptures. Filled with strong religious zeal, he called for the repression of all Japanese traditions (including Buddhist traditions) to be replaced by study of the *Sūtra* (including argumentation justifying state intervention in Religion). His messianic self-conviction and his self-identification with the Buddha was parallel to the Buddha's own self-anointment as ruler, king, and teacher (which appears in the *Lotus*

Sūtra), as well as in line with the strong centrality of the motif of compassion, which defines the Buddha as the father and mother of all creatures. Nichiren did not hesitate to ascribe to himself this image in his writings: 'I, Nichiren, am sovereign, teacher, father, and mother to all people of Japan.'[23] As Habito explains in his article on Buddhist compassion,

> In Nichiren's writings, the Eternal Buddha Sakyamuni is presented as the father of all sentient beings. . . . Nichiren is convinced of the truth of the teaching of the Lotus Sūtra above all other Buddhist scriptures and comes to understand himself as the emissary of the Eternal Buddha. . . . He also comes to assume on himself this heart and mind of compassionate Eternal Buddha, seeing sentient beings, notably 'all the people of Japan', as his own children whom he must save from their predicament.[24]

Thus, Nichiren's commentaries directly link compassion to the image of the ruler-father, as well as imbuing compassion with a clear political connotation, perhaps related to the strong Chinese influence on Japanese Buddhism, with its image of the compassionate ruler/Emperor, sensitive to the suffering of the Nation. But this aside, Nichiren's conception of compassion rests primarily on religious zeal that highlights the mystical and paternalistic aspects of compassion.

A third, less-familiar manifestation of compassion is that appearing in the commentary of another Japanese scholar, Zen Master Dogen (1200–53), Nichiren's predecessor:

> To study and learn the way of the Buddha is to study and learn your own self. To study and learn your own self is to forget yourself. To forget yourself is to be enlightened by the myriad of things of the universe. To be enlightened by the myriad of things of the universe is to let go of your body and mind as well as the body and mind of others.[25]

Dogen's commentary places compassion neither in the world of fantasy and the supernatural nor in the experience of mystical union with the Buddha. Rather it includes compassion in the process of the consciousness, which, as already noted, in its Buddhist sense is a process of deconstruction that enables man to relinquish, first and foremost, his grip on his self-image, both physical and mental. Such a process occurs as the product of basic Buddhist motivation, which, according to Dogen, is an intellectual-rational motivation to know and achieve familiarity and leads to a new and different attitude to the phenomenal world. But of particular relevance to our matter is Dogen's claim that the melting of the self means the emergence of a new possibility with respect to how one relates to the other. This stance argues that relinquishing the self is a condition for knowing the other; it is what enables us to be in the shoes of the other and feel their misery.

Indeed, the emphasis on the conscious basis of compassion, on the one hand, and the identification of Buddhist compassion as a type of empathy, on the other, is a prominent feature of Dogen's approach.[26] And this approach brings us to the next chapter, where I examine of the meanings of Buddhist compassion as a social ideal and its place in Buddhist epistemology, especially Mahayanan.

5
The Buddhist Ideal

Compassion's presence in Buddhist thought, especially in Mahāyāna Buddhism, is integrally related to the Buddhist social ideal of the Bodhisattva:[1] an enlightened being on a long and arduous path to Nirvāṇa, to fulfillment through extinguishing the substantial self and the illusory phenomenal world, to the 'truth', but who vows not to pass into Nirvāṇa until all others have achieved it. The Bodhisattva devotes himself instead to teaching others the truth, of the way to enlightenment, out of *karuṇā* – Buddhist compassion: the awareness of the suffering of others and the desire to release all living creatures from pain and existential distress.

The first Bodhisattva was, of course, the Buddha himself, and he is attributed by the different Buddhist traditions with the decision to attend to the distress of human beings and aid them in their quest for full enlightenment. The Buddha's choice to remain in the Wheel of Rebirth, the world of uncontrolled rebirth, that is, to continue to be embodied in the human reality after his death as the founder of Buddhism, ensured the contemporary presence of compassion in the world. The more human beings succeed in approaching the ideal set by the Buddha, in attaining full enlightenment as Buddhas themselves, the more the circle of compassion expands and both private and overall existential suffering decrease.

In the *Prajña-pāramitā*[2] literature, the Mahāyāna 'Perfection of Wisdom' scriptures, the Bodhisattva is presented as someone who strives beyond enlightenment or, in Buddhist terms, beyond full Buddhahood. According to this tradition, this goal cannot be achieved as part of an egotistical attempt to attain personal liberation – hence the Bodhisattva's vow to remain in the Wheel of Rebirth. Despite the fact that the Bodhisattva attains a high level of liberation and enlightenment, and despite (or perhaps due to) the fact that he is able to see the true reality, he makes the compassionate determination to aid all other living beings.[3]

> Great compassion . . . takes hold of him. He surveys countless beings with his heavenly eyes, and what he sees fills him with great agitation . . . And he attends to them with the thought that 'I shall become a saviour to all those beings, I shall release them from all their sufferings!'. But he does not make either this, or anything else, into a sign to which he becomes partial. This also is the great light of a buddhisattva's wisdom, which allows him to know full enlightenment.
>
> *Prajñā-pāramitā-sūtra*[4]

And in the words attributed to the Buddha explaining the Bodhisattva's intention:

> They should act towards all sentient beings with the mind of equanimity, with the mind of compassion, with the mind that does not create differences, with the mind of humility, with the mind of peace and security, with the mind that does not hate . . . with the mind of a parent, with the mind of a brother, and speak to them like that.[5]

Moreover, the *prajñā-sūtra* states that

> [t]he status of a Bodhisattva is attainable through the mind of compassion, it is not attainable by merely meritorious deeds.

In other words, Buddhist compassion is an intentional state of mind that seeks the good of others. However, this compassion does not manifest itself in routine actions, and indeed, in Buddhism, excessive social activism is even criticized at times. It is precisely the universality of compassion that makes acting for the benefit of a particular creature so difficult, for any such action is likely to cause sadness or pain to another creature – for example, feeding a hungry person could result in that person continuing to hurt others. Thus it is necessary to refrain from excessive activism, at least in situations in which we cannot grasp the picture in its entirety. In terms of the practical aspect of the Buddhist traditions, despite the fact that, as part of their preparation, Buddhist monks are trained for consciousness and action out of compassion, the scope of Buddhist compassionate action is by definition restricted and cannot be understood as sweeping social activism.

The Buddhist, especially Tibetan, endeavor to stress compassi‹
awaken the novice's awareness of its presence in the consciousn
been based principally on a concentration on such feelings as en. ‚ ulıy
and identification with others, accompanied by an insistence on
refraining from similar emotions, such as pity or sympathy, which can
cause suffering to the person experiencing them and thereby increase
the overall amount of suffering in the world. Although such emotions
do incorporate a certain amount of genuine concern for others, they in
fact derive from value judgments of those others as unlucky, or needy,
or 'more wretched than I', which are fundamentally erroneous and
passive. In contrast, compassion is active empathy devoid of any
judgment of others.

The concept of compassion crystallized in Buddhism to the point
where it came to be understood as a yearned-for ideal sought by every
Buddhist. This concept grew out of the world of Buddhist concepts, a
world that embraces compassion and gives it its unique sense of a
desired human ideal. The following are three of the prominent manifestations of compassion relevant to the discussion of *karuṇā* thus far.

Compassion as part of the process of enlightenment

In Chapter 4, we saw that Buddhism, as a transformative process, is
characterized by the fact that it entails a gradual progression – from the
false and illusory consciousness to enlightenment, from a life trapped
in the karmic cycle to a more liberated life of unfettered movement,
from suffering and existential distress to happiness and joy. This
process has always had practical expression in the Buddhist way of life,
both inside and outside the convents and, primarily in the Buddhist
meditation techniques. These techniques are, in general, built on the
meditator's gradual progression from 'regular' states of consciousness
to 'higher' states of detachment from the ego or objects of the
consciousness. In the Buddhist meditative systems, the passage from
state to state is contingent on the meditator's ability to mentally analyze
every physical and mental experience as it occurs, which accentuates
the impermanence and lack of inherent essence of the current stage
(*vipasyana*), and then, through concentration and relaxation (*samatha*),
to progress to the next stage (there are usually a total of eight stages in
most Buddhist meditation techniques).[6]

But how is compassion conceived of in terms of such a process? Is it,
too, a gradual evolution, which Buddhism would regard as the gradual
exposure to the already-present 'truth'?

Relying on ancient Buddhist texts, Ok-Sun[7] offers a rather simple answer to this question. The preparation of the Buddhist novice begins with systematic training for self-restraint and control of his senses through repression of his desires. This control – analogized in Buddhism to the coachman who reins in his carriage – leads to a realization of the needlessness of attachment to objects of desire and to a simple level of liberation from the illusion that is imposed on us by sensual perception. The Buddha himself cautioned many times against excessively radical abstinence and the interpretation prevalent amongst radical ascetics in India, who tended to practice self-inflicted lashings, starvation, and severe self-denial. The Buddha advocated a certain, albeit modest, degree of self-concern and, especially, self-awareness, but taking care not to succumb to the extremism of either hedonism or asceticism. Self-concern, or attention to oneself, enables a person to be aware of both the presence and the essentiality of others, for the Buddhist process of development is grounded in an awareness of mutual dependence amongst all things as constituting the basis of the correct view of reality. Indeed, all things in the world exist in a state of interdependence, and awareness of this reality is the key (particularly in the Madhyamaka tradition)[8] to identifying them as lacking their 'own-being' (*svabhāva*), which, in its precise sense, means emptiness of being or lack of permanent and inherent essence. This Buddhist awareness, claims Ok-Sun, represents an awareness of human beings' dependence on one another and the imperativeness of interpersonal relations, and this awareness, in turn, constitutes the basis of ethical thought. Only upon attaining such insight can the Buddhist novice grasp the wider notion of the human race in general and, subsequently, the concept of additional life forms as well. The type of empathy evoked during this process originates with personal experience: the Buddhist who has experienced personally the great arduousness of self-restraint and the intensity of the attachment to the objects of desire can easily discern and identify with the struggles of others. Thus, the personal transformative experience forms the basis of Buddhist compassion, which, under Ok-Sun's interpretation, serves as the starting point for universal ethics.

First, interpretation of this sort, despite the fact that it can most definitely be derived from the Pali Canon,[9] seems to fall somewhat wide of the mark. To begin with, the Buddhist inclination to eradicate all suffering is already present in the Four Noble Truths, and, from a logical perspective, this inclination precedes every transformative conscious process. Second, this line of interpretation, which places Buddhist compassion at the heart of an ethical system, to a certain extent blurs the anthropological meaning of compassion as a natural, perhaps even instinctual, tendency that is 'released' along with the liberation of the consciousness from the fetters of the illusory reality. And third, it is difficult to accept such a significant attribution of an ethics code based on the self to a tradition whose distinct tendency is to distance itself from any ascription of actuality, permanence, or positive quality of the concept of the self.

At this juncture, it is important to recall that there is an additional way of understanding the appearance of compassion, alongside the regulative ideal of compassion as a sort of yearned-for ideal or even as 'the' Buddhist ideal – namely that compassion is the response to the 'authentic' voice. The moment that a person is released from the illusory grip of reality and the self, regardless of the meaning of that liberation (be it release from social conditioning and conventions or total liberation from reality itself), compassion spontaneously appears. Indeed, it is possible that the Buddhist claim regarding the social quest for overall happiness is in fact an extrapolation of the empiric experience of the actual inability to eradicate completely the suffering of others. It is possible that the Buddhist process of detachment and meditation – a process that systematically teaches the task of 'peeling the onion', stripping the empiric and mental reality of its components layer by layer – is simply incapable of overcoming the basic human tendency to be outraged by the cry of a baby, a friend in distress, a hungry man. This is the very same tendency that cannot be eradicated in the process of the deconstruction of reality, a sort of final and fundamental element of the consciousness that is ever-stable and refuses to fade away. Such an understanding of compassion entails also a different reading of the Buddhist scripture, that compassion is not a condition for the success of the conscious process, in contrast to what is perhaps hinted at in the *Metta Sutta*:[10]

> One who knows the state of well-being, who seeks that place of peace, should live thus: able upright, truly upright, of noble speech, gentle humble. Knowing sufficiency, well-content, with few wants and simple tastes, With senses calmed, discreet, not arrogant, not attached to blood relations, Not pursuing the least thing for which one could be censured by the wise.

Indeed, perhaps this text should be read differently, as Habito suggests:

> The (compassionate and so on) behavior described in the passage can be understood as stemming from the mode of being of one who is

grounded in that place of peace. In other words, rather than an ethical injunction or a moral prescription 'in order to attain a desired end' (that is, the place of peace), the passage can be read as a descriptive one.[11]

Habito's reading, which resonates throughout the Buddhist tradition, sketches the ideal of a person who is already in that very 'place of peace'. This is the form of existence of someone who has gone beyond attachments, beyond familial and personal relations, beyond the egocentricity and personal interests of conventional reality – someone whose compassion and all-encompassing thought encapsulate the world in its entirety. According to Buddhist tradition, achieving this ideal entails long, grueling training, especially in meditation. The different descriptions of the meditative conscious development have forged the conceptual configuration from which the meaning of Buddhist compassion is extracted. The Buddhist ideal, which stresses how the meditator relates to human beings and other creatures, is constructed on four categories of concepts (or values), each one signifying a particular conscious state that is parallel to a meditative stage: *maitri*, which signifies affability, sociability, pleasantness, and (platonic) love for others; *karuṇā*, which signifies a type of identification and solidarity with the pain of others (originally the concept most resembling compassion); *muditā*, which means rejoicing happiness or 'sympathetic-joy'; and *upekśā*, which is generally translated as equanimity, but, according to Habito's translation, means seeing things as they 'really are'.[12]

The relationship between these four concepts can be understood in two ways. The one way is as four values that together represent one conceptual-conscious framework that describes the conscious state of the ideal Buddhist. This is the person who experiences concurrently love and amity toward all, identifies with the pain of all creatures, maintains a joyful vitality and positive, happy outlook – all of which are possible because he discerns things 'as they really are', that is, absent any attachment, desire, or masks and in total serenity, without complaint or judgment.

The second possibility is to understand the four concepts as four different developmental stages of the consciousness during the process of meditative training, as they are presented, for example, by Soonthorndhammathada[13] in his analysis of the *visuddhimagga*. Under this understanding, *maitri* is the conscious state that is characterized by loyalty or even devotion (*pavaṭṭī*) to the welfare and happiness of others. It has a definite practical element of concern and care for others, despite the fact that this 'concern' appears in the text solely as a sort of utterance or even prayer ('If only all were happy'). From a meditative perspective, cultivating *maitri* is very important for dissipating anger and rage. However, the major problem with this conscious state is the ease with which it can turn into sexual attraction and desire. *karuṇā* is characterized by the desire to eradicate the suffering of others ('If only no one would have to suffer'). Its practical implication is ministering to the suffering and identifying with their pain. It is important to note that the text does not advise excessive empathy and cautions particularly against 'burdening' the compassionate person with pain, for this is likely to sadden the observer and thereby undo the achievements of the previous stage and prevent passage to the next stage. *Muditā*, the third stage, is characterized as simple *joie de vivre* and has the practical significance of lack of jealousy of others and genuine rejoicing and appreciative joy at the success and good fortune of others. Indeed, the meditative cultivation of joyfulness is the surest remedy for unpleasantness or even sadness. Finally, *upekśā* is a commitment to regarding equitably all sentient creatures, devoid of any hierarchical conception. It enables viewing all beings equally and with calmness, even apathy, with its meditative cultivation especially important for preventing lust. *Upekśā* manifests not only as a way of treating others, but also as a high conscious state that is beyond the feelings of pleasure or pain (an advanced stage in Buddhist meditation).

The first three states, rather than representing one conceptual complex, are three separate hierarchical stages leading to the fourth desired state. In order to reach the state of conscious indifference, peacefulness, lack of hierarchy, and so on, the meditator must pass through the previous states of consciousness, taking care not to slip into the 'dangerous' states of attachment and illusion. This understanding in fact absolutely binds the compassionate treatment of others to the interest of reaching Nirvāṇa, pointing to a necessary meditative connection (an empiric connection that supplements the logical connection noted in Chapter 4) between a certain type of compassion and achieving the highest, ideal state of consciousness. Soonthorndhammathada's analysis points to the reduction of compassion to an evolutionary process of the consciousness, stripping it completely of its empathic aspect (feeling the suffering of others), for excessive empathy is likely to cause sadness, and, worst of all, even anger. All that remains is the general, formal wish 'If only all were happy', without any accompanying commitment to actual action. And, moreover, the fact that the process culminates in the creation of a 'lucid' consciousness, a correct

view of things 'as they really are', means, from a Buddhist perspective
(at least in certain schools of Buddhism, particularly Theravada
Buddhism), an alienated approach of indifference to others: the other is
exclusively responsible for her actions, and her future state is merely a
reflection of the moral quality of her actions in the past and present. In
other words, there is no real reason to pity her, for she alone bears
responsibility for her actions and fate, and excessive pity is likely only
to cause me pain and distance me from the possibility of achieving the
highest consciousness and peacefulness.[14]

Compassion as self-sacrifice

Chapter 4 described the folklore narrative that shaped compassion in
the form of the god Avalokīteśvara. Similarly, the narrative that links
compassion to self-sacrifice can be found in the *Jatakamala*, which is
the 'Garland of Birth Tales of the Buddha' (*jataka* literally translated is
'birthlet'). The *Jataka* tales, a collection of Indian Buddhist stories,
include the modeling, narrative shaping, and imagery for the ideal
persona of the Bodhisattva as a person who is prepared to practice total
self-sacrifice for the benefit of others. In these stories, the Buddha
appears in his human form in his incarnations as a prince, a king, and a
Buddhist monk, as well as in the form of animals. The stories teach of
his bravery, self-sacrifice, and astounding ability to feel mercy for
others. In his incarnation as a monkey, he saves the life of an ungrateful
hunter; as the King of Antelopes, he risks his life to save the other
animals from danger; in his incarnation as an elephant, he offers his
flesh as food in order to save people starving from hunger; as a parrot,
he hovers in the burning treetops and scorches his wings in order to
save the trapped forest animals; and in his incarnation as a king, he cuts
from his own flesh to feed a dove. The dominant narrative in the *Jataka*
stories is the willingness and devotion with which the hero is prepared
to give up his own life in order to help others – and not only to save
others, but also to provide their needs or lead them to understanding.

The most famous of the *Jataka* stories, frequently cited in modern
commentaries that deal with ethics, non-violence, and Buddhist
altruism, is the story of the tigress and her cubs. In this story, the
Buddha appears in the form of a Buddhist monk, who encounters a
hungry tigress after she has just give birth. The monk's companions on
the journey run for their lives, but the monk, who of course does not
fear for his life, lies down at the tigress' feet. According to one version of
the story, when the tigress refuses to devour him, the monk wounds

himself so that the smell of his blood will waken her appetite. In another version of the same tale, where the Buddha appears as a prince rather than a monk, he sees the tigress about to eat her young cub – an act that, from the Buddhist perspective, exemplifies the destructive power of the illusory existence and the submission to existential despair – and decides to save the cubs and the mother by throwing himself off a cliff and thus turning himself into an alternative source of food.[15]

These stories connect Buddhist compassion to another set of concepts, particularly the concepts of 'absence of the self' and *ahiṃsā* (non-violence and non-injury to others). The high value attributed to self-sacrifice highlights the lack of importance of the self for the Buddhist, while creating a clear association between the attachment to the illusory sense of the self and the presence of interests, lusts, attachments, and connections – all of which necessarily lead to suffering, but not for the Buddhist, who is released from their hold. Relinquishing the illusory life is self-evident for anyone who recognizes this life as suffering, for anyone devoid of a self. But this surrendering of life is carried out without any connection to the attainment of personal enlightenment (which has, in any event, already been achieved), but, rather, in order to advance the well-being of others. In this way it constitutes the successful practical expression of compassion. Such an understanding of Buddhist compassion, as it emerges in the *Jataka* narrative as well as in later Buddhist tales (especially those prevalent in Mahāyāna and Tibetan Buddhism), presents an image of compassion that is in no way instrumental in nature. Here, compassion is not an instrument for achieving enlightenment; it is not a stage on the path to enlightenment or a necessary condition for enlightenment. On the contrary, it is precisely at that very moment when enlightenment is attained or when the Buddhist practitioner approaches it that compassion as a quality of the Bodhisattva appears, but as a byproduct of the conscious process, not a cause. The two different understandings of compassion, as either cause or effect, point to a certain inconsistency in the Buddhist traditions with regard to the status of compassion. Roughly generalizing, in the Theravada tradition, which conceives of Nirvāṇa as a very distant, almost hypothetical possibility that can only be attained by a very few and very rarely appears in history, if at all compassion appears in an instrumental form. It appears as a stage in the overall process of Buddhist advancement, a stage that cancels itself out when enlightenment is attained and removes the actuality of all elements of the human experience, including compassion itself. In contrast, the Mahāyāna tradition, especially, the Tibetan variation, does not conceive

Nirvāṇa so severely, presenting it as a definite possibility, 'here and now'. In this tradition, enlightenment is attained by many Buddhist practitioners; it is one of the clearly definitive qualities of sages and heads of monasteries throughout history, and certainly of the past and present dalai lamas. Thus, in this tradition, it is easier and less complicated to describe compassion as a quality of the enlightened, of the Bodhisattva, and as the promising outcome of a process.[16]

At the same time, the Buddhist narrative weaves the imagery of non-violence, of refraining from any act of aggression toward any living creature, though at times there is a latent recommendation for self-injury (one *Jataka* tale describes in great detail the way in which a Buddhist monk chopped himself into pieces in front of a cruel king, as a didactic act). This linking of compassion with self-sacrifice sets Buddhist compassion in the context of the *śīla*, the Buddhist behavioral code, frequently understood by Western commentators of Buddhism as an ethical code. In practice, this is a set of recommendations for refraining from certain actions, which is an integral part of the Buddhist *dharma*.[17] The *śīla* comprises five instructions: not to kill, not to lie, not to steal, not to be unchaste, and to refrain from intoxicating substances. An interesting interpretation of this seemingly simple (in social or ethical terms) series of instructions places the Buddhist ideal of *ahiṃsā*, refraining from causing injury, in a broad context: the quest for Nirvāṇa and the attempt to be released from the grip of the *Saṃsāra* do not end in the individual desire to disconnect from reality. The *Saṃsāra* is not the exclusive domain of people who hold on to the illusion. Rather, it encompasses a wide range of contacts and relationships, for the mutual dependence of the components of conventional existence prevents existence in solitude. In order to eat, we must pick fruit and harvest wheat and slaughter animals; to be born we must leave our mother's womb in a painful process. In short, our very existence does not begin and end with our own personal suffering; rather it is a sweeping compilation of overall suffering that encompasses the suffering of other people, as well as animals and even plants. This rather ecological outlook, which derives directly from the Four Noble Truths and the principle of mutual dependence, mandates a systematic and radical approach to all life surrounding the Buddhist, which, in the final analysis, emerges as existence in its entirety. This final point under-scores the universality of Buddhist compassion, from an entirely different angle, with compassion understood as a commitment to *ahiṃsā*.

One of the most prominent expressions in the Buddhist tradition of compassion as *ahiṃsā* is the vow taken by Buddhist monks, amongst a series of oaths, to refrain from causing injury at all costs. One of the most cited examples is the text that calls for empathetic treatment of snakes (a counsel attributed, of course, to the Buddha), which was adopted in different places as a sort of incantation, talisman, or supernatural cure against snake bites:

> I have compassion for the Virupakkas and for the Erapatas. I have compassion for the chabyattas and for the Kanhagomatas.[18]
>
> I have compassion for those without any feet and compassion for those with two.
>
> I have compassion for those with four feet and compassion for those with many.
>
> May those without feet not harm me, nor those with two. May those with four feet not harm me, nor those with many.
>
> May all sentient beings, all breathing beings, all living beings, all together see auspicious sights.
>
> May evil come to no one.[19]

Buddhist compassion also has a strong presence in the legends of one of the most famous figures in Buddhism – the Indian philosopher Nāgārjuna who lived around 150 CE. Nāgārjuna was the founder of the Madhyamaka school of Mahāyāna Buddhism and one of the most influential Indian Buddhist thinkers, second perhaps only to the Gautama Buddha. In Buddhist tradition, Nāgārjuna is accepted as the paradigm for the Bodhisattva; the Tibetan tradition even regards him as the incarnation of the Buddha, giving him the name 'the Second Buddha'. Woven throughout the Tibetan folklore stories about his life and death are descriptions of suffering and danger, which are brought to an end only through compassion. This begins with his birth as a sickly baby who is given only seven days to live, but is saved temporarily through the great compassion of his parents and given an extension of seven years of life. The theme continues with the tale of how, as a child, he is sent from his home by his parents when the seven-year extension has ended, but is saved through an encounter with the Mahāyāna deity Avalokiteśvara, the Bodhisattva of Endless Compassion, who takes Nāgārjuna to refuge in the monastery in Nālandā. Nāgārjuna eventually becomes the leader of the monastery, after he spends time in the Kingdom of the Naga ('the Serpents'), and after saving the King of the

Serpents (thereby acquiring the addition of 'Naga' to his name), he brings the *Prajña-pāramitā-sūtra* from the Kingdom to the monastery. However, the essence of the paradigm of Buddhist compassion as self-sacrifice, which is accompanied by a profound awareness of the *Saṃsāra* sphere of suffering and rebirth, is most apparent in the legend of Nāgārjuna's death. Nāgārjuna, a skilled physician, the legend goes, gave King Udayibhadra a potion for longevity, which could only be undone if he himself were to die. The King's son, who sought the King's throne, heeded his mother's advice to bring about the demise of the King by assassinating Nāgārjuna. The prince came to Nāgārjuna's quarters and found him in the shadows in the midst of deep meditation. To his great surprise, when he thrust his sword into Nāgārjuna, nothing happened. Nāgārjuna opened his eyes and, with great serenity and patience, explained to the young prince that in order to succeed in his mission, he must try something else: 'In my youth, I was working in a field with a sickle and accidentally killed a beetle when its head was sliced off by the sickle. It seems that my *karma* is that the appropriate way for me to die is by severing my head with a sickle.' The prince followed Nāgārjuna's advice and beheaded Nāgārjuna with a sickle.[20]

This type of myth, as part of the Mahāyāna didactic folklore (a sort of Mahāyāna responsum to the *Jataka* tales), links self-sacrifice to the causal configuration of the *karma–Saṃsāra*, stressing to the extreme the enlightened Buddhist's apathy toward attachment to the self and the illusory life in general, and binds all of these to compassion. The teacher's understanding of the prince's needs and desires (pathetic in themselves) and his readiness to show empathy for the enemy and assist him in his scheme,[21] while taking full responsibility for his *karmic* fate, serve as a model of enlightened compassion. The very encounter with such radical behavior is of immediate didactic value – if not for the prince, then for the story's audience, which is likely to be motivated to personal transformation by the amazement over such an absurd and unexpected situation.

Compassion and emptiness

The conception of Buddhist compassion as an ideal seems extremely simple and even natural in the contexts of a conscious process, ethics, and self-sacrifice. It is slightly more difficult to understand how the concept relates to the idea of emptiness. The notion of emptiness itself appears in the *Prajña-pāramitā-sūtra*, as a suggestion regarding the ontological status of the *Saṃsāra* empiric reality. The philosophy of the

Prajña-pāramitā-sūtra, as it was developed by the Madhyamaka philosophers (led by Nāgārjuna), asserts that, in this illusory reality replete with suffering, a reality that is no more than convention, it is impossible to find any being with its own essential nature (*svabhāva*).

Entities' lack of an essential nature, an 'own-being', is apparent in the fact (or perhaps what we conclude or derive from the fact, depending on the interpretation) that all things in the world are in a state of mutual dependence and lack autonomous and separate existence. Thus, the only ontological quality that can be attributed to all entities, phenomena, and concepts is emptiness (*śūnyatā*). This quality includes also the 'atomic' components of reality, which are considered by some of the Buddhist streams as concrete and eternal (i.e. as possessing *svabhāva*) but are presented as empty in Madhyamaka philosophy, which, in fact, has been called the 'Theory of Voidness' (*śūnyatā–vāda*).

The philosophical and epistemological advantages of the claim of the inherent emptiness of all entities are clear in relation to the Buddhist intention to create a psychological-consciousness dynamic of extinguishment of the illusory reality and deconstruction of the world constructs. This claim also can form the conceptual basis for imagery of total emptiness that replaces Nirvāṇa as a sort of strived-for regulative ideal and that represents reality as it truly is: a completely empty reality that can be known only through a mystic experience. But the question arises as to how the idea of emptiness relates to compassion. Does the very idea of emptiness not completely undermine the idea of compassion itself? For it is not warned against as an emotion, since it creates a connection or attachment to the suffering person, and as a consciousness, since it lacks 'own-being' and is therefore empty as well.

The answer to this question can be found in Nāgārjuna's famous claim (which became one of the prominent trademarks of Madhyamaka philosophy) with regard to the identification of *Saṃsāra* with Nirvāṇa. This claim puts the notion of abandoning the illusory reality and replacing it with an alternative 'better' or 'truer' reality in a different light: there is in fact no alternative reality, and we are forever living in the same reality. Under this approach, there are two ways of understanding the great Buddhist endeavor to remove the illusion from reality. The first way is to understand this claim as criticism of the idea of Nirvāṇa, in that it is a concept or an ideal that lacks 'own-being' like any other ideal and is therefore empty. In this case, the meaning of the Buddhist quest is that people can exchange their picture of reality only with voidness. That is, they can conduct an absolute deconstruction without any substitute, a sort of mental void that can be most closely compared to a type of unconsciousness or total lack of awareness, a state that, in any event, cannot include compassion, just as it cannot include suffering. This state lacks all meaning; we cannot relate to it even as an ideal. Indeed, we cannot even form a vague notion of it, since any such idea will, in any event, be a convention and, accordingly, also empty. Thus, the entire discussion of compassion, whether as a path to Nirvāṇa or otherwise, is of significance only in the framework of conventional life. Indeed, its appropriate forum is in Buddhist lifestyle, society, and monastic orders, but it bears no greater importance than anything else considered from the perspective of total emptiness.

The second way of understanding the identification of *Saṃsāra* with Nirvāṇa is that, ontologically, the two realities are one, despite the fact that, epistemologically, they represent two different angles from which reality can be observed. Under this approach, a person who succeeds in adopting the vantage point of emptiness vis-à-vis the *Saṃsāra* reality does not completely obliterate it, but, rather, encompasses it in the most perfect way – that is, without becoming attached to any object, without desiring anything, without being chained to illusions and misconceptions, and without having any need to 'solidify' reality's fluidity, to impose simulated order in the chaotic world. What is relinquished here is not the entirety of reality, in all its different layers, but rather the human way of observing it, that is, the conventional observation of the same reality. Someone who succeeds in doing this is rewarded with a special mental and practical liberty, despite the fact that she does not possess a sense of 'self' to which she can attribute that liberty. This second understanding gives compassion greater meaning. From an enlightened viewpoint, one that perceives the emptiness of reality, the human drama appears especially painful since it is based on being shackled to objects, feelings, and thoughts that are all empty and lacking in substance. This state of bondage is not at all necessary and is, therefore, pathetic, and as such, it arouses the compassion of the Bodhisattva. The enlightened Buddhist's capacity for standing in the shoes of others grows as his grip on his private illusory ego loosens, and his ability to be someone else 'momentarily', even when that other person is clearly an empty entity, is infinite. The viewpoint of emptiness also enables the observer to be resistant to developing any connection or attachment to objects of desire, since their emptiness is clear to him. Accordingly, nothing prevents him from exploiting these objects of desire, and it is even advised to do so to benefit others. Indeed, the enlightened person can allow himself to visit the realms of ignorance and illusion, since they do not threaten him – in any event, they are not alien to him, but rather reality itself, which is in a perpetual state of flux and only the ignorant gaze of human beings creates the simulation of order there.

It is possible to discern traces of the two types of understandings of the identification between the two levels of reality in the Madhyamaka Buddhist tradition, passed on particularly to Vajrayāna Buddhism, and correspondingly we can find allusions there to the link between compassion and the ideal of emptiness. Beyond this, however, it is difficult to find one systematic interpretation that coherently unites the two concepts. They are usually only declared as interrelated, just as ancient Buddhism declares a link between compassion and enlightenment.

Chandrakīrti, a seventh-century Madhyamaka philosopher and the greatest commentator on Nāgārjuna, interpreted the emptiness concept in its most radical sense. He maintained that the identification of the two levels of reality in Madhyamaka tradition represents lack of attachment to any philosophical stance (for any such stance would be *a priori* empty), but nonetheless he regarded compassion as the most important basis for learning Buddhism. Chandrakīrti rejected understanding emptiness as an abstract ideal, instead regarding it as a merely linguistic formulation of the empiric-logical phenomenon of the lack of 'own-being' and of the mutual dependence among the different components of reality. Nonetheless, he considered the identification of the two levels of reality an epistemological claim, and his commentary on Nāgārjuna can be understood as mandating compassion. His commentary on the Madhyamaka system (the *madhyamakāvatār* or the *madhyamakāhśāstra*), available only in its Tibetan version, became one of the central learning texts of Tibetan Buddhism: it opens with words of homage to compassion.

The Tibetan commentator on Chandrakīrti was Tsong-kha-pa (1357–1419), who developed the budding theme of compassion, as well as showing its centrality as a Buddhist concept in general, and a Mahāyāna one particularly. His interpretation of compassion in many respects became the classical stance on the concept of compassion in Tibetan Buddhism.

Nāgārjuna's commentary on the *Prajña-pāramitā* was the beginning of a long and multi-staged commentary process, which continued with Chandrakīrti's commentary, built on Nāgārjuna's work, and followed by Tsong-kha-pa's commentary, which developed the ideas of Chandrakīrti. This process, in itself interesting both as a historic phenomenon and as a commentary, is illustrative of the way in which the Mahāyāna concept of compassion evolved: from the starting point of the *Prajña-pāramitā* texts, which, as noted, stress the importance of compassion as part of the way to enlightenment (although it is not at all clear what its fate is after enlightenment has been achieved), through the construction of additional and new meanings of compassion that endow it with a social (perhaps ethical, perhaps ecological) sense, and reaching its pinnacle when the idealization of compassion makes it a clear characteristic of the enlightened person, of the Bodhisattva. In other words, over this process compassion lost its functionalism as the basis for enlightenment and was granted the status of a possible consciousness, revealed in all its glory precisely upon the culmination or at least at the height of the Buddhist transformative process.

Tsong-kha-pa's commentary is in many respects the ultimate example of this kind of evolutionary process. His point of departure was a distinction amongst three types of compassion, which he extracted from Chandrakīrti's tribute to compassion in the prologue of the *madhyamakāvatāra*. The first type of compassion is toward sentient creatures, including human beings; the second is compassion in observing phenomena; and the third is compassion toward the unapprehendable.[22] The first type of compassion relates to the simple and clear way in which people are perceived by the Buddhist meditator. This observation could be understood as an unripened gaze; a gaze that still recognizes people as 'whole', as entities whose impermanent and transitory basic components have yet to be seen by him. Tsong-kha-pa, however, understood this gaze as discerning the way in which people and sentient creatures relate to themselves, that is, as permanent and perpetual entities, which, from the Buddhist perspective, is the suffering and trap of the *Saṃsāra*, the Wheel of Life. Thus, this first type of compassion is the clearest expression of relating to the misery of human existence, and is in fact encompassed in the very observing or consideration of, the encounter with, what are deemed sentient creatures.

But Tsong-kha-pa explains that observing in itself is not sufficient, for if we gaze upon the suffering of our enemy, for example, we are likely to react with indifference or even joy. Our observation of everyone must have the same intention and intimacy that we direct at our family members or even loved ones when they are sick and suffering. Such a gaze will perhaps not change the behavior of the enemy, but this fact cannot serve to allow us to feel estranged from them and to continue to hate them.[23] To train oneself to develop loving intimacy toward people whom it is difficult to love, not necessarily enemies but simply people who are unpleasant and harmful, Tsong-kha-pa recommends a meditative technique of mental study in which the meditator is required to imagine an infinite series of incarnations, backwards and forwards in time, and to discern within this series the logical possibility of every person at some time, in the past or future, being the mother of someone else. The 'memory' of that motherhood, as a conscious state of total and unbiased love and compassion, of complete selflessness and unconditional acceptance, is attributed at first to close friends and acquaintances and then, through the meditative study process, also to enemies or people that the meditator finds repellent. Success in attributing the loving and compassionate mother image to each and every person inevitably leads to awareness of their suffering out of unbounded and total love – that is, to an awakening of Buddhist compassion. The second way of developing the ability to feel loving intimacy toward all people is by means of 'exchanging identities' meditation, in which the meditator is required to adopt, first, the viewpoint of another person and then, slowly turn himself into that person (again, beginning with a close one and progressing to an enemy), in the full sense of the word: to truly conduct a transformation of outlook and personality by means of the conscious act of empathy. Exchanging identities through this technique is the starting point for the arousal of compassion, since it directly exposes the student to the pain of the other.[24]

The second type of compassion is that experienced in observing phenomena. This compassion represents a more sophisticated type of gaze, implying that the observer has reached a higher level of Buddhist training: the observer already can discern the impermanence and perpetually shifting nature of the entities known as human beings. He observes not only humans but also phenomena, that is, the five *skandhas*, the psycho-physical constituents (or 'aggregates') of individuality by which human beings are analyzed in Buddhist phenomenology.[25] This observation reveals the discrepancy between the way in which people relate to themselves as permanent and constant entities and the 'truth' with regard to their relative, partial existence, which is no more than a derivative of the transience of their components. Upon discerning this discrepancy, which signifies the illusion of sequential existence that creates incessant suffering, the observer's compassion is stirred, especially in light of his own experience of exposing the illusion and being released from it. The observer's position and perspective is proof of the non-imperativeness of the illusion of the self and of the possibility of a different state of consciousness. Thus this second type of compassion relates to other people's ignorant and difficult state and their inability to discern an alternative.

Tsong-kha-pa called the third type of compassion 'compassion in observing the unapprehendable', which he explained to be referring to compassion toward sentient creatures that have the quality of emptiness. This type of compassion is, of course, possible in a state of consciousness that already distinguishes the emptiness of all things in the world – including human beings, whose psycho-physical components are even revealed as lacking substance, as non-inherent and devoid of 'own-being'. Existence itself is examined in this state of consciousness from the perspective of emptiness and emerges as no more than a reflection of 'the moon in a puddle' (Tsong-kha-pa's illustration of Chandrakīrti's text): The reflection exists, we cannot claim it does not. But proper observation will discern the paleness of the reflection, that it is an illusion whose fragility is exposed with every small ripple of the water. The illusory and fragile sentient creatures of the world, which cling to their concept of the self, are the objects of the third type of Buddhist compassion.

Tsong-kha-pa's explanation of this third type of compassion is noticeably more ambiguous than its predecessors, with its interpretation resorting to analogy and its formulation discernibly cautious. There are a number of methodological reasons for this. The two most important reasons are, first, the need to avoid arriving at an absurd interpretation – for example, that emptiness itself is the object of compassion (the likely logical deduction of asserting the totality of emptiness), and, second, the intentionally minimal reference in Buddhist theories to the higher states of consciousness, since these conscious states in any event appropriate the 'regular' consciousness usually referred to in the theoretical language. Hence, any difficulty in grasping precisely to what the third type of compassion refers is not indication of anything amiss: we are not supposed to have a precise understanding of this type of compassion, for such an understanding only is attained when this state has already been attained, and then the description itself is superfluous.

What is interesting with Tsong-kha-pa's interpretation of Buddhist compassion is that he succeeds in integrating the meditative system, the process of enlightenment, and the ideal of compassion. The question of whether compassion is a cause or result of the evolution of the consciousness is unequivocally settled by Tsong-kha-pa: compassion *stems* from the process; it is inherent to it; and it is not restricted to any one stage. On the contrary, the further along we progress toward enlightenment, the closer we are to emptiness becoming our outlook of the illusory reality, and the more sophisticated our compassionate gaze on those who remain behind. The Buddhist conscious process, which, in its early appearances in ancient Buddhism, is a process of 'peeling the onion', of liberation from or even eradication of reality, becomes in Tsong-kha-pa's account a constructive process: the empty reality does not cancel out its predecessor, but rather is built upon it and, strangely, even envelops it. The fact that a person has attained a consciousness of emptiness does not change the fact that, elsewhere, the illusion continues to exist; nor does it prevent the enlightened person from being conscious of that illusion, experiencing its presence, and applying his compassion. Here, the *Saṃsāra* reality seems an integral part of the Nirvāṇa reality, compassion becomes the companion of enlightenment, and the two great motifs of Buddhist thought – mysticism and sensitivity to the pain of others – are merged.

Yet adopting this type of interpretation entails a number of rather thorny sacrifices: First, under this interpretation, equanimity – which has always been integral to the general appeal of Buddhist culture – loses its importance to a certain extent. Second, its constructivist outlook discards the empiricist aspect of Buddhist thought – compassion is something to be constructed and it is not at all clear whether it was previously present. And finally, the third price of this interpretation derives from the previous problematic: Tsong-kha-pa's interpretation turns Buddhist compassion into an elite domain. Only those who walk in the path of the Buddha can feel compassion. The ordinary person who is not a Buddhist or, more precisely, who is not a practicing Buddhist monk cannot experience compassion. This final matter will be contended with in the next chapter.

6
Compassion Without Teeth

The Buddhist theme repeated throughout the stories of the life and work of the Buddha stresses significant freedom from social, economic, and political fetters, while directing both implied and direct criticism at these constraints. One example of this is in the Buddha's scrupulous insistence on not favoring the upper class in his homilies and his acceptance of alms from all donors regardless of class.[1] The Buddha treated all people equally and refrained from distinctions based on class, gender, or even age. In one instance he even went so far as to prefer the invitation of the courtesan Āmṛipālī, not only a woman but a harlot of ill-repute, over that of Licchavi lords, men of the upper caste, to dine with them, since Āmṛipālī had invited him first. His fair-mindedness infuriated the aristocratic Licchavis and was considered by all as a great insult.[2] Nonetheless, it is difficult to define the Buddha as a social revolutionary or as tenaciously fighting social and political injustices. The significance Buddhists attribute to the Buddha's work notwithstanding, the general conclusion is that the rebellious social image that emerges from the stories should be understood more in the context of conveying the privileges of freedom enjoyed by the enlightened, holy man than as a message of social change.

The social-political aspect to Buddhism is not uniform and constant, with two contradicting trends apparent. On the one hand, we can easily discern the revolutionary elements of a philosophy of social equality that is critical of the existing reality and offers an alternative that, in principle, is open to all, irregardless of class, ethnicity, gender, or economic status. This proposition combined with the Buddhist implicit commitment to assuaging the distress of the afflicted and wretched produces a formula that would be quite problematic, even dangerous and subversive, for any hierarchic, power-based, tyrannical, racist regime (that is to say, for the majority of the regimes in human history). On the other hand, Buddhism also appears to embody the most radical form of reactionarism in its call to accept life's suffering, poverty, oppression, injustice, and inequality with a stoic equanimity rooted in an attitude of 'in any event, everything is merely an illusion'. Indeed, in certain streams of Buddhism (those coined Kammatic Buddhism by Spiro[3]), it is not rare to hear people say 'In the next reincarnation, I might have a better fate.'

This, in conjunction with the Buddhist tendency to refrain from action, its compassionate universality that sees both the oppressed and the oppressors as victims of the same illusion, produces a very tempting formula for all dictators and despots, who would embrace the idea of sending out Buddhist monks to the rural villages, to poverty-stricken quarters, to minority groups, and to the oppressed to open their eyes and teach the people how to accept their suffering apathetically and fatalistically and to respond to every random decree with *ahiṃsā* (non-violence and non-injury to others).

In fact, the history of Buddhism, in all its various streams in Eastern Asian societies, has witnessed different manifestations of these two conflicting aspects to Buddhism as a social movement. Buddhist monks have frequently stood at the forefront of social struggles; they have joined the ranks of and even led protests against social injustices, and they have done their utmost to contribute to and offer solutions for harsh social distress. Yet, at the same time, Buddhism has also aligned itself with political forces (or been adopted by those forces) to become the State religion, to the point of absolute identification of Buddhism with the State in all its aspect – hierarchy, institutions, aggressiveness, and repressiveness. On the one hand, Buddhism has been, and still is, a populist movement that offers aid and a certain type of salvation to the peasantry, while, on the other hand, concurrently representing an elitist intellectual tradition that has been adopted throughout history by the powerful rulers of mighty empires. In some of these empires, the adoption of Buddhism manifested itself in a softening and, at times, actual change in the approach of the rulers, marked by a shift to tolerance, understanding, pacifism, and even hints of socialism. In other empires, the embracing of Buddhism was no more than a mere pretense of an olive branch offered to the people, actually meant to cover up the belligerent bent of the ruling regime and to facilitate full and legitimized realization of the horrors of the drive to rule.

At this stage, a comprehensive overview of the entire social history of Buddhism would be far beyond the scope and needs of our discussion.

Moreover, this ambitious endeavor has in any event been undertaken by many a talented scholar and is readily available in history and sociology textbooks. Instead, I will analyze only some of the key elements of the Buddhist idea of universal compassion and will identify the notional and practical motifs that have turned Buddhist compassion into a barren wasteland of compassion without teeth.

The problem with universality

The idea of universal compassion presents an immediate challenge for anyone who expects to channel the Buddhist commitment to eradicating human suffering to a practical course. The declared objects of universal compassion are all sentient beings, with no distinction, no order of priority, and no discrimination indicative of judgment on the part of the compassionate person. Any such judgment is an immediate sign of the presence of an ethical, social, or metaphysical theory whose very existence is indication of the person holding on to misconceptions that delay liberation and, in fact, erase any basis to the compassion itself. It follows, then, that a compassionate person does not decide on the objects of his compassion and his compassionate gaze is based on a lack of distinction between victim and victimizer, oppressed and oppressor, coerced and coercer, murder and murdered. Under universal compassion, all are the objects of compassion.

The reason for this absence of discriminative judgment is not related only to the way in which the compassionate person observes others as a person seeking Nirvāṇa. Rather, it derives logically already from the definition of suffering as a fundamental and universal element of human existence, as the substance of life itself. Under this definition, wherever there is life, there is suffering. Accordingly, if we wish to eliminate suffering, we must attack the experience of life itself, and this experience is the domain of all human beings, as well as of animals and plants. Moreover, when we identify desire (or the bonds and attachments that are the products of desire) as the source of pain, we are making a universal statement: it is almost tautological to assert that human beings have desire and that they have intention with regard to the objects of desire. Indeed, this is an elementary definition of life itself and is analytically deduced from the meaning of the term 'to live'. Thus, from these definitions it necessarily derives that all people suffer and since suffering is inherent to the experience of life, there is no possibility of setting a suffering hierarchy.

Two immediate points of criticism arise at this point. First, it is possible to challenge the Four Noble Truths and claim that reality, experience, and common sense do not support the internal logic of the Buddhist model. The identification of life with suffering seems somewhat superficial, despite the fact that the majority of people do suffer and experience pain over the course of most of their lives and despite the fact that Buddhism, like Christianity, is genuinely motivated to help them. From our own life experience we know that sometimes life is freedom, joy, and creativity and that people can lead lives of fulfillment and happiness. The problem is that most people have no possibility to live such a life because they are robbed of their freedom, not that suffering is constitutive of life. It is also difficult to accept that the reason for suffering is desire, even though the elimination of desire can be reasonably assumed to be an efficient remedy for suffering. It seems far more logical to claim that the reason for suffering is usually other people. A great deal of human suffering is caused simply by people's loss of freedom brought about by other people oppressing them, abusing them, subjugating them, and causing them pain. In a certain sense, this is the greatest suffering of all, since it is unnecessary and gratuitous and results in both the oppressor and oppressed losing their humanity. The Buddhist solution of eliminating desire, despite the fact that it seems a successful remedy to suffering, is, in essence, a case of throwing the baby out with the bathwater: it is very possible that autosuggestion leading human beings to a certain type of emotional apathy is likely to mitigate the sense of humiliation and oppression entailed by the loss of liberty. But along with these feelings, a person is likely to lose also his vitality and everything that is worth living for to him. Indeed, this final point was recognized as a quandary by the Buddha himself, who required refraining from both extreme asceticism and hedonism and striving to walk along the middle path.

The second point of criticism attacks the Buddhist stance from an ethical standpoint. Buddhism's presentation of suffering as turning on desire leaves the responsibility for both the suffering and its resolution in the hands of the afflicted individual. In essence, it follows from the Buddhist stance that suffering 'lies in the eyes of the beholder': whether or not we feel suffering is contingent on how we insist on looking at reality. There is no necessary mode of observation – we can look upon reality in a way that prevents us from feeling pain. This is a patently reactionary stance, in that it holds the victim responsible for her meager, poverty-stricken, and painful existence, rather than the person who has created the injustice to that individual. This approach follows along the same lines as the Puritanical philosophy, especially in its

American version, which emphasizes such values as personal responsibility and freedom of choice. People bear responsibility for what happens to them in life: they 'choose' to think negative thoughts, they 'choose' to reach a state of victimization, and the key to change lies in their hands and their hands alone. Changing their lives is not the responsibility of others and certainly not of the establishment. I do not dispute these values *per se*; rather, my quarrel is with those who maintain that people bear responsibility for what others do to them, what institutions do to them, and what is imposed on them against their wills. Is the girl who is raped responsible for her rape? Did she choose to be raped? Is the solution to her distress to detach herself from the grip of her ego? Is the soldier who is killed responsible for his death? Did he choose to die? Is the unemployed man who lost his home when his company went bankrupt responsible for his state? Will relating to reality as an illusion put food in his children's mouths? (Or have I simply forgotten that children have no need for food, since everything is mere illusion and treating children lovingly is no more than an egotistical attachment to the illusory self?) Most of us live life in a reality that places a great many restrictions on us in terms of how and to what extent it is even possible to realize responsibility, let alone freedom of choice, and society's lower classes are, of course, in the worst position in this respect. From the viewpoint of the poor, the capacity to change the way in which they regard reality cannot change the fact of their oppression. Indeed, it can only create the illusion of accepting and reconciling themselves with this reality – the most desirable outcome from the perspective of the oppressor, whether a person or the State.

These two points of criticism bring to light the problematic nature of the Buddhist notion of universal compassion. It appears that this idea, with all its aesthetic beauty aside (and it certainly is a most beautiful notion), emerges under close scrutiny as completely incongruous with the way in which the majority of people feel about themselves and the other. Of course, this is not to say that the Buddhist stance is erroneous. It is very possible that Buddhism is correct in its approach, but human beings, chained to the web of illusions, conventions, and so on, simply are unable to recognize the truth. This notwithstanding, as far as universal compassion forming the basis to a vision for social change, something is obviously lacking. It is possible to convince a person that after a certain number of years of meditative practice, he will feel exactly the same extent of compassion toward a rapist as toward the person raped or that he will feel that a war criminal deserves the same amount of compassion as the starving person who steals an apple to eat. But it seems a significant underrating of human intelligence and common sense to believe that people can be persuaded that it is of vital importance to feel this way and that this is not a manipulation. In order to achieve this, the Buddhist would likely need to supply a clearer and sounder model of compassion. However, the primary thing that the Buddhist has to offer as a response to this ethical problem is his own personal model, his impressive readiness for self-sacrifice – he is always willing to trade places with the downtrodden and endure beatings in their stead. This willingness, when accompanied by *ahiṃsā*, has great force, but this force alone does not offer a solution to the problem or a response to the criticism, for nowhere in Buddhist thought is it explained precisely how these acts are supposed to change reality for the person suffering or lessen human suffering in general.

The universality of Buddhist compassion, therefore, leads to the following conclusions: there is no possibility of admitting to causing pain in the framework of the interpersonal process; there is no possibility of admitting any hierarchy of pain; and there is no possibility of recognizing that the victimizer holds a different position from the victim, despite the fact this position is significant and does not stand in contradiction to the sad fact that victimizers are often deserving of compassion since they themselves were once victims. The totality of this concept creates an *a priori* blindness, for if the reason for suffering is always illusory attachments, then we cannot recognize a cause of pain that is not the product of the illusion itself. And even if the source of the illusion is social, linguistic, or cultural, contending with it must be carried out in the personal sphere and is forever the responsibility of the afflicted and injured. The social ramifications of this approach are clear – there is no possibility of acting to ease the distress of the other: first, because any such action is likely to harm someone other than the person in distress (and, according to the Buddhist approach, it does indeed do so); second, because even if there were such a thing as an action that does not cause harm, it would in no way alleviate distress; and third, even if such action were to bring relief, the person to perform it must be the person suffering and no one else.

Holding the stick at both ends

Elsewhere[4] I have claimed that one of the general features of Buddhist thought is the internal tension produced by its attempt to embrace simultaneously two at least seemingly opposing stances. One the one hand, we learn from Buddhism that the objective of mental analysis and meditative practice is to cease all suffering. But at the same time, we learn that this is the exposure of the truth as to the emptiness of existence. But does therapy necessarily mean finding truth? What if the revelation of the truth leads to despair and suffering? Buddhism teaches us that in order to attain a liberated consciousness, to reach Nirvāṇa, we must abandon all our concepts, judgments, and theories. Yet at the same time, it furnishes us with a new set of concepts and codes of behavior, a new way of life and dogma, and new distinctions between right and wrong, the suitable and unsuitable, and even what is holy and what is impure. Is this not the potential for a new world of concepts? Buddhism teaches us that Nirvāṇa is a state that is beyond all concepts and where language has no application, and therefore it does not lend itself to any description. On the other hand, there is an obvious attempt to define it – as the suitable state, as a regulative ideal that should be strived for. How can foregoing all conceptualization be attempted concurrent to the maintaining of non-conceptualization as a central concept of the culture? We also learn from Buddhism that our conception of the self is a mere illusion that does not withstand either the test of logic or any empirical test, and we learn exercises and meditations to create states of absence of the self. But the Buddhist monks who teach us these things are very real, and they lead lives of remarkable monastic careers, replete with ambition, intentions, self-discipline, and great consistency.

It is important to note that the internal tension that arises from the attempt to hold onto the stick at both ends is not new to the Buddhist, nor is it a feature of only the later commentaries. This phenomenon has been present in ancient Buddhist thought from its outset. Many debates have raged over this tension amongst Buddhist thinkers and philosophers, and it has featured to a significant extent in all the different forms of Buddhist culture. Moreover, this tension bears important implications for the possibility of compassion, especially in relation to its apparent sterility.

Beyond being formally defined as universal, the idea of compassion entails also a process of liberation of the consciousness. As was shown in Chapter 5, the conscious state of compassion is comprehensible in the context of Buddhist epistemology in general. That is to say, there is a link between the conscious state that approaches Nirvāṇa, or is Nirvāṇa itself, and the compassionate consciousness. But in order for the consciousness to approach Nirvāṇa, it must discard all distinctions and strive to attain a state of non-discrimination. It is quite difficult, of course, to define such a state in terms of its contents or experiential features, but it is easily defined from a logical perspective and in terms of what is absent from it. Clearly, for example, in this state, no distinction is made between dichotomous concepts, such as small versus large, good versus bad, and victim versus victimizer. Moreover, it is also clear that the way of observing reality shifts from a focused, intentional gazing upon the object (a feature of the 'regular' consciousness) to a more comprehensive yet detached gaze. This transformation can be analogized to a shift in visual perception – the movement from an intent focused gaze trained on what is before us to a sort of daydreaming gaze, not directed at any particular object. This shift significantly broadens our field of vision, but does not present before us any specific object. We 'see' everything, while not 'seeing' anything in a sense that precedes or is parallel to the term 'to see'. When such a transformation of consciousness is applied to the way in which human beings are regarded, we arrive at an epistemological feature of compassion that relates to all objects, to the entire field of vision, but does not focus on any one object specifically. In essence, it is not at all clear in what sense the compassionate gaze at all discerns what is before it and to what extent the other, who is the object of the compassion, is completely present (and, of course, 'is completely present' has no meaning from the Buddhist perspective, since the other's personality and self have no actuality).

Thus, in Buddhism, we find a twofold circularity with regard to compassion. The first circularity is similar to that found in Buddhist mysticism (attaining a non-conceptual consciousness by means of concepts), the concept of desire (the desire for a lack of desire), and the concept of absence of the self (making a career out of holiness by way of extinguishing the self). In the context of compassion, Buddhism seeks to remedy pain by way of canceling out the causes of the pain. But eliminating the causes entails eliminating the possibility of feeling empathy, which includes an emotional response to the specific distress of the other. The second circularity is embedded in the very concept of compassion: If it is, indeed, a natural concept, then it must be possessed by all. But the Buddhist learning process in fact indicates that it is a concept acquired through long years of training and not available to all.

The loss of focus therefore means the loss of compassion, for the entire meaning of compassion as a basis to the relationship between the self and the other lies precisely in the focus it enables: it exposes us to the presence of the other as a person; it 'forces' us as subjects to feel the experiences of others, to focus on the specific experiences of pain or grief, to gaze upon reality in a specifically focused, narrow, clear, and sharp manner. What, indeed, is the meaning of compassion that is to see the other without looking at her; to feel her pain without feeling sorrow; to identify with her despite the fact that she is not real; to 'be there' without being; to intend with regard to her without having intentions; to be interested in alleviating suffering without having any interests? The answer is clear and has already been hinted at in the formulation of Buddhist compassion: this is an aesthetic experience, devoid of all emotional involvement. It involves no ethical stance, no cognitive experience. It is the outlook of the observer, which is supposedly dependent on the state of the object of observation – the suffering of the other – but in fact rests not on the involvement, but the detachment of the observer. The Buddhist songs of praise for the importance of the uninvolved observer only point to the fact that Buddhist compassion is, at its essence, an aesthetic phenomenon and, as such, does not represent any call for action to reform reality.

Elitist compassion

At the end of Chapter 5, I claimed that the solution proposed by Tsong-kha-pa linking compassion with emptiness succeeds in solving part of the epistemological problem outlined above. Nonetheless, I also noted that one of the prices of this solution is that compassion becomes an elitist action. In fact, during Tsong-kha-pa's period, from the end of the fourteenth century to the beginning of the fifteenth century CE, compassion was already the sole domain of the Buddhist elite and was even definitive of the established social-religious elite. The emergence of the Buddhist elites can be understood both from a historical analysis of the expansion of Buddhism beyond India and from a sociological approach to the phenomenon, which, in turn, illustrate how compassion itself became an exclusionary elitist phenomenon.

The surfacing of a Buddhist elite in Tibet, for example, is rooted in historical and political processes. Tsong-kha-pa, himself a Tibetan Buddhist, in addition to being a highly esteemed and impressive scholar, was also the founder of the Yellow Hat Order (*Dge-lugs-pa*, meaning 'School of Virtue'). This was the reform Buddhist sect and bitter rival of the first generation of Tibetan Buddhism, the Red Hat (*Nying-ma-pa*) sect, especially in South Tibet. In 1409, Tsong-kha-pa founded the first Yellow Hat monastery near Lhasa and developed a system of study and pedagogic philosophy that stresses the imperativeness of a return to the Indian sources of Buddhism and great scholarship as the primary basis to the Buddhist *dharma*. He urged his pupils to go to

India and bring back ancient texts and to even familiarize themselves with what remained of the ancient Buddhist lifestyle in the few places that still maintained it. Tsong-kha-pa's reform had a political facet as well, however. It included also an attempt to revive the strong lamaic tradition of the Tibetan *Sa-skya-pa* Order,[5] which had flourished in the period of the Mongol rulers, especially under Kublai Khan, the great Mongol leader of China. Kublai's instructor, Phags-pa (1235–80 CE), the nephew of Sa-skya Pandita Kun-dga Rgyal-mtshan (1182–1251 CE), one of the most renowned Tibetan Buddhist masters and scholars and head of the *Sa-skya-pa* sect, was granted by Kublai political control over Tibet. This established the tradition of the link between religious-spiritual authority and political-state rule, which, in time, became the trademark of Tibetan Buddhism (not the least due to Tsong-kha-pa's efforts).

By the fifteenth century, the lamaic tradition had been forgotten, and Red Hat Buddhism, that challenged by Tsong-kha-pa, was the dominant Buddhist presence in Tibet. Tsong-kha-pa's Yellow Hat movement arose as a response to the corruption of the Red Hat control, the reform marked by a reorganization of the orders and a return to strong monastic discipline. One of Tsong-kha-pa's disciples, Dge-'dun-grub-pa (1391–1475 CE), a Tibetan master and the first of the line that became the Dalai Lamas, founded the famous Yellow Hat Bkra-shis-lhum-po monastery southeast of Lhasa, in central Tibet. After his death, he was believed to be reincarnated twice in the form of his successors. His third incarnation, Bsod-nams-rgya-mtsho (1543–88 CE), presented Buddhism before the Mongol leader Altan Khan, who was so impressed with its depth of scholarship that he adopted it as the central teaching of the (shrunken) Mongolian Empire and granted Bsod-nams-rgya-mtsho the title of Dalai Lama[6] to honor him. Bsod-nams-rgya-mtsho, who became the first of his line to be called Dalai Lama during his lifetime, was recognized as the third Dalai Lama, with his two predecessors posthumously given the titles of the first and second Dalai Lamas. In the wake of its success in Mongolia, the Yellow Hat sect grew in strength, and in 1641 it was awarded by the ruling Mongol prince temporal and spiritual rule over all Tibet, a birthright that continues to this day. However, this was achieved only after a long period of political struggles, armed disputes, and even bloodshed with the sect's Tibetan rivals – only one small instance of the historical fact that political and power struggles were not unknown to the Buddhist tradition. Throughout the history of Buddhism, the heads of monasteries and even monks could be found deep in the heart of battles for power, accompanied by the consolidation of political and governmental elites.[7]

Compassion, for its part, became one of the most important identifying characteristics of the Tibetan Buddhist scholar. Progression in the
spiritual-political hierarchy was indication of attaining a higher level of
compassion, all the way up to the Dalai Lama, who occupies the highest
spiritual level, which is also that of universal compassion. Furthermore,
it seems that the correlation between the historical process of the
construction of the religious-political hierarchy and the appearance of a
social hierarchy of compassion is not pure coincidence. This correlation
could well give an additional sense to the hierarchical ordering of the
different types of compassion that appears in Tsong-kha-pa's commentary. But what is of relevance to our matter is that compassion, in being
a status symbol, imbued (and still imbues) it with a meaning that
deviates from its philosophical and theoretical sense: it serves as one of
the most important promoters of the popular rule of the Dalai Lama,
ensuring that his rule enjoys maximum support and response from the
people. Being compassionate is the most successful depiction of a leader
from a political perspective, upholding his image as humane, loving,
and paternal.

Another way of examining the emergence of Buddhist elitism is
through a sociological analysis. This type of analysis points, for example,
to the evolution of two different social approaches in Buddhism. First is
the approach toward the Buddhist practitioner, the monks, and the
pupils of Buddhist *dharma* who frequented the monasteries and
devoted their lives to a Buddhist way of life; and the second is toward
the rural community, the illiterate peasants, who were not familiar with
the teachings and were not awarded with the opportunity to be
included in a life leading to enlightenment and liberation from the
Saṃsāra cycle of suffering. Despite the fact the monastic lifestyle was
simple and somewhat ascetic and included a genuine foregoing of the
options of a full life (in entailing celibacy, financial dependence, foregoing
family life, and so on), it offered a great deal of protection and the aura
of holiness and accompanying pride, which bolstered the monks'
motivation and even fostered envy toward them. The division between
the peasant, who was always more of an instrument for monastic life
(primarily as a source of alms, charity, donations, and funds for the
community services provided by the monks), and the monk, who walks
along the Eightfold Path to Enlightenment, in effect created two
different languages, which can be roughly analogized to the two levels
of reality in Buddhist scholarship: the *Samsaric* language, which is
suited to the peasantry and constructed on the world of conventional
concepts in which they live; and the 'higher' language, that of the

official Buddhist texts taught in the monasteries and suitable to life in the Nirvanic sphere or a life striving to reach Nirvāṇa. Monastic elitism was not uniform in all streams of Buddhism; it was more prominent, for example, in the exclusionary Theravada Buddhism than in the more populist Mahāyāna Buddhism. But with respect to compassion, it was and always has been completely clear that compassion is part of the language of the monks and novices. It is not intended for the ordinary people; it is the realm only of those who undergo Buddhist training and reach a high spiritual level. From a sociological perspective, it seems that Tsong-kha-pa's text, for example, was never intended to advocate human compassion in its social sense; rather it is an instructional commentary directed solely at the pupils of Buddhist academia and the Buddhist monks, who train themselves to be compassionate in the framework of their spiritual progression. This is a compassion of the spiritual intellectual elites and seems a long way off from the idea of a 'human', natural, and universal compassion.

As I noted at the outset, the discussion in this chapter is neither historical nor sociological, but rather conceptual. The question then is what is there in the Buddhist concept of compassion that turns it into a property of an exclusive phenomenon? The immediate answer can be found in the historical-social context of the concept, which, as I showed above, points to compassion as a characteristic, a status symbol, an ideal of an intellectual group that was not always above playing power games. But there are also aspects of the Buddhist claim itself regarding compassion that point to its exclusive nature. In order to discern these aspects there is no need to explore the history or sociology of Buddhism, for they are part of the concept itself. One aspect, discussed in the previous section, is the epistemology of compassion, which requires that the compassionate person possess high meditative skills and acquire a certain type of observation that, under the Buddhist conception itself, is not the possible for all people and requires long and arduous practice (including, of course, the correct guidance – personal and textual). The second aspect, also mentioned in the previous chapter, is the ability to minimize the self. This ability is a condition of compassion in two senses. First, it is a condition for the very appearance of compassion since it provides the comparative base-line that highlights the miserable state of the other and of the human race, as Tsong-kha-pa explains in his commentary regarding the second type of compassion. Second, the diminishment of the compassionate person's self is a condition for possibility of empathy. Only someone who can truly put himself aside can truly enter the mind of someone else and feel or imagine their pain. And, similar to first aspect, the extinguishing of the self is a long-term process (according to the Theravada methodology and tradition, for example, it should take sixty years) and, even then, is very rarely successful.

From all this it arises that the 'universality' of the Buddhist model of compassion refers only to the *objects* of compassion, not to the *subjects* of that compassion. 'All sentient beings' encompasses only those toward whom compassion is directed – those feeling compassion are a most rare species. Compassion as first conceived of by Buddhist anthropology as a defining quality, a fundamental feature of humanity present in all people, seems to have disappeared during the evolutionary process of the concept.[8]

Structural impotence

The basic definition of compassion with which I open the book's discussion includes the tendency, desire, or urge to act to alleviate the distress of the other. The Buddhist model seems rather diffident vis-à-vis this aspect of compassion, respecting its translation from an empathetic emotion into a concrete act for the benefit of the needy. This hesitation can be derived, again, from the logic of the Buddhist Four Noble Truths: Suffering has a solution, but only one sole solution – taking the Buddhist path. How the pain, want, and misery appear in the eyes of the person trapped in the *Saṃsāra* is completely irrelevant; this form of existence is in any case illusory. Believing that your suffering was caused by disease, natural disaster, or another person's actions is part of the deceptive illusion of the *Samsaric* reality, for the suffering is the result of your desire and attachments. The only way to be healed is by way of the Eightfold Path to Enlightenment, liberation through the Buddhist way of life. Accordingly, taking action of any kind means progressing only in the *karmic* existence; it is meaningless in terms of alleviating pain and usually is likely to harm both the person for whose good the action is supposedly being taken and the actor himself. Following this logic, it is possible to claim that the very urgency, pressure, and commitment to act amount to a certain type of harmful attachment: the bonding of the compassionate person with the person who is the object of the compassion, and attachments, as we well know by now, lead only to suffering.

This Buddhist disinclination with regard to taking action to ease suffering has a number of manifestations in the Buddhist traditions, two of which I will describe briefly. The first manifestation is related to the way in which the Buddhist ecological outlook (mentioned in the previous chapter) is translated into terms of ethical pragmatism. One of the Mahāyāna *sūtras* tells of how the Buddha, while still a novice, engaged in sexual intercourse with a young girl, who was at risk of losing her mind due to her overwhelming love for him. The Buddha's action was intended to save the girl (motivated by compassion, of course) by releasing her from her obsessive attachment. Williams adds to this story a familiar Mahāyāna tale of the Buddha killing another man because it is the only way to prevent him from causing the deaths of 500 innocent people. As a result of his action, the Buddha sinks into the most hellish of depths.[9] This story appears in a didactic formulation that presents the consequences of the action of the Buddha as a Bodhisattva acting out of compassion. Nichiren (mentioned in Chapter 4), in his attempt to prove the imperativeness of the State subduing rival traditions, made wide reference to accounts of acts of violence in the *sūtras* to demonstrate the legitimacy given by the Buddha himself to the use of force to prevent greater suffering. For example, in the *Mahāparinirvāna-sūtra*, the Buddha recounts how in a previous life he killed a number of Brahmins to prevent them from vilifying Buddhism, thereby also sparing them from the harsh punishments they would have deservedly received had they continued with their actions. In the same *sūtra*, the Mahāyāna righteous are counseled to bear arms and to even ignore the dictates of the *śīla* in order to protect the *dharma*.[10]

But it is precisely these stories of the Buddha's activism and erudition that served as a double-edged sword against the possibility of action. For these stories link every act to future consequences, which are not known to all. How is it possible to act if we cannot know the outcome of our actions in advance? Who will be prepared to take responsibility for an action that is performed out of compassion, but emerges as disastrous in the long term? How, for example, can we save a person who later on is revealed to be a mass murderer? Although we are required to feel compassion toward all people, we must nonetheless always bear in mind that, from a Buddhist perspective, 'taking action' means influencing the overall texture of reality since it changes the order of things that are in a state of mutual dependence. Thus, how can we ensure that an action for the benefit of another will not carry with it great catastrophe for many others and, thus, also for the possibility of liberation for the very person supposedly being helped? It is quite possible that it is preferable for her to remain afflicted and miserable than to be thrown into a worse hell. The actions of the Buddha demonstrate that a Bodhisattva is required to attain a level of comprehensive understanding and knowledge with regard to the future ramifications of every action at the truly global level, in order to act in a way that diminishes suffering and does not intensify it. This type of 'compassion economy' has been prevalent in different periods as well as in internal Buddhist debates. For our purposes, however, its immediate and clear implication is the neutralization of any possibility of easing the distress of others and the placing of the decision of when to act in the exclusive hands of the Bodhisattvas who is able to determine the nature of an action by way of his all-encompassing vision.

The second manifestation of the Buddhist reluctance is related to the problem that is likely to arise in principle, philosophically, and methodologically with regard to the possibility of liberation, in any attempt to rapidly convert an emotion, thought, or mental state into a concrete action. In this context, Mahāyāna Buddhism (which, in Spiro's terminology, would be categorized as Nibbanic, or normative, Buddhism as opposed to Kammatic, or non-normative, Buddhism[11]) is likely to take a rather antagonistic approach to the possibility of action stemming from compassion. In Mahāyāna Buddhism, liberation is a concrete and realistic aspired-for possibility, and one element of that liberation is compassion, as we have already seen. But to take material action means to support the view of the *Samsaric* reality as actuality; that is to say, such an action delays liberation and, therefore, necessarily cannot stem from compassion itself. The fact that the pain of the other leads one to desire to act means that the *Saṃsāra* reality has 'snuck' into their consciousness. Thus if one truly wishes to benefit the suffering person, one must not only refrain from acting, but must also avoid any the connection between empathetic sentiment and action.

These are only two examples of the Buddhist difficulty with the movement from identification with pain and suffering to a concrete, material action to change reality for the afflicted person. These examples highlight the structural character of universal compassion as such that cannot allow for action of any kind. And when we consider this in conjunction with the problematic nature of the Buddhist model as presented above, we cannot help but reach the conclusion that universal compassion is fundamentally impotent or, as one coined it at the opening of this chapter, 'compassion without teeth'.

On its face, the seemingly benign, passive Buddhist model of universal compassion seems the antithesis to the aggressive and instrumentalist approach of Christian divine compassion as it emerged from the analysis in Part I. But both traditions, despite their declared good intentions, not only refrain from social change, but also prevent it.

While Christianity (perhaps) seeks to actively perpetuate suffering in order to attain its egotistical goals of salvation, Buddhism stands by the wayside, calmly and detachedly observing suffering, (perhaps) even fostering it by encouraging those in distress to relate with apathy to their existences. But both lead to the same outcome: the continuation of human suffering and misery.[12]

In stark contrast to these two traditions (both of which have nonetheless secured public regard and even veneration as compassionate opponents of suffering), we find the modern approach to compassion and social activism on the background of the wretchedness of life in the shadow of the cruel and alienating free market mechanism in the wake of the Industrial Revolution. Modernism, discarding the religious notion of compassion, boldly and openly declared its commitment to civil rights and social justice, with the Church's place filled by the nation-state and the legislature in the stead of the compassionate religious leader. Part III of the book will address the marginalization of compassion in modern public discourse, as well as modernism's never-to-be-fulfilled promise to tend to human distress comprehensively and fundamentally.

Part III
Human Compassion

7
The Fragmentation of Compassion

One of the interesting features that emerge from the religious models of compassion, as they have been described in previous chapters, is their comprehensive approach integrating emotional experiences and action into one, all-encompassing general concept. Compassion appears in these models as a concept with an exceptionally wide field of reference, and often it is difficult to understand to what precisely the Christian or Buddhist is referring when he advocates compassion.

The modern approach to the notion of compassion, which, to a large extent, was dictated by empiricist logic, unraveled the conceptual complex forged by Christianity. Compassion underwent deconstruction and fragmentation, collapsing into its fundamental components in accordance with the way in which modernism understood the human mind and the human possibility of sensing the other and acting for his or her benefit. This fragmentation process in fact began with what appeared to be a new and different model of compassion, presented by the eighteenth-century British Enlightenment philosophers in the framework of the philosophical debate over human nature. This group of philosophers utilized the premise of compassion as a natural and elementary human emotion to explain the formation of compassion and its existence in human society – something that seemed to require explanation in light of the liberal outlook that stressed individualism, rationality, and freedom of choice. Countering the Christian-religious conception of compassion, the British moral philosophers proposed a slightly different understanding, one that abandoned the metaphysical and paternalistic aspects of the concept and was not rooted in symbolic acts like charity as expressions of compassion. Theirs was a naturalistic conception of compassion that understood it as a definitive, perhaps even instinctual, human quality.

According to Himmelfarb,[1] philosophers such as Shaftesbury, Francis Hutcheson, and Adam Smith claimed that compassion should be recognized as an innate human 'affection', as the natural – and therefore legitimate – basis for entering into social existence. This was in total contradistinction to their French counterparts, who fiercely clung to reason and rationality as the sole basis to modernism's vision. In contrast, the British philosophers asserted, unlike Locke and Rousseau, that the existence of compassion as a human virtue explains both the need for and the success of human society and civilization, for the act of social organization should not be regarded as an act of reason (a contract or convention) but rather as an act of emotion. This stance was applied by some of the British Enlightenment philosophers, especially Adam Smith, to formulate an optimistic outlook that enables the dulling of the constant economic pressure in modern society: deriving from a moral instinct, humane actions are carried out alongside the cold and sometimes cruel workings of the free market, with certain resources allocated to the underprivileged. Compassion, a 'moral sentiment', was defined by Smith in *The Theory of Moral Sentiment* as

> the emotion which we feel for the misery of others when we either see it or are made to conceive it in a very lively manner...
> ...By the imagination we place ourselves in his situation,...we enter as it were into his body, and become in some measure the same person with him,...[2]

Seemingly inherent to the very notion of defining compassion as a natural (and therefore universal) human sentiment was the potential for constructing a new, modern model of compassion. However, in actuality, this did not occur since the naturalistic ideas of the eighteenth century were an inextricable part of the general cultural rationale of modernism that mandated subjecting every distinction to the terminology and conceptual world of science. This meant that any physical, psychological, or social phenomenon could be understood only through analysis and compartmentalization of its fundamental elements. Under this logic, therefore, if we want to understand compassion or even attempt to justify it, we must first clarify exactly to what we are referring by the term 'compassion'. The philosophical definition of compassion as an emotion was perhaps the first step in the long process of reduction that the conceptual complex of religious compassion underwent: emotions, modern scientific logic asserts, are like any other phenomenon we are used to terming 'mental' – they have material (physical) causes and these causes are known as experiences. At the same time, for emotions to have any significance in a rational world that operates according to the laws of physics, they must also have effects, known as behaviors. Thus, compassion, as an emotion, is positioned between two types of activities about which science has much to say but that are completely, comprehensively, and fundamentally detached from the emotion we know as compassion.

Under modern logic, which prescribed the way in which we understand compassion today, in considering compassion, we must assume a threefold process that is accepted in regard to every conscious act. First, we have an experience; this experience arouses emotion in us; and this emotion is then likely to drive us to act. The logical-causal sequence of experience–emotion–action characterizes both the logical and the chronological structures of how we relate to the distress of others. But this is neither new nor unfamiliar. What is of specific interest in the context of compassion is modernism's fragmentation of the general concept and its reduction to the point of understanding it as 'solely' emotion. Modernism's labels for the three components of the cognizant act are enlightening in this respect, with the experiential and action stages complctcly detached from compassion: the experience is labeled 'empathy', which denotes the experience of entering the mind of the other; the emotional stage remained with the title of 'compassion' or 'mercy', marking the non-rational response to the difficult experience of distress we undergo through empathetic identification with the other; and in the event that the emotion leads to action to alleviate the distress in a way that furthers the interests of the other and not our own, we find altruism.

These two new concepts, empathy and altruism, originated in nineteenth-century Europe, with the realization of the heavy toll taken by the Industrial Revolution – the great poverty, alienation, misery, and distress of a great part of Europe's inhabitants. The new concepts replaced the overly vague and broad concept of compassion. These concepts (which still hold force to this day, albeit not necessarily in their original sense) served as the foundation in constructing the modern approach to the misery of others, to the desire to act to alleviate this misery, and to the social and political significance of such action, while simultaneously upholding the dictate to adhere to scientific terminology.

It was August Comte who, following Smith's ideas, first expounded what is known as the theory of altruism. Comte's theory 'abandoned' the primacy of reason over emotion and proposed a connection amongst the physical structure of the human brain, experiential-emotional processes, and social-ethical behavior. Comte's proposal was to recognize social instinct as forming the basis of human ethics. The four principle assumptions of his theory were: (1) emotion dominates the lives of human beings, and we must accept its preponderance over reason; (2) human beings are controlled by two 'emotional instincts' – the personal, or egoistical, instinct and the social, or altruistic, instinct; (3) the condition for a successful society to exist is the suppression of the impulse of self-love and its subordination to social sympathy; and (4) accordingly, the primary moral principle is the regulative superiority of social sympathy over self-preservation instincts.[3]

But despite the fact that, on its face, the theory of altruism appeared to be a successful replacement for the vague idea of compassion, in fact, it made a significant contribution to the fragmentation of compassion and the shrinking of its significance. The concept of empathetic compassion, which was based on the direct encounter between two consciousnesses, was replaced by the abstract and completely apersonal concept of social sympathy. In order to be altruistic, under Comte's theory, a person does not have to actually witness another's distress; in fact, there is not even any need for 'another' *per se*, for social sympathy is one of the mental qualities of human beings, set in human biology and the structure of the human brain. What is important about the concept of altruism (at least in terms of the way in which it continued to exist in the modern discourse) is that it is understood as circumscribing the entire scope of 'action for the good of others' – in terms of both the motivation to act and the contents and intentional design of the action.

The concept empathy refers to the possibility of people climbing into the mind of the other, to experience her experience, to see through her eyes, and to feel her emotions. The concept first appeared just after Comte's concept of altruism, toward the end of the nineteenth century, in the form of the German expression *einfuhlung*, a translation of the Greek *empatheia*, meaning passion. The expression itself was prevalent amongst the German intelligentsia, particularly in aesthetic contexts: empathy (*einfuhlung*) referred to the way in which a person can sense the deep, hidden emotional meaning of a literary work. The reference to empathy in the context of human relations originated with Wilhelm Dilthey, who, objecting to the application of the dry scientific methodology of empiricism to the social sciences, sought to establish an alternative for researching human sciences and history based on identification-empathy and the inquiry into reality 'through the eyes of the other'. Concurrently, Edith Stein, Husserl's student, proposed a phenomenological model (a modification of Husserl's own attempted model) that describes the way in which one 'radiates' oneself into the inner life of another and experiences her experiences and modifies those experiences.[4]

Empathy lacked the impressive presence in the modern discourse that altruism enjoyed. This, I believe, stemmed chiefly from the fact that empathy was swallowed up into the psychoanalytical discourse, which explained it as essentially an illusion: we imagine ourselves in the shoes of others and believe that we are experiencing the emotions or experiences of others, but what is truly important is not what we think, but the subconscious processes that cause us to think this way. The psychoanalytical logic did not dismiss the importance of the feelings of others, certainly not the importance of identifying with others, but it did raise significant doubts as to our ability to transpose ourselves from our own minds into the minds of others, as will be explained further on.

Thus, the single, all-inclusive conceptual model of compassion – which encompasses the motivation to be aware of the other, the personal experience entailed by such awareness, and the action that is inherent to the encounter (and the predetermined existence of such action in itself) – was replaced, and in its stead came a series of concepts, which, although they logically derive from one another, have no necessary connection. Added to this was the disciplinary fragmentation that characterized modernism from the end of the nineteenth century, which enabled and even encouraged relating to each of the components of any given process as discrete, in accordance with the relevant discipline. Hence, chemistry and biology were detached from physics, geology from geography, and psychology from sociology. This disconnection constituted the final, fatal blow to the broad concept of compassion. The interest in identification and pain became the exclusive domain of psychologists, who investigated the subconscious basis to the individual human experience and human behavior. The interest in compassion as a social sentiment fell into the hands of sociologists who were mortified by the very need to become entangled in something as irrational as emotion, but nonetheless successfully incorporated it into theories explaining the irrational facets of human society. And finally, altruism was happily taken over by biologists and socio-biologists, who sought to refute the idea of an organism that operates against its own survival interests.

All this resulted in compassion, in its modern sense, being squeezed-in between two other concepts, each with its own separate discourse. Compassion (what remained of it after its fragmentation) came to be conceived of as purely emotion. But emotions do not lend themselves to clear description, and if they entail action they clash with modernism's vision of the 'rational man'. Thus, even if we believe that compassion is important and a central element of our lives, under the modernist view, it is not a legitimate basis for appropriate social action, which must necessarily derive only from rational-ethical considerations. Accordingly, the focus of the interest in compassion is how it can be discarded, ignored, prevented, or replaced by something more successful. The pinnacle of the modern discourse on the subject of compassion is very similar to the Bible's premise on the matter: compassion is not advocated for human beings (the Biblical exception being mothers and, even then, in a restricted form), for compassion leads to weakness, clouds judgment, and is perhaps even dangerous.

But what is so terrible about this conception of compassion? Was something important lost with the fragmentation of compassion and its reduction to infinitesimal dimensions? For it is quite possible that the new 'neighboring' concepts of compassion – empathy and altruism – incorporate the best of the important elements of what was once referred to as compassion. Perhaps we must simply switch our terminology and, in our quest for a possible response to human distress, focus on the new possibilities that the new concepts present. And why not take this one step further and examine the way in which ideas such as empathy and altruism are grasped today and shape a new model – Modernism's Model of Compassion?

In order to understand the difficulty in building such a model, it is necessary to consider, along with the process of fragmentation as described thus far, one of the great ethos of modernism, which I term the Egoistic Supposition. This ethos is a cultural presumption – a paradigm of the way in which the ideal 'man' is conceived in the modern age, broken down into a long series of explanatory templates with regard to motivations, emotions, awarenesses, and impulses that are supposed to elucidate every concrete mode of behavior and every given state of affairs in human life. As a paradigm, a cultural presumption has constitutive presence; that is to say, despite the fact that it appears as a description of reality, it also has the power to *create* reality.

The Egoistic Supposition

The Egoistic Supposition is grounded in the contention that human beings are biological creatures that are driven, like all organisms, by the need to supply their essential requirements and this drive is constitutive, determining their development, personalities, and behavior. Since this is an inbred biological need, on which our survival is contingent, it is first and foremost a social way of relating. Moreover, as the elementary and defining characteristic of human beings (and all organisms), this need sets and shapes how we relate to reality, which is the basis for language, consciousness, and our awareness of the other: first as an object that immediately supplies our needs (the mother) and, at a later stage, by means of language and culture, perhaps (if at all) as a distinct and separate subject. The modern roots of this contention can be found in the tractates of Western philosophers, theorists, and psychologists – from Hobbes and Locke to Darwin and Freud.

There has been no lack of opponents to the Egoistic Supposition: Hegel and his followers, Socialists and Anarchists like Proudhon, Marx, and Kropotkin; Pragmatists like George Herbert Mead; and even Liberals such as Smith and Comte. All proposed a range of anthrop-sociological alternatives for understanding human beings as fundamentally social creatures, with the most radical of these alternatives asserting that man's capacity for developing consciousness is contingent *a priori* on his ability to identify the other (per Hegel) or else propounding a softer version of anti-individualism that assumes that, alongside his egocentric tendencies, man also has an inherent 'social sentiment' (Smith and Comte). But these important theories did not stand in the way of the evolution of the myth that became (mainly over the course of the twentieth century) an integral part of the way in which we perceive ourselves and others: as entities that are driven mainly by the personal interest to satisfy their needs. An important factor in the development of this myth is the great dominancy and impressive presence of the psychoanalytical world of concepts and language, on the one hand, and the Darwinist evolutionary conception, on the other. These two approaches (at times completely at odds with the original intentions of their formulators) integrated well into the populist phraseology of the capitalistic and post-modern logic, to the point where the Egoistic Supposition came to be perceived as a self-evident truth, almost an intuition or axiom, with no need to explain or justify it. Today, the victory of the Myth of Egoism is being celebrated on the pages of pseudo-scientific (socio-biological) popular literature, which has transported the debate over sociability versus individualism to the genetic-survival arena and, under the guise of scientific explanations and proofs, seeks to justify life in an alienated, violent, and hostile world, which is presented as a biological necessity beyond human control.

Any attempt to object to this and present a different face to humanity – for example, the theory of altruism – falters as a pathetical and losing battle, clinging to specific manifestations of self-sacrifice for the sake of others and lone and scattered instances of human behavior that contradict individual selfish interest. These examples are intended to refute the dominating egoism myth, but their very use only draws further attention to its presence. And almost always, it is only a matter of time before some 'scientific' or mathematical answer for the discrepancy is offered, explaining the deviation, in the terminology of the Supposition, and safeguarding the social intuition that depicts human beings as self-interested predators.

This overriding presence of the Egoistic Supposition has immediate ramifications for the possibility of compassion in its sense of empathy and altruism. According to the empiricist logic that prescribes the Supposition, there is nothing in the fundamental human experience to support empathy, certainly not compassion, in anything but the most marginal of ways and, of course, bound and subordinate to the satisfaction of personal needs. Therefore, compassion, to the extent that it exists (and, in line with the Supposition, the existence of 'authentic' compassion should most decidedly be regarded with skepticism), originates in one of the two following processes: (1) *One possible source is the external social-institutional process that governs, influences, and shapes us against our 'true' nature.* This is the process by which people are educated to be considerate and have a sense of solidarity and community and indoctrinated to place the interests of others (particularly the general good) before their own needs. Historically, this process has been prominent primarily in the works of the great religions and, in the modern period, also in the social movements, which have sought to generate ideals and ideas that are not part of the basic human experience. Amongst the most ancient tenets of the great religions, for example, we find the premise that man is a creature born into sin (Christianity) or at least a boorish egotist (Buddhism), and only by means of education, indoctrination, external divine intervention, or any other method of suppressing human urges, instincts, passions, and so forth, can man become 'good', enlightened, understanding, and, especially, considerate of others. In sum, compassion is the superimposition of culture onto the egoistical nature of humankind, and any liberal-thinking person who believes natural tendency to take precedence over the dictates of culture must necessarily object to this superimposition (and some would claim that even if such liberal thinkers refrain from objecting, nature will in any event always triumph in the end). (2) *The second possible framework in which compassion can appear is in the human ability to adapt, which facilitates the adoption of the outlook of others when this appears to be beneficial to us (in later childhood, for example) or when it promotes our own interest in power (in business, for example).* We in fact have no direct experience of the other as a subject, but in any event, such an experience is not imperative from the perspective of rationality, since it is likely to impede our achieving our goals and is no more than old-fashioned romanticism. The pain of a fellow human being is actually a nuisance or distraction from the main purpose of our existence and is, therefore, hostile to that purpose. The notion of altruism, of acting in the interest of another, is also no more than a fairytale, created by religious-cultural history and whose didactic purpose is to distance us from our fundamental nature – indeed, deep digging will always reveal the egoistical motivations behind the so-called 'altruism'.

The process of the ascendance of the Egoistic Supposition in the cultural imagination included both the fragmentation of anything appearing to be a rival thesis and the theoreticization of the resulting fragmented components that imbued them with new meaning along the lines of the hegemonic paradigm. In other words, the assertion is not that there was no longer such a thing as compassion – of course compassion continues to exist. Indeed, the empiric data from human history and from life generally show that there are many instances in which people sacrifice themselves supposedly for the good of others; many instances in which people explain their actions as motivated by a sense of sorrow over the distress of another; and many instances in which people seem to subordinate themselves to the egos of others. However, upon closer scrutiny, we find that what people once tended to classify as compassion is no more than an external, social expression, using language and symbols, of culture, internal subconscious processes, urges, and instincts that demand satisfaction, of personal conflicts that demand a solution, or of the inaccessible activity of human genes striving to reproduce. Human beings have a psycho-biological need to create a certain type of identification, and this identification sometimes leads to a feeling of sorrow. The subliminal expression of this need and its realization is effected by means of the idea of empathy, with its softer, less threatening connotations and which enables us to conceive of ourselves and our motivations in a 'cultured' way, more suitable to social existence. Accordingly, an action that appears to the person performing it to be for the good of another is no more than a rationalization of the attempt to realize a personal interest, whether conscious or latent.

At this point, it is necessary to bend concepts such as empathy and altruism to the overall logic of egoism and explain why they are experiences and actions that not only do not represent a genuine encounter with the other, but also are a clear expression of the preservation of the egotistical personal interest.

Identification as a basis for empathy

The narrative pointing to the importance of empathy for the person empathizing, completely unconnected to the meaning of empathy (if it has such meaning) for the person being identified with, is extensive in Freud's writings. Freud was one of the formulators of the modern narrative in general (albeit not always intentionally). His theory, which asserted the subconscious aspect to human experience-action, produced a complex reduction of concepts that signify experiences (empathy, love, anger, frustration) into terms of (essentially biological) instincts and urges that are the background to all conscious experiences and explain them, at times in a completely different way from how the person undergoing the experience is aware of them. According to Freud, in the background of the experience we call 'empathy' lie subconscious processes that can be classified under the category of 'identification'.

Indeed, Freud was the first to link between empathy and identification and, at times, even treated them as interchangeable. Freud's analysis of the processes of identification was presented by Robert Katz, who used it as the basis for his claim for empathy's role in the therapist–patient relationship.[5] Freud's stance, according to Katz, was that the human creature has an instinctual, subconscious predisposition to identify with the other. This tendency manifests itself in a number of ways, since it serves a number of different types of needs of the ego. The three most significant ways are introjection, imitation, and regression, which together form the basis for the sense of resemblance or even identification with the other.

Introjection: Introjection originates in the most basic animal needs of human beings, the essence of which is the need to consume one's environment and to dominate, grasp, and defend oneself from strong and threatening figures. It is linked to what Freud termed the 'cannibalistic instinct', which directs us to 'swallow' or 'absorb' objects in our environment and, at a later stage, to internalize elements of the personality of another person. The process begins with physical assimilation of the object, already present at the instinctual level at birth (the suckling baby who tries to swallow all objects), and continues in the form of the desire to possess objects with no need to 'consume' them, but with the physical absorption changing into a mental introjection. This process reaches its peak in the encounter between one's own ego and another person's ego. The case of twins is most illustrative:

> [O]ne ego becomes like another, one which results in the first ego behaving itself in certain respects in the same way as the second; it imitates it, and as it were takes it into itself.[6]

Imitation: Imitation first appears in early childhood and, at its core, is the desire to take possession and the desire to resemble another and thereby assume one's traits, especially one's power. Under the Freudian method, the accepted expression of identification through imitation emerges deep in the heart of the oedipal complex: when a child senses the threat of castration, feels weak and helpless, and subconsciously assumes the father figure and, thereby, his power. The basic need of the child to move from a state of helplessness and weakness to the preferable state in which it avoids and even conquers its anxieties is the impetus behind the process leading the child, according to Freud, from imitation to empathy.

It is important to note that in Freudian terms identification through imitation amongst both children and adults also is part of the ego's defense mechanisms and is manifested as a shield against anxiety in different situations – for example, the tendency of the weak and defenseless to identify with their aggressors, as in the case of the abused child who adopts the viewpoint of his abusive parent and identifies with that parent. In such a process, the victim in fact imitates the victimizer and adopts the behavior of whom he perceives as a frightening and threatening object, thereby turning himself, as it were, into the very same object. Another manifestation of this defense mechanism appears in the sense of potency that a person derives from the mere belonging to a group she has joined, from merging with a strong group at the price of foregoing some of her sense of individuality.

Regression: Regression in the context of identification signifies a type of retroactive identification with people and images that were significant in one's past and continue to exist in one's memory. This is in fact the recreation of past identifications that were pleasant and confidence-instilling, on the background of problems with identification in the present. The regressive process too is a defense mechanism, related to the self-preservation instinct, the desire to continue holding on, as much as possible, to what one once possessed, what is still perceived as 'mine'. The most familiar example of this is in situations of mourning, when the mourner attempts to continue to hold on to the person she has lost, with part of this effort manifested in the reviving of past identifications with the person. Other manifestations are our ability to identify with previous situations of the ego, our ability to detach ourselves from our present situation and travel into the past to places where we had other identities and different experiences.[7]

There are two interesting aspects to the Freudian approach to empathy that relate directly to the present discussion of compassion. The first is the twofold reduction of empathy: one, a reduction to identification, as a subconscious process that is subject to the dynamics of satisfaction of needs, defenses from anxiety, and survival and, second, the parallel reduction of the concept conveying intention toward another to terms of self-interest, which is expressed at the conscious level as though it were the interest of the other person. Identification and empathy appear here as integral parts of the construction of the self or, in Freudian (and post-Freudian) terms, as serving the ego in the subconscious that determines the way in which we experience reality at the conscious level:

> Without any special reflection we attribute to everyone else our own constitution and therefore our consciousness as well, and that this identification is a sine qua non of our understanding. This inference (or this identification) was formally extended by the ego to other human beings, to animals, plants, inanimate objects and to the world in large, and proved serviceable as long as their similarity to the individual ego was overwhelmingly great.[8]

It follows from this reduction of empathy that the only way in which we can become aware of others is by way of 'importive' empathy: empathy that imports the other, or what we perceive as the other, into our minds. There is absolutely no room to assume the existence of 'exportive' empathy, neither the (perhaps) naïve type that I proposed in the Introduction, nor the type that rests at the base of the original definition of the concept of empathy. Indeed, under this reduction people never detach themselves from the self and climb into the skin of others, since this would contradict our most basic instincts and would pose a most menacing threat to our egos. Even the simplest level of empathy, that which derives from acquaintance with the other, can be only one of two things: either non-existent, and then everything we attribute to it is merely projections of our psyche, or else, alternatively, an experience based solely on our mental needs. I can recognize the pain of another person, but only insofar as it reminds me of my own pain; and if my pain (trauma or psychological complex) is unresolved (a frequent occurrence for most), I will tend to identify with the other person and to express this identification in a (conscious) sense of understanding and sorrow for her distress, although I am in fact relating to my own distress.

The second aspect of the Freudian approach relevant to our discussion of compassion is not part of the theory itself, but, rather, is part of its impact on the scope and content of the modern discourse in general. Freud, himself, did not find empathy troubling at all. On the one hand, he did not regard it as important for understanding mental processes and related to it as merely a byproduct of the subconscious mental process (as he related to every human phenomenon), quite at variance with the original sense of empathy. Yet, on the other hand, as a social theorist he had considerable appreciation for sublimative processes: although it is quite possible that we are merely deluding ourselves when we say that we understand how the other feels because we are able to enter into her mind and feel her sorrow, this is an innocuous and, in a certain sense, even beneficial delusion in that it allows us to perceive ourselves as social creatures. This delusion may be a manifestation of our upbringing or of how our culture, whose values shape the superego, trained us to understand our emotions and motivations at the conscious level, by softening and sublimating the harsh subconscious contents and turning them into something easier to digest. But 'collective delusions' have never enjoyed much legitimacy in the overall narrative of modernism. Culture is a mechanism whose only role is to cover up the truth, and we must expose the deceit and acknowledge our pathetic 'true' natures: if the basis to the way we relate to others is identification that serves the ego, then we are not empathetic creatures who can see through the eyes of others, but, rather, habitual egotists perpetually and only serving our own self-interests, our own urges, and our own personal distress.

Already at the end of the modern period, the original notion of empathy as a legitimate way of relating to the other was revived by Heinz Kohut. In his formulation of the narcissistic aspect of the Freudian developmental theory into a general analysis of the self (the 'psychology of the self'), Kohut presented an understanding of empathy as a process of 'mutual introspection' that explains how a baby develops its sense of self by way of the ability to observe herself through the eyes of those surrounding her, by leaving herself and entering into the mind of her mother gazing at her. This notion of empathy as a type of mirroring, which was proposed also by other psychiatrists (the most famous being Winnicott and Lacan), was expanded by Kohut into a conception that legitimized and even stressed the importance of empathy in the therapist–patient relationship. Kohut's approach influenced the contemporary streams of psychoanalysis, whose followers, in many senses, allow themselves to deviate from the rigid frameworks of modernism and classical psychoanalysis, and it is particularly prominent in the Intersubjective Approach.

The problem with this restoration of empathy, however, was and still is the limited scope of the legitimacy the notion was granted. First, it should be recalled that any sort of authorization for allowing a certain measure of empathy in the therapist–patient relationship threatens one of the most basic tenets of that relationship, that the therapist must strive for maximum control in the therapeutic setting and is obligated to avoid excessive identification and, most certainly, any merging with the patient's ego. This rule serves the notion of faithfulness to the patient's pain and distress, which guides and shapes professional therapeutic work and the rational methodical perspective of the therapist. Kohut, aware of this difficulty, moderated the possibility of therapeutic empathy in accordance with these parameters and did not advocate total empathetic identification, but, rather, empathy in which the therapist constantly – even in the strongest moments of empathy – maintains a certain amount of rational control and awareness of his or her separateness from the patient. The second source of difficulty is that the psychological approach (and certainly the psychoanalytic approach) is still, even in the post-modern period, based on Freudian logic. That is to say, it regards the empathetic process as an expression of the therapist's subconscious impulses, conflicts, and needs: the therapist, through the empathetic process, connects to traumatic or unresolved points in his own mental history. This approach therefore finds empathy problematic in principle, unrelated to the empathetic person. Finally, the third problematic aspect is that the psychological discourse naturally (although at times not consciously) makes a clear distinction between what occurs in therapeutic situations and what occurs in the outside world. What is permissible for the psychologist or psychiatrist to experience and do in therapy is not permitted for others – indeed, this is the essence of the profession. Accordingly, even if empathy is accepted as possible and legitimate, it is restricted to professionals who can control it and develop an awareness and perspective about what it represents and can use judgment, the only thing that can facilitate the eventual alleviation of the patient's distress.

Thus, the rehabilitated idea of empathy, despite the legitimacy that it gives to empathetic identification with the patient's misery, remains an emasculated, partial concept that does not necessarily include the progression from experience to action. On the contrary: under this conception of empathy, it is the experience itself that is the action and is supposed to generate change.

With regard to this last point, it is important to reemphasize the great influence of the psychological logic and language in shaping the cultural reality. The caution and abstinence that characterize therapy (and whose roots, contrary to what therapists tend to think, are not in the mandate of faithfulness to the patient's needs – there is no lack of examples in which psychiatry foregoes this obligation, such as in using drug therapy or psychiatric institutionalization) impact the way in which people understand interpersonal relations in general and how they adapt themselves to the interpersonal dimension of life. This influence is apparent in the current cultural treatment of everything related to the possibility of empathetic identification and can be presented by way of an additional supposition, which I term the 'Cultural Supposition'. This supposition both supplements and expands on the Egoistic Supposition.

The Cultural Supposition

The Cultural Supposition rests on the assertion that to become aware of the other and develop any kind of empathy toward her, we must have a stable and strong sense of self. Our sense of self precedes, both logically and practically, any possibility of being aware of the other. Thus, any way of relating to the other is constructed, first and foremost, on how we relate to our own self. This supposition is built on two theoretical conceptions, both of which have a marked presence in the modern history of ideas. First is the conception regarding the importance of the self as the central axis along which human consciousness and thought is built in general, regardless of the ontological status of the self (for even if it is only a fiction or imaginary construction, the self is still critical to every conscious act). The modern foundations of this conception originate in Cartesian thought, one of the cornerstones of rationalistic thought in general. This conception also appeared in different developments of the concept of the subject in German nineteenth-century ideology; it was in the background of the psychoanalytical attempt to replace the ego with the more comprehensive and complex concept of personality; and it was of critical significance in the evolution of existential philosophy, which has been the theoretical basis of the phenomena of the 1970s and onwards of 'finding one's self', of 'soul-searching' and self-appreciation, so popular in the post-modern era. In fact, the presence of this conception of the self is so overwhelming that it seems almost impossible to object to Descartes' claim that it is epistemologically necessary.

The second theoretical conception on which the Cultural Supposition rests is the developmental psychology approach that a necessary stage in the process of human development is identifying oneself so that one can identify the other as a separate subject. For example, speaking in first person, which appears at approximately age three, is the key to the development of a person's self-awareness as a linguistic subject. This awareness is a condition (or result, depending on the theory) of the development of a consciousness that places that person at the center of reality. From that point onward, she is capable of recognizing that other people may have a different outlook on reality, for they are separate from her, and with time she will learn that they also have their own desires, interests, paces, and so on. This learning process is based on the experience of the ego as a separate, autonomous, and potent entity (as opposed to the impotence of infancy, which is a symbiotic and instinctual state; that is, there is no clear separation between the self and the mother/external world). The appearance of the other in our lives as a concrete and separate entity is possible only after we undergo a separation-individuation process vis-à-vis our surroundings, both logically and chronologically.

The direct linking of these two conceptions makes, in the terms of the Cultural Supposition, our identifying with any experience of the other, and, in general, recognizing that a given experience is occurring in relation to that person contingent on whether our own personal history includes the same experience. Only someone who has experienced pain can recognize the pain of another, and likewise with regard to any other experience. This prerequisite is particularly acute in relation to emotions. One can describe a journey through China, for example, and the listener can identify partially with one's experiences through her imagination. But one cannot convey an experience of terrible rage to someone who has never been angry or enraged.[9]

Moreover, under the Supposition, it is important that we not only cultivate our personal experiences, but also develop a stable ego before the encounter with the other. For a person with a fragmented sense of ego or someone who has a confused self-identity or someone who is lacking in self-confidence, the meeting with the other is likely to be particularly problematic. First, such individuals are likely to be incapable at all of discerning the person standing before them. Their strong inner confusion prevents the development of a coherent experiential database to which they can compare what the other person is communicating and makes it difficult for them to even identify the other person as a subject, since they are not even certain of their own subjective actuality. Second, such an encounter is likely to pose a threat to the vulnerable personality of the observer.

But what is this insisted-on stability of the ego? Who are those 'stable' people, possessors of integrity and a strong enough sense of self, who can allow themselves the luxury of an encounter with the other? In truth, there is no one clear answer to this question. Indeed, the answers that have been offered over time have been guided more by the winds of fashion than a search for a binding definition. In the eighteenth century, stubborn people who did not change their minds were considered 'stable' people; in the nineteenth century, stable people were viewed as those who persevered in an ongoing quest and changed their minds frequently. In the mid-twentieth century, people who underwent psychoanalysis and emerged safely from the journey into 'the depths of the dark soul' were deemed stable people; later on, with the attempt to forego dealing with the self in favor of behavior, it was work and lifestyle that defined stability. And since the end of the twentieth century, when the self has ceased to be such a 'profound' and distant matter and, instead, has become a more familiar and accessible type of consumer product, the disciples of popular self-help literature and television talk shows, who cite the psychological clichés in their sleep, are regarded both by themselves and their therapists as stable with a good sense of self-awareness. However, if we generalize, what is common to all these conceptions of the stable self is expressed primarily in two mandatory qualities: significant reflective ability (known as self-awareness) and the ability to set boundaries between the self and the other at the physical and behavioral levels, the cognitive level (for example, the ability to develop the so-called 'autonomous worldview'), and the psychological level (the ability to differentiate between what is mine and what belongs to others).

Thus, when we attempt to describe empathy as part of the way in which a conscious, responsible, and mature person becomes aware of the distress of the other, the following is the outcome:

> Of course, I know that I am not Anna, that I am not having her experience of feeling sad, and that I am not myself actually feeling sad. These facts distinguish my empathy from other phenomena,

and my beliefs of these facts are presuppositions of my empathy. If I myself start to feel sad, I have crossed the line from *em*pathy to *sym*pathy, feeling *with* the other what she or he feels. If I start to literally share *her* experience, I have crossed the line from *em*pathy to *tele*pathy. If I start to identify too strongly with her experience, if I start to feel likewise just because *she* does, then I have become schizoid, or 'borderline', borderline schizophrenic. And if I start to think I *am* she, then I have crossed over into a form of schizophrenia. In empathy I 'identify' with the other, appreciating her experience *as if* I were going through it, but the boundaries between myself and the other, between my own experience and hers, remain clear to me.[10]

The Cultural Supposition in its entirety represents the second cultural objection to empathetic compassion. The Egoistic Supposition calls into doubt the very existence and justification of compassion toward the other. The second supposition leads to the conclusion that if compassion, in the sense of empathy, does exist, it is problematic and dangerous and suitable only for certain people and in specific situations. Compassion as a type of empathetic experience means entering the mental-experiential world of the other. According to the first supposition, this is an impossibility and perhaps a figment of the imagination that has been provoked by culture. Under the second supposition, even if we assume empathic experience to be possible, it must be restricted to the realm of the imagination, a fantasy in which we imagine ourselves *as though* we are another person and attempt to appreciate, assess, and feel how we would feel *if* we were the other, distressed person. Any extension of this situation to the point of an 'actual' entering into the mental or experiential world of the other is absolutely not recommended, for it is a direct threat to the personal stability of the empathetic person, who might be swallowed into the emotional world of the other and lose her sense of self. In fact, this is likely to be harmful also to the person at whom the compassion is directed. In the event of a pathological problem, it can distance her from assistance, which can be provided only in the framework of a rational-professional process. Moreover, empathy is allowed only for stable people, who know how to maintain boundaries between themselves and others, who are not swept away by emotion and can encompass pain (or anything else) that, during the empathetic experience, they imagine *as though* they are experiencing it, namely only professionals who have been trained to do this.

The best proof of the danger and problems entailed in empathetic compassion, proponents of the two suppositions will claim, can be found in the parent–child relationship, the framework in which compassion and empathy enjoy full cultural legitimacy. Parents tend to be overly involved in the lives of their children and overprotective of their offspring, thereby causing great suffering to themselves and their children. They forego their own lives for what they imagine to be the good of their children, something that inevitably emerges as a regretful evil for all involved. As a result, parents are perhaps the last resort for their children when seeking relief from pain and distress. This clearly demonstrates, supposition advocates will argue, that compassion is a peril best avoided or at least restrained. In fact, under the Egoistic Supposition, empathetic compassion is already checked: those mature people with a stable sense of self and for whom it is 'permissible' to feel compassion, if they do choose to be therapists, in any event have no interest in empathizing with others.

The social problem that arises from understanding compassion as an empathetic experience materializes particularly in the distress of the person feeling compassion. Sorrow is not a pleasant feeling, and when it is accompanied by a sense of impotence, it is likely to generate frustration and may even destabilize the orderly worldview and lead to skepticism regarding the validity of social conventions. In radical cases, this feeling can lead to personal crisis and (even worse, from society's perspective) to a desire to change the world order. The best way to contend with such a distressed state is by means of the rational procedure for dealing with emotions in general: either to abstain from the emotions as much as possible or, if this does not work, to inundate them, talk about them, and be aware of where they originate from – something that should be done with the assistance of a psychologist. This method facilitates identifying the origins of the frustration and understanding one's part in it, which stems from one's private mental history and its contribution to the distress. At the same time, it also enables the person in distress to understand the role played by the person toward whom the compassion is directed in creating the sense of frustration; the distressed person can then recognize that she is, in fact, taking something that does not belong to her. The end result is that she reaches the point where she can refrain from acting compassionately and feel at ease with this.

Compassion as an act of altruism

Altruism is usually defined as the following:

1. Altruism must entail action. It cannot merely be good intentions or well-meaning thought. 2. The action must be goal-directed,

although this may be either conscious or reflexive. 3. The goal of the act must be to further the well-being of another... 4. Intentions count more than consequences... 5. The act must curry some diminution in my own welfare... 6. Altruism sets no conditions. Its purpose is to further the welfare of another person or group, without anticipation of reward for the altruist.[11]

In contrast to the empathy discourse, the discussion of altruism over the course of the twentieth century was intensive and broad, encompassing a long series of disputes over a range of topics, debated by many and various researchers and theorists: from biologists, to Darwinians, to contemporary socio-biologists; from psychoanalysts to behaviorists; from sociologists to journalists and popular science authors; from moral philosophers to cultural historians. All seemed to have something to say about altruism. The literature discussing altruism, particularly from the second half of the twentieth century, covers a far wider spectrum of issues than the present discussion, and thus a comprehensive review of all the various views and topics would be an unnecessary deviation from the course of our current path. Nonetheless, to complete my claim regarding the fragmentation of compassion in its manifestations as empathy and altruism in the hegemonic narrative of late modernism, I will relate briefly to a number of hurdles the idea of altruism has had to contend with, most of which are encompassed in the two suppositions presented above. These chosen points, I believe, are central to considering the reduction of the idea of altruism to insignificant dimensions.

One of the interesting features of the anthropological approach that became prevalent in the twentieth century is the attempt (which has turned into almost cultural intuition) to frame every mental and emotional phenomenon in a biological-material context. This trend, which is totally at odds with the humanistic approach of the Enlightenment and beginning of the modern era, is apparent in almost every area that determines our self-image and the way in which we understand our relationship with our environment and the other. We have become more and more used to the idea that our thoughts and ideas are a function of brain processes, for example, and every time we are informed that a brain equivalent has been found for a mental event, we believe the 'understanding' of that event to be improved. We have come to believe that observing animal life in nature leads to enlightening conclusions regarding human beings as biological creatures, and inferences are drawn from these conclusions regarding social life, culture, politics, and so on. We now 'know' that things once considered to distinguish man from beast and that the idea that culture, language, and the arts are the ultimate indicators of this distinction are parts of an illusion: for human beings are creatures of the animal world and all of their actions are those of an animal. Civilization, in all its aspects, is no more than a byproduct of biological mechanisms; human beings produce buildings, cars, and poetry in complete accordance with the very same process that directs bees to produce honey.

One of the signature marks of biological logic and its application to the conception of human beings is its ground-breaking linking of cause and effect. Eighteenth-century modern logic held (amongst other things) that there are two different and distinct ways of relating to every action: First, according to the action's causes and, at times, in the case of human beings, in accordance with the motivation behind the action; and second, according to its effects or the outcome the action is intended to achieve. Under the evolutionary biological approach, in contrast, the distance between cause and effect narrowed. The cause is predefined by the purpose: the cause for the actions of organisms is survival, and the purpose of the action is survival. The motivation behind their actions is the survival instinct, and the outcome of both their lone actions and the entirety of their activity is survival. Following this comprehensive approach, the idea of altruism, in its capacity as a characteristic of action that encompasses also the 'purposeful causes' (to borrow Aristotle's term) of any action, became an integral part of the evolution debate. Indeed, the term 'altruism' is today specifically a concept of biology.

From this we can deduce that in order to understand any human action, including an altruistic one, we must frame it in biological terms. This can be done in one of two ways. The first is to analogize human beings or human society to different types of animals, in accordance with the type of action or with the explanation we seek to propose. In order to understand human-social behavior, we must find parallels between human society and animals that live in groups, such as dogs or wolves. The 'purposeful cause' of living in a group is the desire to improve the chances of survival of every individual member of the group. Wolves live in packs and act, for example, in a territorial fashion. They perilously guard the pack's different living areas, with a willingness on the part of some of the members of the pack to sacrifice their lives or health for the general good. Arguably, a certain understanding of human sociability can be deduced from this behavior: Human beings live in societies because social life maximizes their chances of survival. Just like wolves, human beings have a territorial instinct, either because they acquired it over the course of their evolution from a simple to complex life form or because this instinct enhances their ability to survive. This comparison can be expanded to the claim that a considerable part of social phenomena, such as territorial wars and even the splitting-up into nations-states, are the result of biological impulses. It can also be claimed that the aggression and hierarchy present in wolf society are proof of the fact that human beings are 'by nature' aggressive and have an innate tendency to construct their social relations along a hierarchy. And as far as altruism is concerned, if some human beings sacrifice their lives for the good of all or act to gratify their leader contra to what appears to be in their personal interest, they must have a biological predisposition to act for the survival of the 'pack'. Acts of aid to others, of which there are abundant examples in nature, can easily be explained as commensurate with the logic of survival, since they increase the survival options of the pack and perhaps even of the entire species. Thus, this is not 'truly' altruism as defined above, but, rather, a biological-instinctive action that stems from a genetic, inbred interest.

This type of explanation presents a number of thorny problems. First, beyond the surface analogical dimension, the basis for the comparison is not at all clear. Why are human beings compared specifically to wolves and not to fish, for instance? To claim that the reason is the great resemblance between human beings and wolves is to beg the conclusion. Second, the comparison is valid only with regard to a small portion of human behavior. For example, a human might commit suicide after failing at a task, whereas no wolf would do so. Moreover, we can assume that at least some of the behavior not covered by the analogy will even clash with that described (for example, human beings behave aggressively in certain situations and completely differently in others). Third, and most relevant to our context, the lone wolf which sacrifices itself for the good of the pack certainly is not conscious of the abstract idea of survival and certainly does not 'know' that its actions improve the mathematical chances of survival for the entire wolf species. Thus, by analogy, an altruistic action on the *individual* level is certainly possible and perhaps even genetically 'guided'. If we take this line of logic one step further, we can claim that some of the so-called 'human genetic heritage', whose essence was perhaps molded by the logic of survival, is no longer relevant, and at times its manifestations are even antagonistic to the survival interest, such as in the case of a territorial battle likely to lead to the eradication of the human race. Thus, human beings could have biological tendencies that are no longer commensurate with the survival interest. And given this, we can most decidedly assume that there are altruistic actions grounded in biology but unrelated to either the personal interest of the actor or the overall interest of the human race.

Thus, biological logic and methodology in fact lead to the conclusion that altruism can be assumed to exist insofar as it is attributable to human genetic heritage. Moreover, altruism is the dominion of private individuals and can in no way be a general trait. Indeed, the very existence of any biological species is the best evidence of the rarity of altruism and its exclusivity, for if it were widespread the entire species would have ceased to exist.

Another way to describe intentional behavior (action) is to remove the motivation (which, in biological terminology, is also the 'reason') for an organism's action from the equation. This possibility arose especially in light of genetic studies that suggested describing an organism as the derivative of its genes. The scientific popular literature (whose viewpoint is of greatest interest to us in this context) describes genes as minute creatures that have all sorts of plans for us, their carriers – they are likened to tiny giants pulling the puppet-strings of what we know as animals and human beings. The logic of biology, which previously was described as guiding the actions of living creatures (that is, toward survival), is transferred here to the genes: the genes want to survive (although the literature always includes a caveat that the word 'want' should not be understood in its literal sense, but, rather, as an allegory), and this survival is contingent on their ability to reproduce themselves. The aspiration (or tendency) of the genes is to continue to reproduce themselves *ad infinitum*. This is a new sense of biological survival, one that fits squarely with evolutionary premises. We can therefore abandon the attempt to describe human behavior from a psychological (motivational) perspective or social perspective and, instead, make a sweeping reduction of the entire living world, in all its complexities, to an alternative, relatively simply world, where tiny genes work to reproduce themselves without any awareness of or interest in, say, architecture or Chinese poetry.

If an organism's behavior is the derivative of the tendency of its genes to reproduce themselves, then, for example, every organism should have a tendency to produce as many offspring as possible. This would mean that a significant part of our social behavior is aimed at ensuring the continuity and perpetuation of our genes. We must necessarily have (genetic) inborn mechanisms that enable us to choose appropriate and fertile mates, and these mechanisms can explain the ways in which we tend to organize our society: toward maximizing reproduction. Given this, however, such phenomena as monogamy, for example, are a tricky challenge for proponents of the genetic hypothesis (primarily sociobiologists). In order to explain simple innovations such as birth control devices, broader survival considerations need to be added to the idea of infinite reproduction. It is with regard to altruism (which, in genetic terms, means increasing the reproductive capacity of the genes of others at the expense of my own) that the genetic proposition is truly challenged, a quandary that cannot be easily resolved. The solutions to the problem of altruism that have been offered can be divided into two types. The first one is to try and minimize the problem to modest proportions, that is, to claim that altruism is very rare and that many people who appear to be altruistic are in fact not. For example, in the case of simple actions of helping others, philanthropy, and so on, even when they entail a substantial loss of income to the actor, they do not necessarily weaken her reproductive ability and, in fact, may even enhance her social status, and thereby contribute to her ability to mate and maximize her offspring. Hence, such actions can be described as non-altruistic. In the case of actions that cannot be presented as non-altruistic, it is always possible to assume that they are 'freaks of nature', evolutionary accidents, or else a type of behavior stemming from a previous state of affairs in which the specific behavior had reproductive advantages that are no longer known to us.

The second type of explanation for the problem presented by altruism is the claim (which has become very widespread, primarily due to the great writing proficiency of one of its advocates[12]) that what we witness in nature is only partial altruism. In the end-run, it does not compromise the genetic reproductive ability of the actor, despite the fact that he is likely to increase the capability of others. This type of explanation is usually accompanied by mathematical calculations aimed at demonstrating how (mathematically) when a person saves her brother from drowning and endangers herself in so doing, she is acting 'on behalf of' the 50 per cent of the genes that she shares with him. When she acts to save her nephew, the genetic imperative is weaker since they share only 25 per cent of the same genes. And so on and so forth. One of the principal debates in this field is the dispute over the correct mathematical model for describing the interest-driven nature of the altruistic act from a genetic perspective; a secondary dispute is whether it is at all possible to reduce human behavior to mathematical models (in almost every experiment performed, it has emerged that people choose a completely different action strategy from that chosen by the computer, which, for example, tends to choose according to mathematical feasibility).

But, to my mind, what is important in all these debates is not so much a matter of who is right and which model correctly elucidates the behavior or of whether it is possible to label and justify an action as altruistic. What is important is that this is a far-ranging, popular, and detailed discourse that has crafted a clear narrative (supposedly) that establishes three set points: (1) What is important is survival, and the struggle for survival is conducted beyond the conscious control of human beings. (2) Altruism threatens and even clashes with survival. (3) In effect, there are no actions that are 'truly' altruistic, for otherwise the human race would have ceased to exist. That is to say, while there are certainly lone acts of altruism, they that are the exception that prove the rule and are exclusive and rare in nature (and so should they be).

To complete this discussion, it is necessary to briefly touch on the other aspect of the modern approach to altruism, the social aspect, on the background of the discussion of the concept of empathy and the definition of both altruism and empathy as compassion. Under the religious models, especially the Buddhist model, the experience of compassion involves no element of judgment or defined intention. Nor is it necessarily based on the personality of the person feeling compassion, but, rather, on her empathic ability and her degree of willingness to 'lose' herself for the moment in someone else's world. The modernist will claim that such a scenario poses no problem or threat for his worldview and approach: if it is at all possible (and, as noted, according to the logic of modernism, this is almost impossible and certainly not desirable) and if there are people who want to lose themselves in the experiences of others, so be it. However, the problem arises when action is warranted to alleviate the pain of the other. Then we are diving into the area that deviates from interpersonal interaction, that is, straight into the social sphere, the public territory in which strong forces operate to sow formidable wariness of anything that even hints at the possibility of change. The modernist logic – which represents, amongst other things, an alignment of powers and interests seeking to preserve the social order – therefore necessarily includes the tools for undercutting any possibility of significant action for the benefit of others.

Necessary to the progression from an experience, especially an emotional one, to action is a person who processes the experience, envelops it, arranges it in her previous picture of reality, takes a stance with regard to the experience, arrives at an intention, and, finally, performs a concrete and material act. This complex process thus requires, first and foremost, the presence of a person. Since one of the possible outcomes of empathy is a sense of sorrow for the other person, it is not at all clear whether the future action is an emotional one – that is, an action whose purpose is to respond to the emotional distress sensed by the compassionate person – or an act motivated by cultural conditioning, by the world of norms and values, or perhaps by ethical considerations derived through a rational process. In order to define the nature of the action for the benefit of the other so that the social danger is neutralized, the motif of 'aid to the other' must be removed from the action and the 'agent' of the action isolated.

Modern society has set forth a three-stage process to accomplish this: The first stage is to define every action as interest-driven. This definition of actions is encompassed in the Egoistic Supposition, according to which there is no such thing as an action for the benefit of another that does not entail an either open or hidden personal interest of the actor. Thus, we can kill two birds with one stone: in effect, when we relate to the agent as bearing a personal interest in the action, there is nothing problematic in a discourse with him regarding the matters of people who are suffering, abused, hungry, or 'simply' miserable. Moreover, due to his vested interest, he can be allowed to act, albeit under restricted conditions – that is, to take action that does not threaten the social order and, in the long run, even supports its perpetuation.

The second stage of the process is professionalization, which is encompassed in the Cultural Supposition, namely the treatment of distress should be limited to professionals, both because modern logic and methodology stress the imperativeness of professionalism in every field and also because the existence of professionals resolves well the problem of responsibility for the distress of others. (Who is responsible for a child abandoned in the street? The social worker, the psychologist, and so on.) These professionals can work under the aegis of the establishment, something that is even desirable since the establishment can thereby control their activity, on the one hand, and present itself as the benefactor of the wretched and misfortunate, on the other. The additional advantage to the professionalization mechanism is the banishment of all sorts of 'do-gooders' from the arena, as well as the rest of the charlatans who claim to have the ability to help others. Such people simply are not licensed to help others and operate outside the law.

The third stage, which is the necessary derivative of the previous two stages, is a familiar and integral part of the modern industrial democratic State: the institutionalization of social services whereby the State is defined as the body that responds to distress (and, accordingly, functions in a moral fashion), while, in the name of 'professionalism', seeking to leave as much responsibility as possible in the hands of those who act on its behalf. This institutionalization seals the control of the State and institutions working on its behalf over any possibility of action for change. The people working for the State undergo long training processes, in which they learn to translate their desire to help and change into the terms of the Cultural and Egoistic Suppositions (an area that is generally referred to as the 'social' sciences). They enter an institutionalized work system that sets long and detailed procedures and practices (for this is professionalism, is it not?), which delineate and delimit the scope of change that they can achieve in line with the parameters of the institutional interest. And finally, they are subject to constant supervision and regulation, which forces them to 'toe the line': refrain from any social protest and, commensurate with the capitalistic logic of the modern State, be loyal to the entity paying their wages – the Establishment.

8
Compassion Revisited

In the previous chapter, I described the fragmentation of compassion in the Modern Era. This process did not occur in a vacuum. It was part of the social-historical course of modernism, during which a number of endeavors were made to dispose of the ideal of compassion and replace it with rational-scientific, 'objective' procedures by which it would be possible, at least presumably, to alleviate the distress of human beings.

With the rise of nation-states and parliamentary democracies in Europe at the height of the Industrial Revolution came the accompanying liberal, humanistic, and, particularly, socialist demand to protect the weak, oppressed, and downtrodden through legislation that would guarantee social justice and some degree of equality for all citizens of the State. Thus, religious charity was replaced with social justice, paternalistic compassion with legislated rights. Society, in taking responsibility for its members' social welfare and the eradication of suffering, released individuals from any need or drive to feel compassion toward the suffering and neutralized any chance of individual social activism.

The erosion of compassion during this period did not produce a social void. There was no lack of social practices for easing distress, poverty, want, or suffering – on the contrary. The obsolete conceptual composite of compassion, translated in the Judeo-Christian tradition into charity, was replaced by modern European ideas such as the aspiration for social justice and civil rights. The compassionate works of the Catholic and Protestant churches and Jewish communities were replaced by State-sponsored social welfare; the religious leader and saint were replaced by the legislator and bureaucrat. This happened across the globe, regardless of regime – in the Western industrial democracies and socialist and communist European states, as well as in the imperial states of the

Far East. The twentieth century witnesses an intensification of this socio-political process, with the consolidation of the social-democratic trend in Europe and its goal of mitigating the horrors of capitalism through socialist reform. The height of this movement was epitomized in the creation of the modern welfare state in the 1960s and 1970s, the flag-bearer of State responsibility for the weak and needy. The European model (and North American variations of) the welfare state set as its primary and supreme task legislating and establishing social services unprecedented in scope and range, including social security, public health, welfare, and aid services, sanitation and police services, and, of course, state education. All of these services operate in line with the bureaucratic logic, that is, in a rational, supposedly impartial manner, in accordance with uniform criteria. Moreover, they attend to the needs of broad sectors of society that previously had never enjoyed protection and welfare. On the face of things, it appeared that the poor, weak, and needy were no longer dependent on the paternalistic pity of the rich and contented and the benevolence of corrupt and anachronistic religious institutions.

The welfare state certainly has had its share of critics, however. The socialist line of criticism accuses it of serving as a tool in the hands of world capitalism. Socialists claim it to be an ideological supra-structure and moral camouflage for the continued exploitation of the working class by promoting trivial and marginal improvements in their standard of living – especially in light of the fact that this so-called 'progress' was attained through the economic subjugation of Third World countries. This critique exposes the cynical face of the modern welfare state, as controlled by capital and giant corporations and whose institutions are constructed to perpetuate class reproduction rather than improve the state of the individual. Moreover, as argued by critics of modernism in general, the welfare state is the epitome of an age characterized by materialism, selfishness, and shallowness, by social disintegration and an absence of spirituality. The modern response to the distress of the individual, some claim, was overly superficial and hollow in focusing on material needs while neglecting human beings' need for spiritual and mental support through social frameworks that give meaning to the life of the individual and without which there cannot be any relief of human pain and suffering.[1] Criticism has also been forthcoming, of course, from political right wing, conservative corners, the 'natural' opponents of the welfare state. These critics have attacked the welfare state for its economic unfeasibility, waste of resources, and suppression of the free market, as well as its centralism, practiced under the slogan of 'State responsibility'. Other critics have pointed to the great discrepancy between the welfare state's intentions and legislation, on the one hand, and their problematic execution and implementation in practice, on the other. Moreover it has been a resounding failure in providing solutions to such social plagues as social disparity, inequality before the law, protectionism, congested bureaucracy, a politicized public service, and the latent control by commercial interests.

Much of this criticism is well-founded, casting doubt on the fitness of the welfare state to offer an alternative to compassion. Nonetheless, in the context of the present discussion, it seems unnecessary to delve into these critiques at any great length, perhaps even improper to speak ill of a social phenomenon on its deathbed. In any event, the rise of neocapitalism[2] has marked the downfall of the welfare state, after many years in which classical capitalism withstood (by and large appalling) socialist attempts to halt its domination. The final barrier fell with the demise of the Soviet and Eastern European regimes, the collapse of social collective bodies (such as the Israeli *kibbutz* structure) or else their conversion into economically motivated enterprises, and the crumbing of the social security, health, and welfare systems. 'Socialism' has become a term of derision, while the ideology dictated by the Reagan and Thatcher regimes in the 1980s has risen to the so-called objectively scientific status of 'exclusively right' economics. Capitalism has taken on the more sophisticated, battle-ready, liberal form of neocapitalism, which steadfastly gnaws away at the last outpost of social values: the fading welfare state.

Not only is the welfare state reaching its end – the (hazy and problematic) notion of social justice is also passing from this world. This is not because the welfare state has any exclusivity over promoting social justice. Though the notion does lie at its ideological foundation, the aspiration for social justice did not originate with the welfare state; indeed, as we have seen, the quest for social justice arose long before the Modern Era, in some of the religious traditions of compassion, such as Judaism.[3] Rather, the decline of social justice is related to the psychosocial aspect underlying social welfare policy in general; that is, the fact that the welfare state, beyond being a political-economic form, also represents a moral value stance rooted in the objection to injustice, repression, suffering, and poverty. This stance has lost all of its force in the postmodern, neocapitalistic age, for how indeed can we defend justice in a reality characterized by an absence of moral values? How can we justify social institutions in an aggressive commercial world that always favors immediate and fast profit? How can the piercing cry of poverty have any meaning or impact in a political reality with the moral values of pimps? Indeed, the social reality of a great part of the Western world has been that the waning of social justice is accompanied by a return of charity to its traditional position: once again the poor, hungry, and downtrodden are reliant on the benevolence of the lord and philanthropist, once again softhearted, merciful, 'bleeding heart' citizens are asked to open their wallets and save the needy.

The neocapitalist age has also closed the gates to any possibility of justifying the State's responsibility for ensuring equal education, since this prospect would apparently not be profit-yielding. Neocapitalism has stripped bare the promise to guarantee the physical and mental welfare of all citizens (never mind their happiness), equal opportunity, and the rectification of historical injustices to deprived populations.

But within this reality lies a hidden, radical potential, which can be revealed by re-examining the source of such notions as social justice and charity. It is my claim that these two seemingly conflicting concepts share a common source: the human empathetic ability to feel the pain of the other and the perhaps instinctive inclination to act to ease that pain. This claim is essentially anthropological in nature as it rests on a premise regarding human nature, similar to how the British Naturalists sought to present compassion in the eighteenth century and how the Buddhist epistemologists understood compassion.

I have presented two models of compassion as a central element in the narratives of Christian culture and Buddhist culture from ancient times to this day. The importance of compassion in these cultures derives from, amongst other things, their need to provide an optimistic promise and vision for their followers or, in sociological terms, a theodicy. The analyses of these two models revealed the gap between the level of declaration and intentionality and the possibility of the given culture fulfilling its promise at the practical level. When the discussion moved to compassion in the framework of the intellectual history of European-American modernism, which was not bound by the requirements of theodicy, we saw that compassion underwent fragmentation and was replaced by concepts that meet modernity's demands, receding, in the long run, into the periphery of the general cultural narrative.

The question of interest at this point, as the final part of the discussion, is whether it is possible to propose an alternative model of compassion, one that describes human tendencies better than these three preceding ones. I argue that such an alternative is most certainly possible, in the form of a model with a link to certain elements of the religious concepts of compassion but that applies certain premises present in modernism's theories that did not achieve primacy. It should be noted that in the last few decades, quite a number of attempts have been made in the psychological, sociological, and philosophical literature to present a more optimistic picture of human behavior or at least of the motivations behind that behavior. These efforts generally took the shape of a defense of the possibility for empathy and/or altruism and to a great extent relied on the discrepancy between Modernism's two Suppositions (the Egoistic Supposition and the Cultural Supposition) and reality as it unfolds in practice. The empiric data seem to indicate that the ruthless, alienated, and oppressive dynamics of humanity during the twentieth century have been accompanied by numerous manifestations of humanity, love for the other, and willingness to make personal sacrifices to alleviate the distress of others. These latter phenomena seem, both at the personal level and at the social level, to mandate a change, or at least a significant modification, of the modern assertion regarding the innate egoism of the human race. The conception I will propose belongs to this intellectual-research trend, but calls for a deeper revision of the current reality, resting on a broad model of compassion that entails (albeit not necessarily) both empathetic and altruistic acts.

In order to describe this model, I will make three basic premises that will serve as counterweights against the hegemony of Modernism's two Suppositions: the Egoistic Supposition, which assumes individuality and egocentricity to be inborn human qualities, and the Cultural Supposition, which assumes the self to be a mental construction whose presence is a prerequisite for recognizing the other and the sole basis to the human ability to feel empathy. There are three reasons to counter these Suppositions. The first reason is that although both Suppositions have an impressive presence in modern culture and deep roots in ancient traditions (the Judeo-Christian and Hindu traditions), they in actuality block any possibility of understanding compassion as an actual, empiric, day-to-day, universal human phenomenon. It seems that the infrastructure of the broad conception of compassion – that promised by divine compassion and, especially, universal compassion – offers different and far better possibilities for understanding compassion than the narrow modern conception.

The second reason for rejecting the Suppositions is the fact that they acquired the majority of their force at the height of the capitalist age, concurrent to the shaping of what came to be known as the modern nation-state, many of whose institutions (especially its social ones) were intended to respond to the needs of the poor, weak, and deprived, as well as to set rational procedures of 'professional' services for any subjective sense of pain or suffering. For physical pain, there is a doctor; for mental pain, there is a psychologist; for social pain, there is a social worker; and so on and so forth – and, importantly, all function in line with rational (that is, professional) procedures, free of any emotional or empathetic bias. These so-called 'professionals' undergo strict qualification processes to train them to suppress and repress such emotions as empathy and identification, the appearance of which is deemed evidence of 'unprofessionalism'. The institutionalization of aid activities that accompanied the fragmentation of the broad universal concept of compassion should, in my opinion, be regarded with great suspicion. And this suspicion deepens when we consider the tremendous difficulty encountered when trying to describing empathy, one of the most widespread and mundane phenomena in the human mental life, as well as people's great difficulty in the current era in translating this mental phenomenon into concrete action for the good of others.

Third, and most critical, the two Suppositions must be rejected if we wish to formulate a counter-narrative in the current reality, where personal experience unites with the established narrative and shapes us by way of an obsession with the self, which is too easily translated into marketing and consumer terms and actions. The critical analyses of the various models of compassion have shown, I submit, the theoretical importance of such a counter-narrative, with regard to both the religious models and the modern narrative, which claims to encompass these models, but thereby neutralizes them.

The First Counter-Premise: Instead of assuming that human beings are biological creatures driven only by need-satisfaction, let us assume that we are biological creatures driven *also* by the need to attend to the interests of someone else. This alternative assumption, which I term the 'Supposition of Altruism', presumes people to have an inclination to respond to the distress of the other. Socio-biologists would, perhaps, describe this inclination in survival or genetic terms or perhaps not at all[4] – but the choice of label is irrelevant for our purposes. What is important is the presumption that all human beings have an inclination to 'climb into the skin' of the other and experience reality through her eyes and attempt to help her through concrete action if she is in distress. This premise is in no way novel; as already noted, it has had many serious advocates in both Buddhist philosophy and Christian theology, as well as amongst the Scottish moral philosophers at the outset of the Modern Era. Moreover, this premise does not necessarily clash with the Egoistic Supposition: it is certainle possible to assume that a person has two, conflicting tendencies, like two ends of a rope pulling in opposite directions. This also is commensurate with human behavior as we know it from personal experience. When we see a truck about to run over a person crossing the road, most of us experience two conflicting reactions: on the one hand, we are driven by an urge to jump into the road and save him, while, on the other hand, we are also driven by the desire to protect ourselves and avoid danger. These two opposing urges pull with equal force, and the outcome, in most cases, is paralysis, which generally characterizes the existence of two such urges. And since most people tend to experience such paralysis in the face of danger, distress, or a problem requiring intervention for another's good, it seems logical to assume that human beings do, indeed, have two concurrent conflicting urges with regard to acting to ease the distress of others.

The Second Counter-Premise: Under the second counter-premise, instead of assuming that a stable self is necessary to identify and sense the other, we assume that sensing the other is a precondition for the self's stability or even its very existence. One implication of this premise is that the mental construction known as the self is the product of interaction with the other. A second implication is that the construction of the self in an intersubjective process is contingent on a person's ability to identify how the other observes us. Thus, one must be capable of climbing into the skin of the other and feeling her emotions and observing through her eyes. Or, in other words, a certain level of empathy is a prerequisite for human beings to form a self-image, to possess a self.

But why and how does climbing into the skin of the other facilitate forging the individual sense of self? The explanation can be drawn from two phenomena that characterize the empathetic process. One phenomenon is the exiting of one's own body, as it were, and entering into someone else's mind. This mental act enables us to observe ourselves from without, through the eyes of the other with whom we are identifying. According to the second counter-premise, this conscious possibility of externally observing ourselves holds the key to constructing a separate and actual self, which exists in the world through the eyes of another. The second phenomenon is the acquaintanceship with the self of another, which transpires when we enter into her mind. This encounter with a way of observing a very different, yet completely familiar reality forms the empiric-experiential basis for generating an autonomous self. The experience is particularly intense in the encounter with the pain of the other, since pain is the key catalyst to separation ensued by individuation of the self from one's environment and other people. Indeed, pain, especially the mental experience of pain may have even greater importance in the context of the synthesis of the self than usually ascribed to it: people tend to experience themselves as different, separate, and distinct from those surrounding them most particularly in times of pain. These moments of pain generate the experience of uniqueness and even the desire to distance oneself and withdraw from the world (in contrast, for example, from the experience of happiness, which produces a desire to share and socialize with others). Experiencing the pain of the other enables the compassionate person to become acquainted with the former's distinctness and uniqueness, in precognitive, intuitive ways that create the emotional and experiential basis for generating the latter's own sense of self.

The Third Counter-Premise: The third counter-premise to Modernism's two Suppositions is founded on the combination of the first two counter-premises: namely, that both the personal and general experiences involve (intuitive, conscious, judgmental, and emotional) acquaintanceship with the distress of the other and in this acquaintanceship lies the desire or inclination to alleviate that distress, as an integral part of the experience. I assign the general term of compassion to this acquaintanceship and claim that it represents a fundamental, primitive, and indivisible phenomenon. This phenomenon does not appear in human beings as part of a long and ongoing process of experience-emotion-action, but, rather, as a complete, unified, and simultaneous composite whose different elements can be distinguished only in retrospect. Accordingly, compassion cannot be described as an experience, feeling, or consciousness, simply because it is in fact a conglomerate of all three and because all (or at least some) appear simultaneously, in no hierarchical order and without any necessary casual connection. Those instances in which compassion entails an imperative to act to change reality for the suffering person (and not just an inclination to ease the distress) I term 'radical compassion' – a private instance of general compassion.

Compassion and empathy

As an experience, compassion can appear as empathy. That is, it is what happens to us when we leave our own bodies, our self (assuming we have one), and find ourselves either momentarily or for a longer period of time in the mind of the other.[5] We observe reality through her eyes, feel her emotions, share in her pain. This experience is not uniform in nature, and at least three different types can be conceived of. The first is *imaginary empathy*, which is identifying with the distress of another by means of the imagination. There are two possible modes of this type of identification. One is to imagine that the other is in distress, even though it is not at all clear what she is 'truly' feeling. In such a case, the distress is the product of the compassionate person's imagination and the entire process transpires within him, including the virtual entry into the mind of the other. The second mode of imaginary identification is identifying with the pain of people present only in our imaginations. We envisage their situation and, using our imaginations, experience pain that seems to us to be their pain (for example, when we hear of a disaster and imagine ourselves in the place of those who were injured). This type of identification – climbing into the skin of an imaginary other – is commonly described in the context of watching movies, reading books, and in instances of general social distress.

The second type of empathetic experience is *allegorical empathy*. This refers to identification with the other's emotional contents, based completely on the experiential history of the compassionate person. The feeling will be described as 'I felt exactly the same way when...' or 'it does hurt when...' and so on. With this experience, there is only a partial, safe entry into the mind of the other, since there is no merging with her self or loss of a sense of our 'original' self. We take on the vantage point of the other, but equipped with our own self – not only do we not lose that self, we use it to observe or imagine the experience of the other.

These two types of empathetic identification most certainly may be part of the phenomenon of compassion; they also are in line with the modern logic that 'concedes' the possibility of partial empathy. The type of empathy I term 'imaginary' was first proposed in the phenomenology of the turn of the century; the modernist D. W. Smith recently revived it with his novel conception, described in Chapter 7, asserting imaginary intentionality toward the other as the only legitimate possibility of empathy and rejecting any deeper identification as clearly dangerous and psychotic. Allegorical compassion, for its part, appears frequently in reference to compassion in the religious models. Moreover, according to Smith and even Kohut, one of the great advocates of empathy in psychoanalysis since the 1970s, it is an inseparable part of imaginary empathy since it is a precondition to the possibility of activating one's imagination with regard to the state of the other (which, in my opinion, more closely resembles what is currently termed 'sympathy').

But the problem with these two types of empathetic experiences is the simple fact that despite the fact that they do exist in the framework of interpersonal relations, they do not suffice as descriptions of the empathetic phenomenon and, therefore, do not succeed in describing the empathetic aspect to compassion.

Let us imagine a person watching a film in which the hero's one true love is tragically killed, and he expresses his great grief with a heart-wrenching cry. The viewer 'identifies' with the hero and bursts into tears. What exactly has transpired? Under the imaginary empathy model, the person watching the film activated his imagination, while thinking 'What would I feel were I the hero and my beloved had just been killed?' His imagination enabled him to envision himself in the hero's place and thereby experience his pain. But this account in no way resembles what happens at the time the film is being watched. For in fact, the viewer's imagination is not operating at all, because he is being guided by the progression of the film, by the *director's imagination*. And, moreover, when the identification occurs, the person watching the film does not differentiate between himself and the hero as advocated by D. W. Smith – he does not maintain a boundary between himself and the on-screen character. In fact, what actually happens is that the viewer *becomes* the hero, completely losing any sense of the presence of his own self. He does not 'feel' – the hero is the only 'person' feeling! The only defense in such a situation – which Smith refers to as a state of schizoid psychosis[6] – is the temporariness of the moment, which ensures the return to what seems to the viewer to be his 'original self', as soon as the film ends. But is this day-to-day occurrence, familiar to most of us, indeed, a psychotic experience? If we take this logic one step further, we can claim that, in effect, during most moments of our lives, we do not experience ourselves as present, but rather as merging with others through talking, encounters, and interaction with our environment. This outlook combined with the second counter-premise noted above raises the possibility of additional types of empathetic identification.

This leads us to a third type of empathy, that characterized by an experience of total identification, merging, or even complete loss of the sense of the self, which is connected to the entry into the mind of the other. The totality of this experience is so fundamental that it is not at all clear to whom it actually belongs: Is it the experience of the person suffering or the person feeling compassion? And what if any meaning can an 'experience' of the compassionate person have if her self is not present during that experience? Indeed, with the entry into the mind of the other, his self is left behind or completely relinquished, at least for that moment. This type of experience of compassion has been the subject of much social criticism and is commonly presented as dangerous and undesirable, although psychoanalysis acknowledges its existence and importance, at least in infants at the stage of symbiosis with their mothers. This aside, however, if we accept my three counter-premises, then this type of empathetic identification with pain (that is, compassion) is the most authentic representation of the link between us and some of those people surrounding us, for it forms the basis of our ability to forge the mental structure of the self, as well as appropriately defining the general self–other relationship.

The presumption of our ability to 'become' other people is not a new one. A description of this phenomenon appears in the work of William James, who tried to show the absurdity of the assumption of a stable and set self by describing the different ways in which we both assume and discard identities on a day-to-day basis as part of the conception of stream-of-consciousness.[7] Another familiar illustration of this ability appears in George Herbert Mead's theory of 'The Social Self', as the basis of our ability to construct social relations on empathy. I propose a similar, but more radical presumption: that we are able to become and actually do become other people on a daily basis. There is no reason why I can 'become' Superman while watching a movie, yet not become the person suffering stomach pain in a hospital.

However, empathetic identification and the exchanging of identities and situations with others in no way exhaust the phenomenon of compassion. Compassion often emerges in us spontaneously and unintentionally; it does not always entail a journey into someone else's mind and can occur in the absence of any real contact with the other. A person can experience compassion from merely reading dry statistics on global hunger, without any undernourished African child appearing even in her imagination.

Thus, our search for an accurate description of compassion must take another avenue: the alternative model of radical compassion, which explains the spontaneous and emotional aspects of compassion, as well as manifestation of compassion as action.

The spontaneous aspect of compassion

The first counter-premise proposed considering the phenomenon of compassion as coexisting with the survival instinct. Elsewhere,[8] I have noted that compassion, especially in its radical form, manifests itself as an impulse. This manifestation stands in stark opposition to the underlying premises of the Darwinist theories, which regard the survival instinct as determining human behavior, as well to the Freudian logic of the Pleasure Principle, which refutes any supposedly natural tendency on the part of human beings to act against their own interests and proposes viewing such an inclination as the product of cultural conditioning. In contrast, I propose one of two alternatives: either the egoistical-survival instinct is accompanied by an opposing instinct that directs us to immediately and automatically respond to the distress of the other, at odds with the tendency to preserve ourselves or, alternatively, the Darwinist-Freudian description is simply erroneous and the reverse of what actually occurs – our immediate instinct is to help, but culture trains us to refrain from such action and to instead behave egoistically.

But in the context of the current discussion, the causality behind the manifestation of compassion is irrelevant. For our purposes, we need only take note of the simple fact that compassion appears spontaneously, similar to the appearance of what we call 'instinct'. That is, it appears automatically, completely unconnected to conscious will or desire, within a short, even infinitesimal, period of time, in the framework of the encounter with the distress of the other. Even in retrospect, no conscious discursive process can be discerned as preceding the appearance of compassion, nor the activation of the imagination.

Imagine that we are looking through a one-way mirror at a seven-year-old child unaware of our presence. The child has just learned to read, and the first story he comes upon is Andersen's *The Little Matchstick Girl*. As we watch the child reading the story, he bursts into tears. What exactly transpires in this scenario? First of all, something happens to us as observers. We are filled with compassion for the weeping child. Our response is automatic; this is how we usually respond when we encounter a crying child – for some of us, it is sufficient to hear only the sound of crying to arouse a feeling of sorrow, as well as the desire 'to do something' to stop the crying. It is difficult to claim that, in such situations, we activate our imaginations in a type of intellectual process of first trying to picture in our mind's eye, or recall, what it is like to be a seven-year-old, then trying to remember and imagine the sad feeling we experience when reading a tragic story, and, lastly, transferring that feeling into the seven-year-old's world we first imagined. Such a process is simply not part of the phenomenon. We respond to the open pain of the small boy, in a spontaneous reaction that resembles the protective instinct awakened in us in any encounter with children (or people in general) whose helplessness and vulnerability are evident. It could be argued that the reaction is spontaneous simply because we are adults who have been subjected to conditioning or who respond automatically based on our own experiences, which enables us to take short-cuts around the imagination straight to the reaction. But this claim is clearly groundless: children also respond immediately and spontaneously to the pain of others, despite their lack of experience in an imaginary return to similar situations.

A second occurrence in the above scenario is the child's experience. But what precisely is this experience? What happens to him? Can we say that he identifies with the matchstick girl? Does he fly away with his imagination and imagine himself a little girl selling matchsticks? The experiential world of a seven-year-old boy does not include acquaintanceship with people who sell matchsticks, certainly not children. Nor has he ever been a small girl or experienced bone-chilling cold; indeed, perhaps he does not even know that people can die from cold (if he even already has any idea of death that he can conjure up). But nonetheless, he feels the tragedy of the story; he recognizes the emotional force of the situation – despite the fact that the story does not describe feelings! He not only feels himself a small, lonely girl, shivering from the freezing cold, but also experiences something beyond this – a feeling of great sorrow and pain in the face of an unnecessary, atrocious state of affairs.

In fact, a certain type of judgment of reality is present in what happens to both the observer and the boy – a judgment that the state of affairs before them is simply unjust, inappropriate. A sort of inner voice is heard by the boy declaring it to be unthinkable for a little girl to be all alone and die from cold in a deserted stairwell. The same voice is heard by the observer declaring that it is not right for a tragic tale of death to be the first story a seven-year-old reads. Of course, no actual voice is heard speaking. Indeed, we already determined that the reactions are spontaneous and appear to lack any discernible discursive aspect. But we can nonetheless distinguish here a considerable extent of judgment supposedly transpiring at the precognitive level. Why, however, is the situation adjudged problematic compared to something terrible? For such a judgment to occur a comparison must be made against some internalized set of values, norms, or perhaps ethical code, according to which, for example, it is forbidden to abandon children, children are defenseless and must be protected, and so on and so forth. These determinations supposedly lie in the (conscious or subconscious) background of our judgments, but where did they come from? It is completely clear that the adult observer has many sets of such determinations, and it is also clear that they are almost always the background to our responses, even though the latter seem automatic to us. But what about children? What about the child who reads the story of the little matchstick girl? Does he adjudge the situation to be intolerable? Or perhaps he makes no judgment, and instead the situation he reads about reminds him of his worst fears – to be left all alone and shivering from cold. Perhaps we have here a type of 'natural morality', by which human beings are able to distinguish intuitively between good and bad, suitable and unforgivable.

In the framework of this mental exercise, whose purpose is limited to only a description of the phenomenon of compassion, we do not need to determine the answer to these questions. We need only consider the features of the phenomenon, which include spontaneity and judgment that seems to appear almost self-evidently, without any deliberation. These features of compassion are most prominent in the different manifestations of radical compassion, which is the extreme and concrete realization of the call, or summons, a person hears when he feels the pain of the other. This call represents both the cry of the reality and the context in which the distress is set as well as the inclination to act to change that reality. In effect, radical compassion is tantamount to taking what is a unique stance: one that is not founded on the judgment and categorizing of the other person, but rather of the situation in which that person is. This stance does not lean on a causal analysis of the reasons for the distress. On the contrary – it is a purposeful stance directed at a future situation in which the distress will disappear, totally independent of the cause of the distress. Radical compassion is the refusal to come to terms with a given state of affairs with regard to the other, which is translated into intentional action to change that reality. At the immediate, spontaneous level, radical compassion is founded on the imperative to change the reality of the suffering person, with this imperative appearing spontaneously, like an impulse, as well.

The emotional aspect of compassion

Most particularly today, the conventional way of understanding the term 'compassion' is as a feeling of sorrow. The object of this feeling of sorrow is the other, and the sorrow felt by the compassionate person relates to the bad luck, pain, misery, and so on, of that other person. The problem is that from the counter-premises set out above, and the discussion of compassion as a phenomenon thus far, it emerges that a great deal of confusion exists regarding the emotional dimension of compassion. It appears that two different sets of emotions exist, both connected to the emotional experience of compassion. The first set belongs to the person suffering, and it includes her feelings of her own pain, deprivation, and suffering. This set of emotions is supposedly not included in the scope of the concept of compassion, but rather falls under the category of 'distress'. The second set of emotions is that of the compassionate observer. This includes his feelings of sorrow, empathy/sympathy, and so on, which, in the present context (as opposed to how they were described epistemologically), must be considered types of emotions, even though it is not completely clear what these emotions are (but that is the nature of emotions in general). A causal link supposedly exists between the two sets of emotions, with the first the clear reason for the emergence of the second. Thus for our purposes, we need only to surmise, or identify, the site of the process of merging of consciousnesses: Does it occur in the imagination of the compassionate person or is there actual contact between the two consciousnesses, as I assumed earlier?

It is at this point that a number of problems become apparent. First, a pre-existing or parallel system of distress is not always attached to the feeling of compassion. There are many instances in which we feel compassion toward people who most certainly seem happy and light-hearted. The most extreme model of this phenomenon is described by Buddhist universal compassion, which assumes *a priori* pain and suffering even if the 'sufferer' does not feel them. But the basic situation is familiar to us all – for example, the compassion felt for a person with a brain injury, who, happy and laughing, exhibits no feeling of distress. Here, the distress is entirely theoretical in nature and is imposed on the situation by the observer. Second, it is not at all clear what happens on the emotional plane in the event of radical empathetic identification. When an exchange of identities or merging with the other takes place, there is no way of distinguishing between the two sets of emotions. Indeed, in such cases, only one emotional system is present, that of the suffering person, which the compassionate person joins, simply feeling the suffering of the other, as Adam Smith described in his definition of compassion cited in Chapter 7. Can we call this 'compassion'? Perhaps the feeling of compassion should be attributed to a later stage – when the compassionate person returns to his 'original' mind, recalls the experience, and then feels compassion. But there is also the possibility described by D. W. Smith, who explained that for an empathetic person in situations of compassion, the greater the identification the more his sense of his separate self is preserved, making the coexistence of two separate emotional sets perfectly feasible.

In the framework of this exercise, I propose the following as the appropriate answer – all of the above! For indeed, each option describes actual occurrences that are familiar to us all from our own personal experiences. This exemplifies perfectly the emotional complexity of the phenomenon of compassion and its multifaceted nature: perhaps it is a composite of emotional phenomena, rather than one clear, distinct emotion – an observation that would meet with the approval of both the Buddhist and the Christian.

This insight does not complete our quest for an exhaustive description of compassion. We have determined that compassion is not comprised only of a feeling of sorrow. If we give serious weight to the judgmental element of what appears as 'compassionate intuition', it is clear that the emotional complex of compassion includes emotions such as anger and rage. It is possible that these emotions (which the religious models systematically seek to isolate and repress) are part of the fundamental emotions of compassion: the anger and sense of injustice we feel in witnessing the distress and suffering of the other. This possibility may, in fact, be the key to understanding compassion. Compassion often entails a sense of misery, impotence, and frustration. One of the most intense manifestations of these emotions is when a child's pain arouses in the parent a sense of helplessness; the parent's immediate impulse is to 'trade places', as it were, with the child and feel the pain in her stead. Thus, in addition to sorrow, compassion possibly involves a considerable amount of rage, frustration, and helplessness.

Again, these emotions are particularly discernible in radical compassion. As we will see throughout history, radical compassion has stood in the background of the demand and struggles for social change and, thus clearly, has entailed a strong emotional timbre of considerable anger and frustration.

Compassion as Praxis: The passage from imperative to activism

A person can find himself in a state of distress for many different and complex reasons. We tend to think that only by identifying the causal process and attending to the causes can we affect the outcome. The causal logic, standard in therapeutic models, is derived from the mechanistic-scientific conception of reality and has great explanatory force. On the practical level, however, it is more limited. Usually there is no simple way of pointing to a specific reason for specific distress, unless it is distress born of a physical event (someone is beaten by someone else and the outcome is pain). For most emotional states of distress, there is a wide range of reasons related both to what has happened recently in the physical reality and to the way in which what happened is interpreted by the suffering person – that is, to the complex emotional dimension, in part hidden and in part rooted in events in the more distant past, but, either way, inaccessible. If we further consider that the people involved almost always maintain a variety of contradictory explanations for the immediate causes of the distress in practice, we see just how problematic taking a stance with regard to another person's distress is if we rely on a causal analysis. Yet against this complexity, we find the compassionate person with a clear sense of the inappropriateness of allowing the situation of distress to continue and his inability to accept the situation.

Throughout I have assumed the imperative to act to be a part of the phenomenon of compassion. The question that arises is just what action this imperative directs us to take. It has been asserted that the imperative is to create a reality in which there is no pain, in which suffering disappears, but just what precisely is such a reality? The nature of a situation where suffering has disappeared will vary in accordance with the type of pain involved, with the specific circumstances, and with what the involved individuals have to contend with. Thus is it at all possible to generalize about compassionate action? There is a multitude of possible expressions of compassion as action, and we assume a correlation between the act and the imperative. The assumption that compassionate action is the derivative of the imperative to act in the face of distress and of the actor's judgment as to the most accessible and effective option for diminishing that distress produces an infinite amount of possibilities for acting in an infinite amount of possible situations of compassion. But history in fact shows that compassionate activism is a rarity, which, of course, clashes with the universality of the imperative to act. It is in fact generally possible to identify only three accepted modes of action for easing distress, all of which are usually identified with the three models of compassion I have described. I will give a brief description of these three modes of action, in order to explain why they only partially respond to radical compassion's imperative.

The first mode of action is based on the premise that empathetic treatment of the other is the best action for easing distress. Under this approach, prominent in the history of compassion and enthusiastically embraced by Modernism, empathy alone is the correct and successful response to the distress of another. The fundamental rationale that has traditionally underlined this approach stresses the power of empathy as a form of therapy and for easing loneliness, the sense of being misunderstood, and alienation – which are, in any case, some of the most dominant factors of human distress. Clearly, this does not satisfy the imperative for concrete, material action to change reality.

Viewing empathy *per se* as a mode of action for the good of the other that fulfills the commitment of the compassionate person toward the person for whom she feels compassion is identified with the religious models of compassion, as well as with modern therapeutic approaches. This approach is not altogether unthinkable in the framework of the radical compassion model; indeed, empathy can be understood as an important (albeit very partial) possibility for easing distress, given the second counter-premise presented above, that a person consolidates her self-identity by way of the gaze of the other. If we add to this an additional premise,[9] that self-identity is shaped by the sense of *being of value* in the eyes of another, we arrive at a rather reasonable formula for regarding empathy as a way of shaping reality for the other. A person who receives empathy from another person, who feels that the other is willing to draw close to her, to create intimacy with her to the point of actually entering into her world, benefits from an immediate sense of value. And since this feeling is constitutive of her self-image, it is of great benefit and can, indeed, change reality for her. In other words, the fact that another person has seen and discerned one person, has erased themselves and identified with one's pain, means that, in their eyes, the one is of value. And without a doubt, such acknowledgement has great potential for diminishing distress.

The most compelling claim against understanding empathy as action is that it is a state of consciousness, an emotion, and lacks the ability to change any aspect of the material reality. Moreover, in situations of compassion, empathy is in any event present; there is no necessary connection between empathy and decreasing distress unless the distress stems from alienation, humiliation, contempt, or a sense of lack of worth. This notwithstanding, it is also important to recall that much of the distress experienced as personal by underprivileged and minority groups is also social distress that is characterized by social exclusion and a psychological sense of lack of value in the eyes of others. In such situations, empathy has a more important role than generally thought as the basis for creating a renewed sense of value, and it can even manifest as real action.

The second recognized type of compassion action is the act of giving. This mode of action, the pillar of the divine model of compassion, developed into a veritable art in the monotheistic traditions. It is most closely identified with Judeo-Christian religious compassion, which translates the imperative of compassion into a powerful economic system, stretching across the world, which often also saves lives. This system is skilled at giving, especially basic material needs, such as food, shelter, and clothes, as well as medical treatment and education. Indeed, according to the Judeo-Christian Scriptures, the lack of these items is the greatest, most accessible distress of all and those who endure this distress will inherit the earth. This system teaches the rich to give to the poor; it has tried repeatedly to translate compassionate action into action for changing the allocation of resources; and it has preached, and still does preach, exploiting the psychological advantages of the act of giving as creating a sense of fulfillment and joy for those who perform it, in addition to being the basis for improving the state of the needy. Moreover, the religious traditions expanded the reach of the act of giving into the emotional sphere. They offered a type of 'relief for the soul' in the form of confession and prayer, which, in certain times, was particularly attractive, replacing the mystical powers of the saints in the past. Saying a prayer for someone is a form of giving that especially suits the divine model of compassion, mainly because it connects the person suffering with the compassionate divinity. It means that I plead your case before the divinity, as well as giving you divinity itself in the form of the compassion of the Creator, Savior. Giving as compassionate action also has been adopted by the modern welfare state, in terms of both the physical aspects of aid it provides and social services such as education.

The first problem with the phenomenon of giving is that it does not merely respond to distress, it also defines it. Under this model, distress is always necessarily the product of want, physical or emotional, and the imperative of compassion is therefore satisfied through the act of giving. Thus, anyone whose distress is not rooted in a lack of something, but rather is 'merely', say, being abused by one's spouse, is excluded from the scope of compassionate action and compassion in general (although this person's distress may be responded to by means of the law, for example). The second problem is that before they specialized in giving, these systems of giving specialized primarily in taking. Their critics show that from an economic perspective, they clearly still take more than they give, for otherwise they could not continue to exist. Thus it is not clear just to what extent the religious social systems and the social system of the modern state execute the imperative of compassion, and to what extent they act simply to survive and amass power. The third problem with giving as a mode of compassionate action is that it does not respond to the impulse to change reality. Radical compassion, which is aroused in the encounter with the poor, lonely, or afflicted, is not directed at giving charity or replacing shabby clothing with clothes donated by a middle-class family. It is directed at changing reality itself, at effecting a radical change in the global agenda, not at providing immediate and modest material relief, which suspends the encounter with distress and enables donors to sleep well at night, with the knowledge that they are Good Samaritans.

The third accepted form of compassionate action is acts of rehabilitation. Rehabilitation is particularly suitable as a reaction to some of the more painful situations in the human experience, for example instances of trauma, personal tragedy, and terrible pain from loss, disaster, and war. Under the rehabilitative logic, the compassionate desire to 'turn back the clock' upon encountering such horrible distress is impossible to realize, and therefore it should be translated into maximizing the good of the suffering person, by returning him to proper functioning and society's embrace. Under this logic, society, with all its values and economic-occupational procedures, is the warmest and sanest haven for restoring a person's will to live in the most balanced and fairest of ways. And even if it does not succeed in so doing, rehabilitation is the best available option that society can offer the individual in distress. Rehabilitative action confers a significant part of the responsibility for the rehabilitation to the person herself, on the basis of the assumption that only by summoning and mustering her own strength can her functioning be restored and can she be reintegrated into society.

The problem with this mode of action is threefold. First, a rehabilitative action is not a full realization of the compassionate imperative. Moreover, it is subject to the rational analysis of possibilities versus desires, realism versus fantasy (of course, there are those who would regard this as an advantage, not disadvantage, but in the present discussion we must remain faithful to the perspective of compassion and the interests of the compassionate person). Second, this mode of action rests on the assumption that human society is healthy and that people in distress are 'deviant', sick, or flawed and must be set back on the 'right' track. The problem is, of course, that human society, in all its concrete historical manifestations, whether in antiquity, the Middle Ages, or the Modern Era, has never been 'healthy', has never been a safe and warm refuge, and has never been nor tried to be fair. The third and most acute problem of all is the fact that this type of action, again, defines distress in a very emasculating way. Is the slave beaten by his master in need of rehabilitation? Is there any need at all to rehabilitate someone who has been humiliated? Or, should the humiliation first be terminated and only then its harm investigated? Under this model, a person who cannot benefit from the rehabilitative action is completely excluded from the scope of human compassion in general.

With these three familiar modes of action as background, I want to point to the possibility of a fourth mode of action, one that suits primarily the imperative of radical compassion, namely action for social change, or what is commonly referred to as social activism. As noted, this imperative rests both on the unwillingness to accept a given state of affairs in relation to the other and on the need and call to change reality for that other. The imperative of radical compassion is expressed as intentionality toward reality, toward the atrocious injustices we encounter in the world through compassion. It is not directed at changing the person who is suffering, since her suffering is felt by the compassionate person precisely from that place where she is victim – of circumstance, of coincidence, of arbitrariness, and, especially, of other people. Indeed, the imperative, as was shown, does not relate to the causes of the distress; these become relevant only at a later stage. The anger vis-à-vis the unacceptable situation arises already at the immediate, spontaneous stage of identification. This anger leads the compassionate person to the sense of being unable to come to terms with such a reality and of having to turn the world upside down to change it.

Thus, radical compassion encompasses the imperative for concrete action to change the distressful reality in which the other exists. Looking through the eyes of the other entails experiencing an often intolerable, impossible, and painful reality. The unwillingness to tolerate this reality is at times more intense than the way in which the compassionate person conceives his own reality: people are often willing to endure a very high level of arbitrariness and injustice directed against them, but refuse to bear this when it is directed against others (the simplest example of this is the noted context of parenthood). This social-psychological situation has led, over the course of history, to the emergence of the radical social movements, despite the fact that they themselves often denied the compassionate nature of their activities, preferring to regard themselves as 'rational' or 'scientific'.

Radical compassion translated into action for social change is oftentimes found in the margins of the official social discourse. It is distinct to groups of world-reforming revolutionaries and religious missionaries who take 'too seriously' the idea that it is possible to change the world and help human beings. Yet radical compassion is also implicitly present in most of us, despite the fact that it almost never rendered into a lifestyle or even lone concrete action.

What is unique about radical compassion as action for social change is the fact that it in no way entails a 'profound' understanding of the overall causes of social distress. It is not the product of a call for social justice, of an organized ideology, or of a coherent model of possible utopia. It is simply and entirely the concrete response to the distress of the other. My claim is that once people are able to realize their basic capacity for radical compassion, they in any event will have to contend with complex realities and will attain at a more analytical view of the reasons for distress, and the imperative that mandates effective action will lead many of them to choose strategies of change that deviate from the conventional patterns of the official social discourse. The combination of a conceptual evolution and development of strategies of concrete action leads to the shaping of a language game, of a reality that diverges in many of its parameters from the present neocapitalistic reality as well as from past realities dictated by the different traditions of compassion.

But it is rather inconsequential how a person arrives at radical compassion in social activist form. Many embark on their activity for social change out of a commitment to a religious conception of compassion, but the way of life and the exposure to the reality of the lives of the poor, oppressed, and outcast inevitably lead them down the path of calling for overall social change and of radical stances with regard to themselves and reality, even if this stands in opposition to or deviates from the original discourse from which they originated. The manifestations of this phenomenon are so numerous, stretching far and wide across time, culture, and geography, that it is quite impossible to touch on even a small part of them. I will mention only some of the more well known examples, certainly not representative of the phenomenon in its entire scope, but rather the mere tip of the iceberg.

Many familiar figures associated with radical social activism can be found in the history of Christianity, in both the Catholic and the Protestant streams,[10] and it is not difficult to discern the clear connection between the exposure to distress and the awakening of the urge to act. Such was the case of the thirteenth-century Saint Raymond of Piacenza, a pilgrim in his youth and later a wandering preacher who embraced holy poverty and committed himself to aiding concretely and materially the weak, poor, and ostracized. Similarly, Antonio Vieira (1608–97), the seventeenth-century Jesuit missionary and great classical master and writer of Portuguese prose, was drawn into the battle against the colonial horrors and slavery as the result of his work with the

Amazon Indians in Brazil, eventually fighting the very Church that had sent him on his mission. There were also the Methodist priests in eighteenth-century England and nineteenth-century United States whose direct work with the communities that bore the terrible price of the Industrial Revolution sent them to the forefront of the struggle for social rights;[11] and, in the same vein, there were the twentieth-century educators (of which Ivan Illich is the most famous) whose work in Third-World countries led them to form a radical pedagogical outlook that was translated into action to change the global agenda on education. Also of note in this category is Father Joseph Wresinski, the French priest of Polish descent who founded the Fourth World Organization originally as a movement of people committed to living with people in extreme poverty, but which became over the years committed to fighting for social change through, amongst other things, legislative reform.[12]

Buddhist history, as well, has no shortage of impressive examples of social activism that depart from the passive paradigm of the Buddhist model of compassion. One contemporary and well-known example is the work of the Buddhist practitioners whose compassionate works led them to recognize the criticality of concrete, material action within the framework of Engaged Buddhism.[13] The concept 'Engaged Buddhism' was coined by Thích Nâht Hãnh, a Vietnamese Buddhist monk, whose work for peace in Vietnam was boycotted by both sides in the conflict, forcing him into exile in France in 1966. His innovative interpretation of the directive of Buddhist compassion as a commitment to social change established him already in the second half of the twentieth century as a leading figure in the global social struggle. His words illustrate poignantly the process and experience of radical compassion:

> When I was in Vietnam, so many of our villages were being bombed. Along with my monastic brothers and sisters, I had to decide what to do. Should we continue to practice in our monasteries or should we leave the meditation halls in order to help the people who were suffering under the bombs? After careful reflection, we decided to do both – to go out and help people and to do so in mindfulness. We called it engaged Buddhism. Mindfulness must be engaged. Once there is seeing, there must be acting. Otherwise, what is the sense of seeing?[14]

Other prominent social activists include Luangphaw Charoen Parnchand, the Abbot of the Tambrabok Monastery in Thailand who declared all-out war against the drug plague both inside and outside his country, and A. T. Ariyaratne, the founder of the Sarvodaya Organization in Sri Lanka, which specializes in grass-roots community development projects based on social justice. Also worth noting in this group is the Jewish-American Zen Master Bernie Glassman, who gave up his life as an engineer to become a social activist and initiator of social-economic projects for the needy.

Finally, in this context, it is of course most apt to mention one of the most prominent models of radical compassion, a model supposedly grounded on the traditional paradigms of compassion and represented by of two of the greatest socio-political leaders of the twentieth century, Mohandas Karamchand Gandhi and Martin Luther King, Jr. These two leaders established a model of social activism based on altering the harsh social reality through brotherly love and compassion, claiming their work to rest on, or even revitalize, traditions of compassion.

Gandhi, a Hindu (Vaishnavist with a strong tinge of Jainism), put forth an ideology of active non-violence, which he attributed to the ancient Indian sources: Jainism, Buddhism, and the traditional Indian philosophy of the *Bhagavad Gītā*.[15] But Gandhi's manifest of non-violent activism and change, the *satyagraha* (translated as 'civil disobedience', 'passive resistance', or 'truth force') in no way resembled the Buddhist idea of *śīla*, the radical Jainist concept of *ahiṃsā*, or Krishna's words of counsel to Arjuna in the *Bhagavad Gītā* to ignore the moral dictate and hesitance and to wage a bloody war against his own family. The Gandhian ideology seems to have rested primarily on an inner truth and deep self-conviction that derived from the direct contact with the pain and suffering of the Indian people. It is not representative of the universal model of compassion, nor of any other tradition of compassion other than radical compassion.[16]

Martin Luther King, Jr, a Baptist minister, was greatly influenced by Gandhi. He constructed an argumentation that grounded the struggle for civil rights on the biblical idea of Christian love (although the terminology he used in his sermons was Baptist and Methodist), but in practice, his activity was based on modern social-democratic values and concepts of rights, freedoms, and equality, which were combined with a philosophy of non-violent activism and protest taken straight from Gandhi's doctrine. Clearly King's was also a personal-political, activist, and radical manifest that wore the mask of a traditional model, whether for didactic purposes or out of loyalty to his cultural origins.[17]

Finally, even in the heart of the modern establishment (the modern, or postmodern, industrial democracy), an astounding number of people emerged whose close contact with human pain and suffering led them to feel the imperative to act. Doctors, social workers, psychologists, teachers – all with a drive to engage in radical change of the oppressive, cold, exasperating reality that holds so much misery and pain for so many. The list of social activists includes those hundreds and thousands of devoted people for whom radical compassion is a way of life, whether in the framework of an organized movement or on an individual level, whether openly or privately. In responding to the inner voice calling for commitment to fight the distress of the other by means of concrete, physical action, these people have recognized the crucial need for overall social reform, as opposed to philanthropic acts, for example, which do not entail any real action and are in fact constructed to *protect* the philanthropist from radical compassion. What all of these social activists have in common is the fact that their work is the product of a direct acquaintanceship with distress and suffering and is aimed at bringing about a change in reality, not in the person in distress.

* * *

There are three senses to the radicality of radical compassion. The first is that this is fundamental, primary, and essential human compassion. It is the root – the radical – of our humanity. The second sense is that it is indicative of activism, of an attempt to translate consciousness into action and not to leave it as a 'game' of emotions and concepts. The third and, to me, most important sense of the radicality is that it hints at the nature of the action: action to change reality for the other. That is to say, radical compassion is an intentionality toward the other that includes an unraveling of a reality of distress and an identification of the elements whose alteration will lead to an easing or complete disappearance of the distress. This is compassion that is not satisfied with the feeding of the hungry person, but rather requires a change in reality to eliminate any possibility of hunger.

The concept of radical compassion also encompasses the call to act to change the world order. Radical compassion distinguishes between a reality of distress that requires change and a reality of distress that does not mandate intervention. I already noted above that, presumably, the imperative to effect change is tantamount to a normative stance based on and deriving from a value judgment of the compassionate person with regard to a given reality: it does not derive from the sense of compassion itself. This is most apparent when we consider the application of the Buddhist universal compassion model to poor and rich alike, without distinction: the notion of acting to change the situation of the pauper, especially if at the expense of the rich, is a social-moral (or ideological-political) stance, absolutely unrelated to compassion.

My claim, however, is that the separation of the social stance from compassion is absolutely wrong. Indeed, radical compassion is in itself a social stance! In principle, there is a difference at the epistemological level between the ways in which compassion is aroused in each of us. Not every instance of compassion is accompanied by a call to change reality. For example, an encounter with a homeless person lying in the street is likely to awaken radical compassion directed at changing that person's life, whereas the encounter with an industrialist frustrated by the disappearance of a million dollars from their bank account is likely to generate a different kind of compassion in us, in no way radical in nature for it will not be directed at changing reality for them. Similarly, an encounter with a well-fed child who is frustrated because she received 90 and not 100 on an exam will arouse compassion in us but, again, not of the radical type. A different compassion will be aroused by contact with a hungry, illiterate child: for such a child, we must change the world, and this is the true sense of radical compassion, of the call to act to bring about change.

Conclusion

The discussion in the book has presented and critiqued three traditions of compassion – the divine model, the universal model, and the human model – and closed with a proposed fourth, alternative model: radical compassion. To conclude, I will revisit for a brief analysis the first two traditional models on the background of Modernism's two Suppositions and, then, all three models in light of radical compassion.

When we consider the Egoistic and Cultural Suppositions in relation to the Christian model of compassion, it is apparent that there is correspondence, or at least no antagonism, between the two. Both models accede that human compassion is a rare, confused, and certainly dangerous commodity. It is not at all clear why it is necessary or what it serves, and its dismal nature in fact drives us to continue to look to another source of compassion (heavenward, for example). The wretchedness of human compassion stands in stark contrast to the power and beauty of the compassion of the Savior, which can constitute an excellent supplement and source of hope in our cynical, cold, technocratic, and rational world, a world of predators and quarry. The extent to which the divine compassion of God/Jesus can generate a change in reality is contingent solely on man himself: on the ability of the sinners and unenlightened to embrace the Gospel. And in the face of the limitations of this ability, with success hardly guaranteed, this model provides an excellent, ready explanation for the unremitting presence of suffering in the world and the tragic fact that, despite centuries of Christian rule in major parts of the world, no relief for suffering has appeared.

A different conclusion emerges when we consider the modern conceptions in the framework of the Buddhist model of compassion, for it appears to be far more compatible with the counter-premises to the Suppositions presented in the previous chapter. Buddhism seems to promote the idea of natural compassion, viewing the ability to diminish the sense of self both as the basis to an empathetic capacity and the cognitive-emotional potential for eliminating suffering. Buddhist anthropology, which is inherently optimistic, also incorporates an explanation for the continued presence of suffering in the world: while Buddhist compassion is universal and it can offer a certain response to pain, human beings are trapped in an illusory reality dictated by the dynamics of desire and attachment to its objects. This cycle cannot be broken solely by means of compassion, but rather entails the adoption of the Buddhist lifestyle and practice. Only when the entire human race has embraced the Buddhist Eightfold Path to Enlightenment will suffering be vanquished. But Buddhism cannot take responsibility for ensuring such a change of reality because it is not a missionary culture in the sense that it does not operate on the basis of divine dictate. The choice of the Buddhist lifestyle is an individual one, connected to the overall, uncontrollable *karmic* contexture.

In contrast, the modern concepts of empathy and altruism are not at all intended to explain the presence of suffering in the world. Under the modern approach, suffering is an empirical fact, and it is not at all clear if it is possible, desirable, or even necessary to act to eliminate it. The desire to eradicate all suffering is, to a certain extent, related to sentimentality rooted in modern tolerant and socialist culture, but from a scientific perspective, this culture is no more than a tempering of the 'true' nature of human beings: egoistical, competitive, and survivalist. This approach asserts that people are not, and will never be, equal and that society should be organized like nature into hierarchical power structures. Given such harsh preliminary conditions, it is telling of the greatness of the human race that in the midst of the great struggle for survival, it manages to find the time and energy to compose music and poetry and to paint works of art – and, more astonishingly, to harness the daunting forces of Nature by means of ethical-rational codes and legitimizing certain sentiments, of which compassion is but one. In fact, under close scrutiny through the spectacles of Modernism, compassion is exposed as no more than lip service paid to cover social manipulations. However, how can we fault this if doing a philanthropic deed is what enables people to sleep well at night by distancing them from the victims of the existential jungle?

The picture changes somewhat when we consider the Christian and Buddhist models in light of the abbreviated typology of empathy I presented in the alternative model of compassion. It appears that the allegorical and imaginary types of empathetic identification are generally compatible with the Christian model, whereas the third type – the experience of total identification, merging, with the other and the loss of the sense of the self – is not. The Christian logic does not point to a conscious extinguishing of the self, nor to a total relinquishment of any attachment to the self for the good of the other, although there is no lack of anti-egoistic preaching in Christian rhetoric and, as a rule, Christian culture can certainly be characterized as calling for the foregoing of personal pleasure and interests and even significant self-sacrifice for the good of all. However, this notwithstanding, the Christian concept of compassionate love, similar to the Jewish variation, was grounded from the outset on self-love as a condition for loving the other. The idea of holy self-mortification and *imitato Christi* to a great deal turns on the willingness to withstand all physical temptation. But in terms of compassion, this is not tantamount to a merging with the other, for this would constitute holy desecration and would be counter to the concept of the soul as a divine possession. The appropriate form of self-sacrifice in the context of compassion is the provision of a personal-experiential base through which it is possible to grasp and identify with the suffering of the other. Through his own suffering, the Christian believer or saint creates his ability to identify with the suffering of the other and thereby make himself a candidate for the status of Good Samaritan. As opposed to its manifest difficulty in justifying an intense experience of identification, the Christian model sets a high standard with regard to the second sphere of the process of compassion: compassionate concrete, material action for the good of the afflicted and suffering. It is actually the relative paucity of the emotional dimension (which stems from the fact that all compassion is in fact Jesus' compassion and man is no more than a medium by which the Savior's love is channeled to the suffering person) that turns Christian compassion into a type of praxis and not an emotional experience.

In contrast, it seems that the Buddhist perspective would have absolutely no difficulty accepting the third type of compassion. For a culture that devotes a sizeable part of its education, goals, and modes of action to the systematic diminishment of the status of the self, the empathetic merging with the suffering other is not only feasible, it is almost an imperative. There are two noteworthy qualifications to this, however. First, the Buddhist will always seek to refrain, as much as possible, from allowing the sorrow of the other to be transferred to the compassionate person, since such grief is likely to hamper the possibility of progressing to liberation, to Nirvāṇa. Yet avoiding such a situation seems impossible without foregoing the experience of total identification. Second, the

Buddhist logic could emerge as being even more radical than what I present as the third possibility of empathy: it is very possible that the state of absence-of-self, which, for the Buddhist, is in all events a desirable state, will not be limited specifically to the encounter with the other and is likely to persist beyond this experience. In such a case, it will be problematic to complete the course of compassion and arrive at action. Buddhist compassion is likely to always remain in the empathetic experiential sphere.

With regard to the second type of empathetic experience, allegorical identification, where the identification with the pain of the other is based on the past personal experience of the compassionate person, there is a considerable amount of support in the Buddhist literature for the suitability of this type of identification to the general model of universal compassion. Especially compelling are the references to the Buddha's compassion, whose personal experience with suffering led him to recognize the suffering of others and which, in fact, forms the basis to the Bodhisattva's commitment to leading others to the Path of Enlightenment.

Imaginary identification, the first type of empathetic experience, is presented convincingly and in detail in Tsong-kha-pa's commentary (described in Chapter 5); and it appears that, over the years, it was in Tibetan Buddhism that the greatest technical skill in developing this type of experience was attained. In fact, the most important and interesting aspect to the Tibetan Buddhist development of the Buddhist meditation technique in general is its perfection of the means for activating the imagination, developing an assortment of techniques for guided imagination.

It is in the passage from experience to action that the weakness of the Buddhist model lies, as discussed in Chapter 6. But this aside, it seems that Buddhism would embrace the idea of change by means of empathy, for it is a great advocate of the notion of giving. In fact, Buddhism is likely to accept most elements of the model of compassion put forth in the previous chapter, including its fundamental premises, but, nonetheless, likely to reject the radical aspects of compassion, especially the positive role attributed to anger, rage, and the impulsive inclination to impact reality without any ability to assess the outcome.

As far as radical compassion is concerned, if we were to ask the Buddhist and Christian their views on such a model, both could be expected to express great reservations, albeit on different grounds. From the Buddhist perspective, the passage from empathetic experience to actual action would seem overly hasty and resolute. Moreover, many of the emotions entailed in the compassion process under the radical compassion model are objectionable from a Buddhist perspective, such as rage and the sense of injustice. The unequivocal Buddhist dictate is that all reform – even with regard to an injustice – must be conducted in a state of equanimity, serenity, and sympathy, since hostile and the so-called 'negative feelings' only increase suffering and do not lead to any good outcome. Thus, the first three modes of compassionate action that I noted (empathy, giving, and rehabilitation) are likely to be accepted in principle by Buddhism, but it would never advocate the fourth mode of action. It is reasonable to assume that the Buddhist response to the desire to act would be to insist on an ad hoc consideration of each case, consideration of the picture in its entirety and context, and wariness with regard to the illusory power of the action and its consequences vis-à-vis the general fabric of reality. For there are an infinite number of ways to act, but only one clear way to put an end to suffering.

Christianity, for its part, would likely accept the claim with regard to the existence of fundamental human compassion. However, the foregoing of the compassion of the Savior as the paradigm of 'true' and all-embracing compassion would be regarded as the Achilles' heel of the radical model. In fact, the Christian will claim, the shortfall of a model that fails to include divine love manifests itself in every one of the model's aspects. In such a model, the compassionate person loses himself in an experience of irresponsible identification and ends up in a state of anger, which leads him to seek to change the world order, including those arrangements that are the sole dominion of the Lord. Thus, such compassion is not only partial and feeble in being exclusively human in nature; it is also likely to lead to heresy. The Christian believer, who revels in the compulsory practicability of the divine compassion model, will be satisfied by – and will even defend – the legitimacy of the first three modes of compassionate action, but will unequivocally reject the fourth type.

The salient common denominator shared by the three traditional approaches to compassion, against the background of the alternative model I have proposed, is the great rarity and measured exclusivity that they attribute to compassion as a phenomenon. Let us try, for the moment, to estimate the scope and presence of human compassion in our lives: if we reconsider the abundance of possibilities for different types of compassion – empathetic and remote, emotional and intellectual, spontaneous and rational, judgmental and non-judgmental, constitutive and a derivative of us, soft and raging – if we consider all those instances in which we have felt identification, allowed ourselves to feel the misery of someone else, cried when watching a film, delighted in a book, and so on and so forth, we will perhaps arrive at the conclusion that human compassion is a common and widespread day-to-day phenomenon and even an integral and constant experience in our lives in general. Nonetheless, we cannot overlook the fact that, every day, we pass by the homeless in the streets and look away, that we have become totally estranged from the friend who was paralyzed in a car accident, that whenever we watch the news and see children with stomachs swollen from hunger, we say 'This time I must do something!' but do nothing. The list goes on – of disasters, wars, and injustices about which we are certain we will take a stance but never do.

It therefore seems appropriate at this point to regard somewhat suspiciously the claim of impotence regarding the ability to realize of the imperative of compassion. Not surprisingly, this so-called 'helplessness' seems to be the feature of people who are not genuinely interested in improving the state of the suffering. And since a considerable part (if not, the majority) of human suffering in general is caused by other human beings, especially those in positions of power and influence, the difficulty in moving from identification to action appears to serve most the interests of the socio-economic class status quo. This status quo preserves the social power structure and, through mechanisms of social reproduction, hinders any possibility of change and perpetuates the poverty, degradation, alienation, and social oppression of a significant proportion of the world's population. From this wary vantage point, the claim that cultural norms and values, and not compassion, bear the determinative weight in establishing the motivation to take action hints at the existence of a smokescreen intended to distance us from our natural, simple, and immediate instinct to ease the suffering of others.

Two questions arise in the context of the possibility of understanding compassion as a natural, universal, and binding human inclination, as it appears in the radical compassion model. The first is this in fact a solely theoretical premise or perhaps a possible empiric description of reality? And second, how are the models of divine compassion, universal compassion, and modern compassion connected to radical compassion, given that the latter refutes premises that originate in European Modernism and proposes a completely different model of compassion?

The answer to the first question is related in a rather interesting fashion to the second. In order to present the above mental exercise assuming compassion to be a general and natural human instinct as a description of reality, two obstacles must be overcome. The first one is empiric – to what extent is the counter-narrative I suggest anchored in the human life experience? To what extent is it possible to explain human behavior in light of the premise of radical compassion? Following the speculative line I take in this final part of the discussion, I argue that this first obstacle presents absolutely no challenge. First, the two Suppositions of Modernism have absolutely no empiric advantage to the counter-premises I raise (perhaps even the opposite is the case). Second, there is absolutely no empiric difficulty with the model of radical compassion, which, in any event, exists only in the margins of our current social reality (and in the margins of history in general).

The second obstacle is more serious. How can we assume the necessary presence of compassion as a universal and widespread phenomenon, the domain of all human beings, and even argue in favor of radical compassion when we see right before us the cold human-social reality that is exploitative, class-dominated, alienated, and oppressive, whose historical manifestations completely refute the notion of human beings as compassionate creatures? The challenge in this second question places us in a very interesting position vis-à-vis the alternative model of radical compassion. In order to maintain that this model describes an actual reality, or at least an actual human possibility, we must explain why compassionate action – especially radically compassionate action – has not found a more empiric, concrete expression or, alternatively, why it has manifested itself only negligibly. In other words, if human beings are as compassionate and willing to act for the good of the other as claimed, why is the human reality so cruel and harsh? In order to give an account for this seeming anomaly, we must assume the existence of powerful social forces that systematically and perpetually repress any possibility of giving expression to this natural tendency that, under radical compassion, is constitutive of human beings. This assumption is not a simple and straightforward one. On the one hand, it is completely clear that radical compassion poses a threat to social stability and the social status quo. It encompasses everything that every institution, every wielder of power and means, most fears: change, and particularly change that benefits the wretched and oppressed in a way that is likely to impact the world order. This is not a theory or an anarchistic ideology – this is genuine rage and an imperative to bring about real change, here and now. On the other hand, it is also clear that if compassion is a natural human tendency and the basis to people's ability to forge a self-identity and function socially, then it is not possible, nor desirable, to repress it absolutely. Thus, compassion should be contained, especially in the form of radical compassion, and then re-routed to benign channels from a social perspective.

The practical ramifications of restraining compassion are, on the one hand, the identification of social-cultural outlets for people to give expression to their desire to be compassionate toward the needy and weak and, on the other hand, the certainty that no real and meaningful change will actually transpire and that the compassionate establishments are provided with the appropriate rhetoric for explaining why such change cannot occur. This logic points to the possibility that religious compassion, in its different forms and models described in this book, has served throughout history and still serves as a smokescreen for the socio-political establishment (to which this form of compassion belongs). It also emerges that the types of compassion presented by Buddhism and Christianity not only differ as models of compassion from the alternative I propose, but also constitute expressions of the suppression and delegitimization of human compassion. But the most remarkable conclusion relates to Modernism: Camouflaged as belief in man and as scientific and transparent, Modernism wrote the destructive narrative that teaches us to live in complete denial of our most fundamental experiences. It propagated the great myth that translates all our outrage at the distress of the other into terms of an 'ego-trip' that should be a source of shame. It created the procedures and practices for action that ensure the channeling of any desire to render change into controllable, rational institutional action. And it intensified and amplified, to horrific dimensions, the sense of impotence and inability to bring about real change, as well as stripping compassion of all meaning.

Notes

1 The compassionate god

1. Emphasis added. Unless otherwise noted, the source for all passages cited is the King James Version.
2. This point is relevant and important in every discussion of the problem of theodicy. The problem arises in light of the empiric reality that there are righteous who truly suffer and wicked who prosper. The Bible itself does not offer any conclusive resolution to this quandary, providing only partial solutions such as that only the 'truly righteous' enjoy the possibility of being rewarded or, alternatively, that it is, in fact, impossible to be truly righteous and everyone is a sinner, including Moses. Other solutions were later offered by Christianity, the most familiar of which is the promise of eternal life in Paradise for the righteous.
3. '[A]nd the children of Israel sighed by reason of their bondage, and they cried, and their cry came up unto God by reason of the bondage. And God heard their groaning, . . .' (*Exodus* 2:23–2:24).
4. This version of the passage is taken from the New American Standard Bible, which represents the closest translation of the Hebrew original. In the King James Version, the Hebrew word *hemla* is translated as mercy rather than compassion.
5. In Hebrew, the words compassion (*hemla*) and absolution (*mehila*) are morphologically similar, comprised of an identical set of Hebrew consonants.
6. New King James Version (emphasis added).
7. The entire set of Hebrew divine commandments is directed at action and not emotion – this is the most significant heritage of the legal ethos of the Bible. In fact, there is only one instance of a commandment formulated in terms of emotion: 'Love thy neighbor as thyself.' However, though this appears to be a requirement for some sort of emotional involvement, a close reading of the passage 'Thou shalt not avenge, nor bear any grudge against the children of thy people, but thou shalt love thy neighbour as thyself: I [am] the Lord' (*Leviticus* 19:18) reveals that this is actually a commandment requiring a certain type of social behavior, directed specifically at the People of Israel, with no universal application.
8. The analogy between the relations between God and the People of Israel and the father–son relationship is problematic due to its strong pagan overtones and the association with the idol-worshipping religions of the ancient Middle East, as well because this type of relationship poses a direct threat to the idea of the biblical covenant and the emphasis on choice in biblical theology.
9. A long series of appellations appear in the rebukes of the prophets, such as 'wayward sons', 'mischievous sons', 'imbecilic sons', and so on.
10. As in when God shows love and mercy toward Ephraim, who has acted like a wayward son, in *Hosea* 11 and in *Jeremiah* 31:17–31:20. See A. Goshen-Gotshtein, *Elohim ve'Yisrael ke'Av ve'Ben: BaSafrut HaTannait* [*God and Israel*

as Father and Son in the Tannatiic Literature] (Hebrew University of Jerusalem, 1987) p. 219.

11. New King James Version.

12. The literal translation of the word *Torah* is 'a teaching', whereas the *Torah* is generally known as the Five Books of Moses or the Pentateuch. In traditional Judaism, the Five Books are considered a reliable and exact record of the word of God as relayed to Moses. They describe the creation of the world, the main events of the first 2000 years of Jewish history, the origins of the nation that was to become the Jewish People, their exile and slavery in Egypt, and their redemption, and culminating with the giving of the *Torah* at Mount Sinai. The *Torah* also includes some very limited details of the 613 divine commandments. In Jewish tradition, both the Oral *Torah* and the Written *Torah* (the oral law and the written law) were given to Moses at Mount Sinai during the forty years in the desert and were taught to the Israelite Nation. Both are essential to fully understand traditional Jewish teaching and thought. The Written *Torah* mentions each of the commandments only in passing or by allusion, whereas the Oral *Torah* fills in the gaps.

13. In 188 CE, Rabbi Yehudah HaNasi compiled a basic outline of the Oral *Torah* into a series of books called the *Mishnah*, considered the cornerstone of Judaism. Its sixty-two tractates, divided into six parts, provide the background for every subject of Jewish law found in the Oral *Torah*, and it was intended to serve as a memory aid so that it would be easier for students to remember the oral law. It is primarily a very brief outline of the oral law, with no in-depth analysis or explanation of the laws. Such explanations are compiled in the *Gemara*: the rabbinical commentaries and analysis on the *Mishnah*, undertaken in the rabbinical academies of Palestine and Babylon over a three-hundred-year period until about 500 CE. The *Mishnah* is the core text, whereas the *Gemara* is the analysis and commentary that completes the *Talmud* (see note 16, *infra*).

14. *Tosefta* literally means 'supplement' and is a second compilation of the oral law from the period of the *Mishnah* (200 CE). It contains explanations and discussion not included in the *Mishnah* and is organized along the same six divisions. Materials in the *Tosefta* are attributed to rabbinic authorities in the first and second centuries CE, the same ones cited in the *Mishnah*, and as such the *Tosefta* is crucial to the study of formative rabbinic Judaism and early Christianity. The *Tosefta* offers authors' names for laws that are anonymous in the *Mishnah*; it also supplements the *Mishnah* with additional glosses and discussions.

15. About 300 years after the completion of the *Mishnah*, it was feared that the *Gemara* would be forgotten. The Jewish sages in Babylonia compiled the *Gemara* into a written work as a commentary on the *Mishnah*. This completed work is the Babylonian *Talmud*, which is made up of six sections and is the complete collection of the *Mishnah* and the *Gemara*. Somewhere between the completion of the *Mishnah* and the Babylonian *Talmud*, the rabbis of Israel had begun work on a Jerusalem *Talmud*, an important part of the Jewish library but, due to Roman persecution, never completed.

16. *Hassidic* Judaism is an ultra-orthodox religious movement founded by Israel ben Eliezer (1700–60), also known as the *Baal Shem Tov*. *Hassidism* formed in

a time of persecution of the Jewish people and when European Jews had turned to *talmudic* study. Many Jews felt at this time that most expressions of Jewish life had become too academic and that there was no longer any emphasis on spirituality or joy: *hassidism* was a reaction to this situation and aimed at changing it.

17. Under a more radical, Spinozean interpretation, autonomy from the capriciousness of God as well.

18. *Halakha* is commonly used to refer to the collective corpus of Jewish law, custom, and tradition regulating all aspects of behavior. It constitutes the practical application of the commandments in the *Torah* as developed through discussion and debate in the classical rabbinic literature, especially the *Mishnah* and the *Talmud*.

19. The *Midrash* is *talmudic* literature containing legends based on biblical verses with homiletic exegesis of the *Torah* and its paragraphs that relate to law.

20. The adoption of a text that is sacred to one religion by a religion that is evolving therefrom is an interesting phenomenon in and of itself and, I believe, unique to Christianity.

21. J. Rogerson, 'The Old Testament and Christian Ethics', in R. Gill, ed., *Christian Ethics* (Cambridge: Cambridge University Press, 2001) pp. 32–3.

22. This is also the second part of the Jewish ritual prayer 'Hear O Israel' (*Shema Yisrael*), which are the first two words of the *Deuteronomy* passage (6:4), affirming faith in God: 'Hear O Israel the Lord our God the Lord is One.'

23. It is not clear whether and to what extent the newly forming Christian myths had an influence on Jewish thought, but similar themes appear in the early centuries CE in Judaism as well: *Midrash Ruth Rabba* [*Great Commentary on the Book of Ruth*], Chapter 3; *Agadat Ha'Olam Ha'Hafuh*, Masechet Psachim 50:71.

24. This appears in a slightly different form in *John* 15:12: 'This is my commandment, That ye love one another, as I have loved you.'

2 Human divinity

1. Hillel the Elder, also known as Hillel the Babylonian, is considered the greatest sage of the Second Temple period. He lived from the end of the first century BCE to the beginning of the first century CE.

2. *Midrash Eicha Rabba*, Chapter 24.

3. In the Jewish tradition, it was ruled in the later periods of the *Talmud* and thereafter that, in the event of any dispute, mercy must be the guiding principle in the determination as to how to proceed.

4. The idea of a suffering God is more complex than what is presented here. The idea has not always had the popularity it has enjoyed in the theology of the past two hundred years, and it raises a not inconsiderable amount of difficulties, which impacted, amongst other things, the formulation of the dogmas already in the early stages of Christianity, at the First Council of Nicaea, for example. The idea itself has ramifications for Christian theodicy, which will be addressed in the next chapter.

5. The identification of compassion with agape and of both concepts with charity recently appeared in the excellent analysis by T. P. Jackson, *The Priority of Love: Christian Charity and Social Justice* (Princeton University Press, 2002).
6. 'A Christian man is the most free lord of all, and subject to none; a Christian man is the most dutiful servant of all, and subject to every one.' M. Luther, *Concerning Christian Liberty* (1520). Translated by R. S. Grignon in 1910, in C. W. Eliot, ed., *The Harvard Classics*, 36 (New York: PF Collier & Sons, 1910) p. 345. The view of the human duty (prescribed by both Luther and Calvin) to serve all people – the public, the community, and so on – as a principal Christian objective highlights the detachment of the idea of neighborly love both from the divine sense of the notion, which Jesus gave it according to the Catholic interpretation, and from the sense of compassion, which I present above.
7. Here I refer, of course, to Maimonides' well-known distinction between social commandments and commandments relating to the relations between God and man. This distinction enabled him to develop a broad and detailed conception of charity, as a continuation of the legalistic conception of compassion noted in the previous chapter.
8. This discussion is not the appropriate forum for expanding on this model, but I will refer to it indirectly in Chapters 7 and 8.
9. The Old Testament model for this sort of saintly compassion and supernaturalness appears in the Bible in the form of the Prophet Elijah, in a story frequently cited in the Christian sources, which stresses the importance and power of a miraculous act as a type of salvation and healing by the holy person:

> And it came to pass after these things, [that] the son of the woman, the mistress of the house, fell sick; and his sickness was so sore, that there was no breath left in him.
>
> And she said unto Elijah, What have I to do with thee, O thou man of God? art thou come unto me to call my sin to remembrance, and to slay my son?
>
> And he said unto her, Give me thy son. And he took him out of her bosom, and carried him up into a loft, where he abode, and laid him upon his own bed.
>
> And he cried unto the LORD, and said, O LORD my God, hast thou also brought evil upon the widow with whom I sojourn, by slaying her son?
>
> And he stretched himself upon the child three times, and cried unto the LORD, and said, O LORD my God, I pray thee, let this child's soul come into him again.
>
> And the LORD heard the voice of Elijah; and the soul of the child came into him again, and he revived.
>
> And Elijah took the child, and brought him down out of the chamber into the house, and delivered him unto his mother: and Elijah said, See, thy son liveth.
>
> And the woman said to Elijah, Now by this I know that thou [art] a man of God, [and] that the word of the LORD in thy mouth [is] truth.
>
> 1 *Kings* 17:17–17:24

10. At this point, it is difficult to accept the distinction, prevalent in sociology, between folk religion and established religion, each with its own interests and dynamics. For indeed, established religion is much closer to what is referred to as folk religion, which, in any event, is a vague and perhaps even redundant concept; moreover, all the established religions in general have a clear interest in the persistence of folk sentiments and in presenting them as objecting to or contradicting the official doctrines.

11. An analysis of this literary genre can be found, for example, in A. Kleinberg, *Prophets in Their Own Country: Living Saints and the Making of Sainthood in the Later Middle Ages* (University of Chicago Press, 1992).

12. Cited in K. B. Wolf, *The Poverty of Riches* (Oxford: Oxford University Press, 2003), taken from R. J. Armstrong, J. A. Hellmann, W. J. Short, eds, *Francis of Assisi; Early Documents* (New York: New City Press, 1999–2001).

13. 'Lay not up for yourselves treasures upon earth, where moth and rust doth corrupt, and where thieves break through and steal: But lay up for yourselves treasures in heaven . . .' (*Matthew* 6:19–6:20).

14. 'Take therefore no thought for the morrow: for the morrow shall take thought for the things of itself' (*Matthew* 6:34).

15. R. Brooke, ed. and trans., *Scripta Leonis, Rufini et Angeli Sociorum St. Francisci* (Oxford: Oxford University Press, 1970) p. 171.

16. The bond between compassion and sin is not so clear. It can most certainly be claimed that there are two parallel yet different narratives that characterize the history of Christianity: the one, loving, compassionate, and accepting; the other, judgmental, strict, and accusatory. The point that is most important for our purposes is that both narratives make use of the terminology of compassion.

3   Seeds of anti-compassion

1. An interesting attempt at doing just this can be found in C. Smith, *Disruptive Religion; The Force of the Faithful in Social-Movement Activism* (Routledge, 1996).

2. The *Legend of the Three Companions* is a joint narrative of St Francis' life compiled by Leo, Rufino, and Angelo, three intimate companions of the saint.

3. For a discussion of the symbolic and social meanings of leprosy, see S. N. Brody, *The Disease of the Soul; Leprosy in Medieval Literature* (Ithaca, NY: Cornell University Press, 1974).

4. K. B. Wolf, *The Poverty of Riches* (Oxford: Oxford University Press, 2003) p. 14.

5. R. Brooke, ed. and trans., *Scripta Leonis, Rufini et Angeli Sociorum St. Francisci* (Oxford: Oxford University Press, 1970) p. 240.

6. The Church was at the height of its power during this century, and despite the fact that the writing was already on the wall, the battles with the European monarchs had yet to diminish its power.

7. The practically classic analysis of this process is P. Braun, *Power and Persuasion in Late Antiquity; Towards a Christian Empire* (Madison: University of Wisconsin Press, 1992) pp. 71–117.

8. An interesting discussion of this point can be found in Wolf, *The Poverty of Riches*, pp. 77–90.

9. Hitchens explains that Mother Teresa had always been completely frank regarding her lack of intention to heal people and instead to share in their torments, which she compared to the torments of Christ. C. Hitchens, *The Missionary Position: Mother Teresa in Theory and Practice* (Verso, 1995).
10. Hitchens, *The Missionary Position*, in his critical book on Mother Teresa, cites this conversation she had with a journalist after she was rebuffed in her attempt to visit a slum neighborhood in Washington.
11. P. Berger, *The Sacred Canopy* (New York: Anchor Books, 1969) (repr. 1990) p. 58.
12. Ibid.
13. Ibid., pp. 55–6.
14. A. Camus, *The Rebel* (NY: Vintage, 1956) p. 34, cited by Berger, *The Sacred Canopy*, p. 77.

4 Indiscriminate compassion

1. S. Radhakrishnan and C. Moore, eds. *Source Book in Indian Philosophy* (Princeton: Princeton University Press, 1957) p. 93. Cited in Berger; P. Berger, *The Sacred Canopy* (New York: Anchor Books, 1969) (repr. 1990), p. 66. The *Upanishads* are the most basic and important Hindu scriptures, discussing primarily philosophy and meditation and constituting the basis of the doctrines of most schools of Hinduism. The *Maitri Upanishad* is one of the principal and later *Upanishads*.
2. Berger, *ibid*, pp. 63–68. Berger conducts his discussion following the Weberian analysis as it appears, for example, in *The Sociology of Religion* (1920).
3. The *Laws of Manu* (or *Manava Dharma Shastra*) is one of the standard books in the Hindu canon and a basic text for gurus to base their teachings on.
4. See note 2, *supra*.
5. See note 1, *supra*.
6. Karl Potter, for example, suggested in the 1960s an interpretation of Indian philosophy according to which liberation is the central concept around which all Indian systems of logic developed. K. Potter, *Presupposition of India's Philosophies* (New Jersey: Prentice Hall, 1964).
7. Cited in Berger, *The Sacred Canopy*, p. 67, from Radhakrishnan and Moore, *Source Book in Indian Philosophy*.
8. The term 'rationalization' has a different meaning here from its previous sense, in the context of the rationality of the Indian *karmic–Samsaric* system, which rests on the definition of rationality as logical coherence. In the present context, rationality means the demystification of the picture of the world that Weber attributes to Buddhism.
9. The Pali Canon is the first Buddhist scripture to be put into written form and (supposedly) the closest to the authentic word of the Buddha.
10. Berger, *The Sacred Canopy*, p. 68.
11. This idealistic tendency characterizes a considerable part of Indian thought and is a thread woven throughout the *Upanishads* as well as in the more ancient Vedist literature. In certain respects, the idea of presenting reality as consciousness-contingent is not specifically Buddhist, but rather an almost necessary derivative of the *karmic–Samsaric* configuration itself.
12. D. Anderson and H. Smith, eds and trans., *Sutta Nipa-ta* (London: Pali Text Society, 1913) nos 143–52, cited in R. L. F. Habito, 'Compassion out of

190   *Notes*

Wisdom', in G. S. Post, L. G. Underwood, P. J. Schloss and B. W. Hurlbut, eds, *Altruism and Altruistic Love* (Oxford: Oxford University Press, 2002) p. 363.

13. This translation of the passage from the *Majjhima-Nikāya*, or 'Middle-Length Discourses of the Buddha' is taken from P. Soonthorndhammathada, *Compassion in Buddhism and Puranas* (Delhi: Nag Publishers, 1995) p. 93.

14. *Aṅgūttara-Nikāya* is an important source book on Buddhist psychology and ethics, which provides an enumerated summary of all the essential features of the theory and practice of the *Dhamma* – the teachings and doctrines of the Buddha.

15. P. Soonthorndhammathada, *Compassion in Buddhism and Puranas*, p. 120.

16. Ibid.

17. W. Rahula, 'The Social Teachings of the Buddha', in F. Eppsteiner, ed., *The Path of Compassion* (Berkeley, CA: Parallax Press, 1988) pp. 104–5.

18. Ibid., pp. 111–12.

19. E. Conze, *Buddhist Wisdom Books* (New York: Harper Torchbooks, 1972) p. 79. The five *skandhas* are the psycho-physical constituents (or aggregates) of individuality by which human beings are analyzed in Buddhist phenomenology.

20. Kumārajīva's translation was only one of a long series of translations into Chinese of texts supposedly written originally in Sanskrit, but this is the most prevalent version and has had the greatest impact.

21. P. Williams, *Mahāyāna Buddhism* (UK: Routledge, 1989).

22. Ibid., pp. 231–2.

23. P. Yampolsky, ed. and trans., *Selected Writings of Nichiren* (New York: Columbia University Press, 1990) p. 146.

24. Habito, 'Compassion out of Wisdom', p. 372.

25. Passage taken from the *Shobogenzo*, translated by Habito, ibid., p. 370.

26. In Chapter 7, I present a completely different outlook on compassion, the modern view, which entails preserving and holding on to the self as a condition for empathy.

5   The Buddhist ideal

1. *Bodhisattva* literally means 'enlightenment being' in Sanskrit.

2. The translation of the word *prajña* as 'wisdom' is not simple. In fact, the term represents in Buddhism a conscious state that is attained by means of rational and logical analysis, through insight meditation (*vipasyana*) that strives for an understanding of the true nature of reality. According to the Mahāyāna tradition, especially the Madhyamaka philosophy, a significant part of what is termed 'wisdom' under other streams of Buddhism and non-Buddhists is in no way *prajña*, but rather an assortment of prejudices and misconceptions. The process of the enhancement of wisdom, which is intended to reveal the complete emptiness of the *dharmas* (the simple components of reality), of the self, and so on, is indicative also of the possibility of an intuitive and perhaps mystic insight, and indeed later streams in Chinese Buddhism and Zen Buddhism thus understood the idea of enhancement of *prajña*.

3. Williams warns against a simplistic understanding of the Bodhisattva as someone who defers enlightenment to a later stage. This type of understanding

is more acceptable in the later literatures of Chinese and Japanese Buddhism, but is not in line with ancient Indian Buddhism and certainly not with the Tibetan variation, which would never accept that the Bodhisattva is not actually already enlightened. P. Williams, *Mahāyāna Buddhism* (UK: Routledge, 1989) pp. 43, 52.

4. This is taken from Conze's translation of the *Prajña-pāramitā-sūtra*, E. Conze, *The Perfection of Wisdom in Eight Thousand Lines and Its Verse Summary* (Bolinas: Four Seasons Foundation, 1973) pp. 238–9, cited by Williams, *Mahāyāna Buddhism*, p. 50.
5. *Smaller Prajña Sūtra*, VI, Taisho, VIII, p. 563c, in J. C. Cleary, trans., 'On Temporal and Spatial Adaptability of the Buddhisattva Percepts', in C. Wei-hsun Fu and S. A. Wawrytko, eds, *Buddhist Behavioral Codes and the Modern World* (London: Greenwood Press, 1994) p. 7.
6. R. Gimello, 'Mysticism and Meditation', in S. Katz, ed., *Mysticism and Philosophical Analysis* (London: Sheldon Press, 1978).
7. Ok-Sun An, *Compassion and Benevolence: A Comparative Study of Early Buddhist and Classical Confucian Ethics* (New York: P. Lang, 1998).
8. Madhyamaka is the 'Middle Path' school of Mahāyāna Buddhism.
9. The Pali Canon is the first Buddhist scriptures to be put into written form and (supposed to be) the closest to the authentic word of the Buddha. It is made up of three books, the first is the *Vinaya Pitaka*, the Book of Discipline, which includes the rules of monastic discipline given by the Buddha during his lifetime. The second is the *Sutta Pitaka*, a collection of the Buddha's discourses, containing the essential teachings of the Buddha, accounts of his enlightenment experience, and instructions on morality and meditation. The third book is the *Abhidhamma Pitaka* or Higher Teachings, an intricate analysis of the nature of mental and physical existence.
10. The *Metta Sutta* is a mantra found in the Pali Canon and is considered the Buddha's teachings on *metta*, usually translated from the Pali as 'loving-kindness'.
11. R. L. F. Habito, 'Compassion out of Wisdom', in G. S. Post, L. G. Underwood, P. J. Schloss and B. W. Hurlbut, eds, *Altruism and Altruistic Love* (Oxford: Oxford University Press, 2002) p. 364.
12. Ibid., p. 366. The literal translation of *upekśā* is 'close to the eye', which, from the Buddhist perspective, is analogous to a lucid view of things without any illusory covering.
13. P. Soonthorndhammathada, *Compassion in Buddhism and Puranas* (Delhi: Nag Publishers, 1995) pp. 110–16.
14. Ibid., p. 115.
15. A. N. D. Haksar, trans., *Jatakamala: Stories from the Buddha's Previous Births* (India: Harper Collins, 2003); P. Khoroche, trans., *Once the Buddha Was a Monkey: Arya Sura's Jatakamala* (Chicago, IL: University of Chicago Press, 1989).
16. It is interesting to note, for example, the difference between the way in which Williams describes the Buddhist approach to Nirvāṇa as a real, 'here and now' possiibility following his encounters with modern-day Tibetan Buddhists (Williams, *Mahāyāna Buddhism*, p. 53), and, in contrast, the way in which Bunnag describes the Thai Buddhist monks' outlook, which in no way regards Nirvāṇa as a realistic possibility. J. Bunnag, *Buddhist Monk, Buddhist Layman* (Cambridge, 1973).

17. The *dharma* is one of the three 'jewels' that constitute the basis of Buddhist life in general: the Buddha, the *dharma* (the dogma, way, and teachings of the Buddha), and the *sangha* (the Buddhist order, monastery, and community).
18. These are four types of snakes.
19. P. Soonthorndhammathada, *Compassion in Buddhism and Puranas*, p. 98.
20. Of course, the story does not end here and there are a great many other stories about the fate of the decapitated head that continued to appear and influence reality during the next centuries in different places in India and the Himalayas.
21. This ability to feel empathy for the enemy earned Nāgārjuna the second part of his name – Arjuna, after the mythological warrior hero of the *Mahābhārata*, whose moral qualms prior to the war and his unwillingness to harm the enemy are at the core of the classic text of the *Bhagavad Gītā*.
22. J. Hopkins, *Compassion in Tibetan Buddhism* (New York: Snow Lion, 1980), with translation of Tsong-kha-pa's commentary on Chandrakīrti's *Madhyamakāḥśāstra*.
23. Ibid., p. 87.
24. A. Weiman, *Buddhist Insight* (Delhi: Motilal Banarasidas, 1990) pp. 101–2. From the way in which Weiman analyzes Tsong-kha-pa's practical suggestion, it emerges that Tsong-kha-pa did not attribute great importance to the warning in the *Prajña-pāramitā* of the importance of refraining from feeling the pain of others.
25. These five constituents are: (1) *rupa* or 'form' – the material body; (2) *vedanā* or 'sensation' – the receipt of information through the senses; (3) *samjanā* or 'perception'; (4) *saṃskāra* or 'volition' – mental habits; and (5) *vijñāna* or 'consciousness'.

6   Compassion without teeth

1. The latter requirement was particularly radical in traditional Indian terms, for a substantive part of the definition of the caste hierarchy lies in the prohibitions on giving and receiving between the upper and the lower castes.
2. R. A. Ray, *Buddhist Saints in India* (Oxford: Oxford University Press, 1994) p. 93.
3. M. E. Spiro, *Buddhism and Society: A Great Tradition and Its Burmese Vicissitudes* (Harper & Row, 1970).
4. K. Lampert, *The Philosophers of the Mystical* (Ph.D. Dissertation, Tel Aviv University, 1997).
5. The *Sa-skya-pa* Order is one of several Tibetan schools of Buddhism that came into being during the eleventh and twelfth centuries CE and traced their lineage back to certain Vajrayāna saints who had lived in India some centuries earlier. It is one of the most prominent of these orders and, during the course of Tibetan history, gave rise to many other orders.
6. *Dalai* means 'ocean' in Mongolian, and *Lama* means spiritual leader in Tibetan.
7. P. Williams, *Mahāyāna Buddhism* (UK: Routledge, 1989) pp. 191–3.
8. It is only fair to note at this juncture that the fact that compassion requires training in order to be manifested does not contradict the claim that it is a

fundamental quality of all people. It is most certainly possible to assume that every person has the potential to be compassionate, which is hidden by the illusory life of the *Samsaric* cycle and only through purification and practice can this potential be realized. This type of argument has been raised in different places in the Buddhist literature, one example being its appearance in *Ta-ch'eng ch'i-hsin lun*, the Chinese version of the Mahāyāna text attributed to Aśvagosha (erroneously, of course). See Y. S. Hakeda, trans., *The Awakening of Faith* (New York: Columbia University Press, 1967) p. 83.
9. Williams, *Mahāyāna Buddhism*, p. 145.
10. Ibid., p. 161.
11. Spiro, *Buddhism and Society*.
12. At this point it is important to stress that I do not claim that Christians or, alternatively, Buddhists have not worked and do not work tirelessly to alleviate human suffering. On the contrary, as I will argue in Chapter 8, a great deal of the history of social activism is closely tied to those people who grew up on the religious traditions of compassion. My claim is that their work was in no way part of the traditional models of compassion (divine compassion, universal compassion). Rather, these people in fact deviated from the model dictated by the given tradition and acted out of what I term further on 'radical compassion', which often stood in total contradiction to the policy of the Church or the Order.

7 The fragmentation of compassion

1. G. Himmelfarb, 'The Idea of Compassion: The British vs. the French Enlightenment', *The Public Interest*, 145 (Fall 2001).
2. A. Smith, *The Theory of Moral Sentiment* (D. D. Raphael and A. L. Macfie, eds, Oxford: Clarendon Press, 1976) (1759) Part 1, Section 1, Chapter 1.
3. G. Lenzer, ed., *August Comte and Positivism: The Essential Writings* (Transaction Books, 1997).
4. D. W. Smith, *The Circle of Acquaintances: Perception, Consciousness, and Empathy* (Dordrecht: Kluwer, 1989) pp. 117–18.
5. L. R. Katz, *Empathy: Its Nature and Uses* (London: Collier-Macmillan, 1963).
6. S. Freud, *New Introductory Lectures on Psycho-Analysis* (W. J. S. Sprott, trans., New York: Norton, 1933), quoted in Katz, *Empathy*, p. 72.
7. Katz regards this as our ability to feel empathy. Katz, *Empathy*, p. 74.
8. S. Freud, *The Unconscious* (1915), in J. Strachey, ed., *The Standard Edition*, 14 (London, 1957) p. 169.
9. C. D. Batson, S. C. Sympson, J. L. Hindman, P. Decruz, R. M. Todd, J. L. Weeks, G. Jennings and C. T. Burris, ' "I've Been There, Too": Effect on Empathy of Prior Experience with a Need', *Personality and Social Psychology Bulletin*, 22 (1996) 474–82.
10. Smith, *The Circle of Acquaintances*, p. 117 (emphasis in original).
11. K. R. Monroe, *The Heart of Altruism* (NJ: Princeton University Press, 1996) pp. 6–7.
12. R. Dawkins, *The Selfish Gene* (Oxford: Oxford University Press, 1990). The great operational contraction that biological reductionism imposes on complex concepts such as compassion is clear in innumerable scientific articles

over the last few years. See, for example, C. D. Batson and T. Moran, 'Empathy-induced Altruism in a Prisoner's Dilemma', *European Journal of Social Psychology*, 29(7) (1999) 909–24.

8 Compassion revisited

1. The leading critics in this context were the prominent Protestant theologians of the twentieth century, such as Paul Tillich and Reinhold Niebuhr. See, for example, R. Niebuhr, *Moral Man and Immoral Society: A Study of Ethics and Politics* (Westminster: John Knox Press, 2002).
2. I use the concept neocapitalism in two main senses. The first one refers to radical capitalism – capitalism where the gloves have come off and there is no longer any pretense of morality or self-righteousness. Its sole interest is profit, and activities to maximize profits are conducted openly, in broad daylight, completely shamelessly. The second sense is what Mandel coined 'Late Capitalism' and which Jameson adopted. E. Mandel, *Late Capitalism* (J. de-Bres trans., London: Humanities Press, 1975); F. Jameson, 'Postmodernism or the Cultural Logic of Late Capitalism', *New Left Review*, 146 (1983) 53–93.
3. It seems both reasonable and logical to identify the Jewish tradition of legalistic interpretation of the biblical commandments as the historical origins of social welfare. This tradition gained great force in Maimonides' extremely influential commentary from the Middle Ages, where he distinguished between social commandments (amongst men) and religious commandments (between man and God). Thus Maimonides laid the foundation for communal responsibility to attend to the distress of individuals without waiting for Heavenly benevolence, as it were. At the same time, the commentary also developed the idea of legal responsibility by means of the idea of charity (Maimonides lists a hierarchy of eight different types of charity).

   This aside, it is important to recall two relevant matters. First, social welfare is an ancient notion, discernible in different cultures across the world even prior to the appearance of traditions of compassion. For example, the role of the Emperor in Ancient China was defined as attending to the welfare of the nation. Already in twelfth century CE, the Duke of Zhou declared that as a condition for receiving the 'mandate from heaven' (*T'ian Ming*), the cosmic legitimacy for the emperorship, the ruler must care for the welfare of the farmers and protect them against natural and human harm. In the *Arthaṣastra*, an ancient Indian text from the fourth century BCE, its author, the Hindu sage Kautilya, counseled the great Indian Emperor Chandragupta to adopt a welfare policy as the basis to the stability of the Kingdom and as the necessary definition of the role of the Emperor. Finally, while the biblical commandments are usually credited with the appearance of social welfare in the Judeo-Christian culture, there were already signs of social legislation in Ancient Egypt and in Hammurabi's Code in Mesopotamia, which, without a doubt, influenced the biblical narrative.

   Second, during the period of the *Mishna* and the *Talmud* (see notes 13 and 15 to Chapter 1), charity and benevolence became central community practices with set forms and institutions, such as community funds, cauldrons, lodgings, burial, aid to mourners, and charity for the needy (orphans, widows, ransom funds). These arrangements persisted and even continued to evolve over the generations and across the Jewish Diaspora. Despite the fact that the extensive Jewish tradition of charity constitutes a type of model of social welfare in Medieval Judaism, it is important to note the discrepancy between the *Midrash* (see note 19 to Chapter 1) and what was done in practice, between the laws and declarations and actual implementation. This discrepancy is apparent, for example, in the inconsistency between Maimonides' assertion that he had 'never heard of nor seen' a Spanish community without a charity fund and the fact that, apparently, only in fourteenth century CE, about a century after Maimonides' death, was care for the poor included in the explicit aid policy of this community.

4. There is actually no way of explaining complex concepts such as empathy, love, compassion, and justice by way of biological reductionism. All attempts to do so have usually been completely dismal, falling into one of the following categories: either the explanation is tautological (we are empathetic because our genes seek survival and the proof of this is that we are empathetic) and suffers from the empiricist problem (which has existed since the days of Locke) of a lack of a sufficient explanation in moving from the empiric level to the abstract concept or, alternatively, the explanation foregoes strict reductionism and uses external concepts from philosophy, religion, and the like, as was standard in evolutionary psychology. See A. Lampert, *The Evolution of Love* (Westport: Praeger, 1997).

5. Of course, 'find ourselves' is used here metaphorically, since in this experience it is not at all clear that we continue to sense ourselves as having separate existence or as completely merging with the other; what we 'find' is the experience of someone else.

6. D. W. Smith, *The Circle of Acquaintances: Perception, Consciousness, and Empathy* (Dordrecht: Kluwer, 1989) p. 117.

7. Cited in J. R. Harris, *The Nurture Assumption* (New York: Touchstone, 1999) p. 56.

8. K. Lampert, *Compassionate Education: Prolegomena for Radical Schooling* (MD: University Press of America, 2003) p. 175.

9. I have presented this premise in greater detail in ibid., pp. 103–7.

10. B. P. Stone, *Compassionate Ministry: Theological Foundations* (Orbis Books, 1 February 1996); S. C. Mott, *Biblical Ethics and Social Change* (New York: Oxford University Press, 1982).

11. A superb historical analysis of the work of the Christian churches and organizations, as well as of the naïve enterprises of social activism in the nineteenth century can be found in G. Himmelfarb, *Poverty and Compassion: The Moral Imagination of the Late Victorians* (Vintage, reprint edition, 27 October 1992).

12. On the work of the Fourth World Organization, see J. M. Rosenfeld, *Artisans of Democracy* (MD: University Press of America, 2000).

13. M. Batchelor and K. Brown, eds, *Buddhism and Ecology* (London: Cassell, 1992); C. K. Chapple, *Nonviolence to Animals, Earth, and Self in Asian Traditions* (Albany, NY: State University of New York Press, 1993); K. Kraft, ed., *Inner Peace, World Peace: Essays on Buddhism and Nonviolence* (Albany, NY: State University of New York Press, 1992); F. Eppsteiner, ed., *The Path of Compassion: Writings on Socially Engaged Buddhism* (Berkeley, CA: Parallax Press, 1988); K. Jones, *The Social Face of Buddhism: An Approach to Political and Social Activism* (London: Wisdom Publications, 1989).

14. Th. N. Hānh, *Peace Is Every Step: The Path of Mindfulness in Everyday Life* (Bantam Reissue Edition, 1992).
15. The *Bhagavad Gītā*, meaning the 'song of the Lord', is a core sacred text of Hindu religion and philosophy and a summation of Hindu thought: the Vedic, Yogic, Vedantic, and Tantric philosophies.
16. An attempt to examine Gandhi's philosophy on the background of Indian metaphysics and Western philosophical ideas can be found in G. Richards, *The Philosophy of Gandhi* (New York: Barnes and Noble, 1982).
17. D. Halberstam, *The Children* (New York: Random House, 1998).

Bibliography

Akers, K. *The Lost Religion of Jesus: Simple Living and Nonviolence in Early Christianity* (New York: Lantern Books, 2000).

Anderson, D. and Smith, H., eds and trans. *Sutta Nipa-ta* (London: Pali Text Society, 1913).

Armstrong, R. J., Hellmann, J. A. and Short, W. J., eds, *Francis of Assisi; Early Documents* (New York: New City Press, 1999–2001).

Batchelor, M. and Kerry, B., eds, *Buddhism and Ecology* (London: Cassell, 1992).

Batson, C. D. 'Sociobiology and the Role of Religion in Promoting Prosocial Behavior: An Alternative View', *Journal of Personality and Social Psychology*, 45 (1983) 1380–5.

Batson, C. D. and Moran, T. 'Empathy-induced Altruism in a Prisoner's Dilemma', *European Journal of Social Psychology*, 29(7) (1999) 909–24.

Batson, C. D., Sympson, S. C., Hindman, J. L., Decruz, P., Todd, R. M., Weeks, J. L., Jennings, G. and Burris, C. T. ' "I've Been There, Too": Effect on Empathy of Prior Experience with a Need', *Personality and Social Psychology Bulletin*, 22 (1996) 474–82.

Berger, P. *The Sacred Canopy* (New York: Anchor Books, 1969; reprntd 1990).

Braun, P. *Power and Persuasion in Late Antiquity; Towards a Christian Empire* (Madison: University of Wisconsin Press, 1992).

Brody, S. N. *The Disease of the Soul; Leprosy in Medieval Literature* (Ithaca, NY: Cornell University Press, 1974).

Brooke, R., ed. and trans. *Scripta Leonis, Rufini et Angeli Sociorum St. Francisci* (Oxford: Oxford University Press, 1970).

Bunnag, J. *Buddhist Monk, Buddhist Layman* (Cambridge, UK: Cambridge University Press, 1973).

Camus, A. *The Rebel* (New York: Vintage, 1956).

Cleary, J. C., trans. 'On Temporal and Spatial Adaptability of the Buddhisattva Percepts', in Wei-hsun Fu, C. and Wawrytko, S. A., eds, *Buddhist Behavioral Codes and the Modern World* (London: Greenwood Press, 1994).

Conze, E. *Buddhist Wisdom Books* (New York: Harper Torchbooks, 1972).

——. *The Perfection of Wisdom in Eight Thousand Lines and Its Verse Summary* (Bolinas: Four Seasons Foundation, 1973).

Chapple, C. K. *Nonviolence to Animals, Earth, and Self in Asian Traditions* (Albany, NY: State University of New York Press, 1993).

Dalai Lama and Carrière, J.-C. *Violence and Compassion* (New York: Doubleday, 1996).

Davis, M. H. 'Measuring Individual Differences in Empathy: Evidence for a Multidimensional Approach', *Journal of Personality and Social Psychology*, 44(1) (1983) 113–26.

Dawkins, R. *The Selfish Gene* (Oxford: Oxford University Press, 1990).

Eisenberg, N. 'Empathy-related Emotional Responses, Altruism, and Their Socialization', in Davidson, R. J. and Harrington, A., eds, *Visions of Compassion: Western Scientists and Tibetan Buddhists Examine Human Nature* (London: Oxford University Press, 2001) pp. 131–64.

Eppsteiner, F., ed., *The Path of Compassion: Writings on Socially Engaged Buddhism* (Berkeley, CA: Parallax Press, 1988).

Freud, S. *New Introductory Lectures on Psycho-Analysis* (W. J. S. Sprott, trans., New York: Norton, 1933).

——. *The Unconscious* (1915), in Strachey, J., ed., *The Standard Edition*, 14 (London: Hogarth, 1957).

Gardner, E. C. *Justice and Christian Ethics* (Cambridge: Cambridge University Press, 1995).

Gimello, R. 'Mysticism and Meditation', in Katz, S., ed., *Mysticism and Philosophical Analysis* (London: Sheldon Press, 1978).

Goshen-Gotshtein, A. *Elohim ve'Yisrael ke'Av ve'Ben: BaSafrut HaTannait [God and Israel as Father and Son in Tannaitic Literature]* (Jerusalem: Hebrew University of Jerusalem, 1987).

Habito, R. L. F. 'Compassion out of Wisdom', in Post, G. S., Underwood, L. G., Schloss, P. J. and Hurlbut, B. W., eds, *Altruism and Altruistic Love* (Oxford: Oxford University Press, 2002).

Hakeda, Y. S., trans. *The Awakening of Faith* (New York: Columbia University Press, 1967).

Haksar, A. N. D., trans. *Jatakamala: Stories from the Buddha's Previous Births* (India: Harper Collins, 2003).

Halberstam, D. *The Children* (New York: Random House, 1998).

Hānh, Th. N. *Peace Is Every Step: The Path of Mindfulness in Everyday Life* (New York and Toronto: Bantam Books, 1992).

Harris, J. R. *The Nurture Assumption* (New York: Touchstone, 1999).

Himmelfarb, G. 'The Idea of Compassion: The British vs. the French Enlightenment', *The Public Interest*, 145 (Fall 2001).

Hitchens, C. *The Missionary Position: Mother Teresa in Theory and Practice* (London: Verso, 1995).

Hopkins, J. *Compassion in Tibetan Buddhism* (New York: Snow Lion, 1980) (translation of Tsong-kha-pa's commentary on Chandrakīrti's *Madhyamakāhsāstra*).

Jackson, T. P. *The Priority of Love: Christian Charity and Social Justice* (Princeton: Princeton University Press, 2002).

Jameson, F. 'Postmodernism or the Cultural Logic of Late Capitalism', *New Left Review*, 146 (1983) 53–93.

Jones, K. *The Social Face of Buddhism: An Approach to Political and Social Activism* (London: Wisdom Publications, 1989).

Katz, L. R. *Empathy: Its Nature and Uses* (London: Collier-Macmillan, 1963).

Katz, S., ed., *Mysticism and Philosophical Analysis* (London: Sheldon Press, 1978).

Khoroche, P., trans. *Once the Buddha Was a Monkey: Arya Sura's Jatakamala* (Chicago, IL: University of Chicago Press, 1989).

Kraft, K., ed., *Inner Peace, World Peace: Essays on Buddhism and Nonviolence* (Albany, NY: State University of New York Press, 1992).

Lampert, A. *The Evolution of Love* (Westport: Praeger, 1997).

Lampert, K. *Compassionate Education: Prolegomena for Radical Schooling* (MD: University Press of America, 2003).

Lenzer, G., ed., *Auguste Comte and Positivism: The Essential Writings* (New Brunswick and London: Transaction Publishers, Fall 1997).

Luther, M. *Concerning Christian Liberty* (1520) trans. Grignon, R. S., in Eliot, C. W., ed., *The Harvard Classics*, 36 (New York: PF Collier & Son, 1910) p. 345.

Mandel, E. *Late Capitalism* (de-Bres, J., trans. London: Humanities Press, 1975).

Monroe, K. R. *The Heart of Altruism* (NJ: Princeton University Press, 1996).

Mott, S. C. *Biblical Ethics and Social Change* (New York: Oxford University Press, 1982).

Niebuhr, R. *The Nature and Destiny of Man: I. Human Nature* (New York: Charles Scribner's Sons, 1941).

Ok-Sun An, *Compassion and Benevolence: A Comparative Study of Early Buddhist and Classical Confucian Ethics* (New York: P. Lang, 1998).

Post, G. S., Underwood, L. G., Schloss, P. J. and Hurlbut, B. W., eds, *Altruism and Altruistic Love* (Oxford: Oxford University Press, 2002).

Potter, K. *Presuppositions of India's Philosophies* (NJ: Prentice-Hall, 1963).

Radhakrishnan, S. and Moore, C., eds, *Source Book in Indian Philosophy* (Princeton: Princeton University Press, 1957).

Rahula, W. 'The Social Teachings of the Buddha', in Eppsteiner, F., ed., *The Path of Compassion: Writings on Socially Engaged Buddhism* (Berkeley, CA: Parallax Press, 1988) pp. 103–11.

Ray, R. A. *Buddhist Saints in India* (Oxford: Oxford University Press, 1994).

Rinpoche, Th. *A Guide to the Bodhisattva's Way of Life of Shantideva: A Commentary* (Delhi, India: Sri Satguru Publications, 2002).

Rogerson, J. 'The Old Testament and Christian Ethics', in Gill, R., ed., *Christian Ethics* (Cambridge: Cambridge University Press, 2001) pp. 32–3.

Rosenfeld, J. M. *Artisans of Democracy* (MD: University Press of America, 2000).

Smaller Prajna Sūtrā, VI, Taisho, VIII, p. 563c, in Cleary, J. C., trans. 'On Temporal and Spatial Adaptability of the Buddhisattva Percepts', in Wei-hsun Fu, C. and Wawrytko, S. A., eds, *Buddhist Behavioral Codes and the Modern World* (London: Greenwood Press, 1994) p. 7.

Smith, A. *The Theory of Moral Sentiment* (Raphael, D. D. and Macfie, A. L., eds, Oxford: Clarendon Press, 1976) (1759) Part 1, Section 1, Chapter 1.

Smith, C. *Disruptive Religion; The Force of the Faithful in Social-Movement Activism* (New York: Routledge, 1996).

Smith, D. W. *The Circle of Acquaintances: Perception, Consciousness, and Empathy* (Dordrecht: Kluwer, 1989).

Soonthorndhammathada, P. *Compassion in Buddhism and Puranas* (Delhi: Nag Publishers, 1995).

Stone, B. P. *Compassionate Ministry: Theological Foundations* (New York: Orbis Books, 1 February 1996).

Taylor, J. L. 'Social Activism and Resistance on the Thai Frontier: The Case of Phra Parajak Khuttajitto', *Bulletin of Concerned Asian Scholars*, 25(2) (1993) 3–16.

Webb, S. H. On *God and Dogs: A Christian Theology of Compassion for Animals* (NY/Oxford: Oxford University Press, 1998).

Wei-hsun Fu, C. and Wawrytko, S. A., eds, *Buddhist Behavioral Codes and the Modern World* (London: Greenwood Press, 1994).

Weiman, A. *Buddhist Insight* (Delhi: Motilal Banarasidas, 1990).

Williams, P. *Mahāyāna Buddhism* (UK: Routledge, 1989).

Wolf, K. B. *The Poverty of Riches* (Oxford: Oxford University Press, 2003).

Yampolsky, P., ed. and trans. *Selected Writings of Nichiren* (NY: Columbia University Press, 1990).

Index